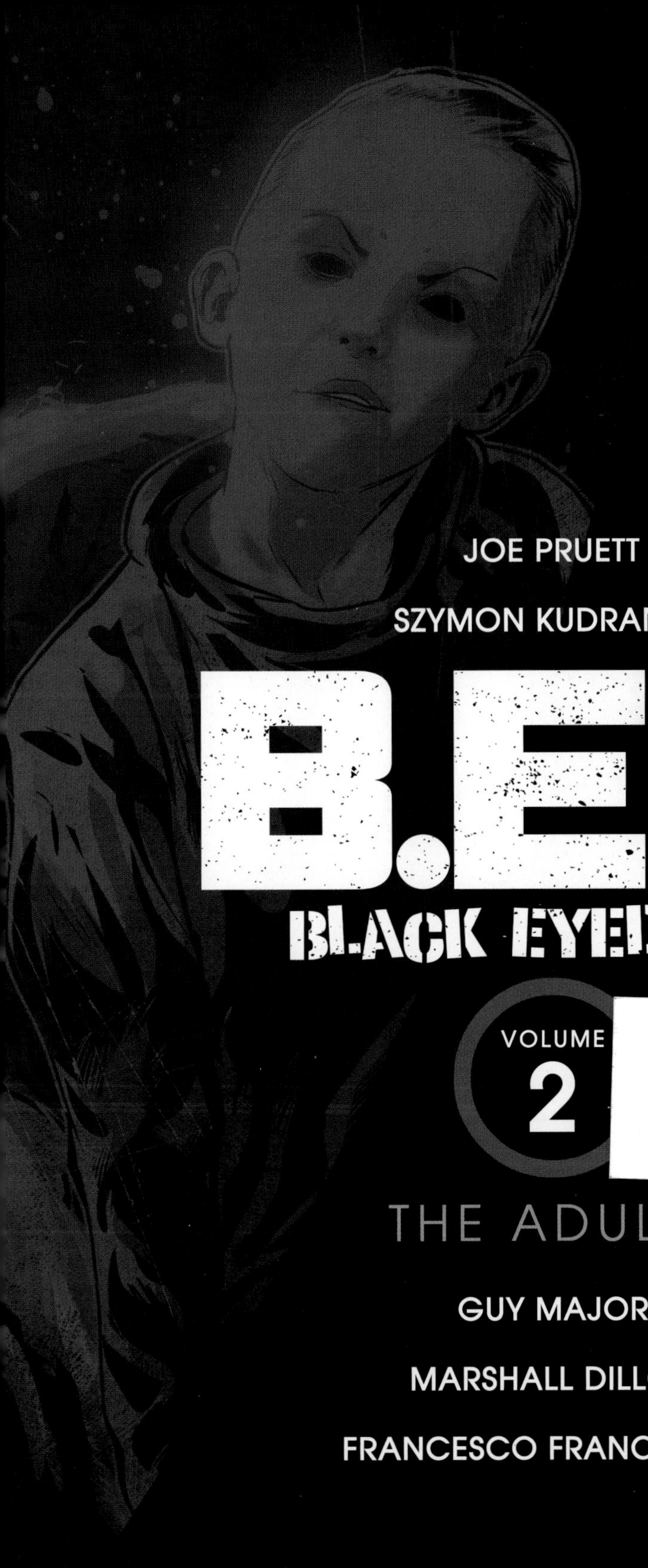

JOE PRUETT

SZYMON KUDRANSKI

B.E.K.
BLACK EYED KIDS

VOLUME 2

THE ADULTS

GUY MAJOR

MARSHALL DILLON

FRANCESCO FRANCAVILLA

AFTERSHOCK

BLACK

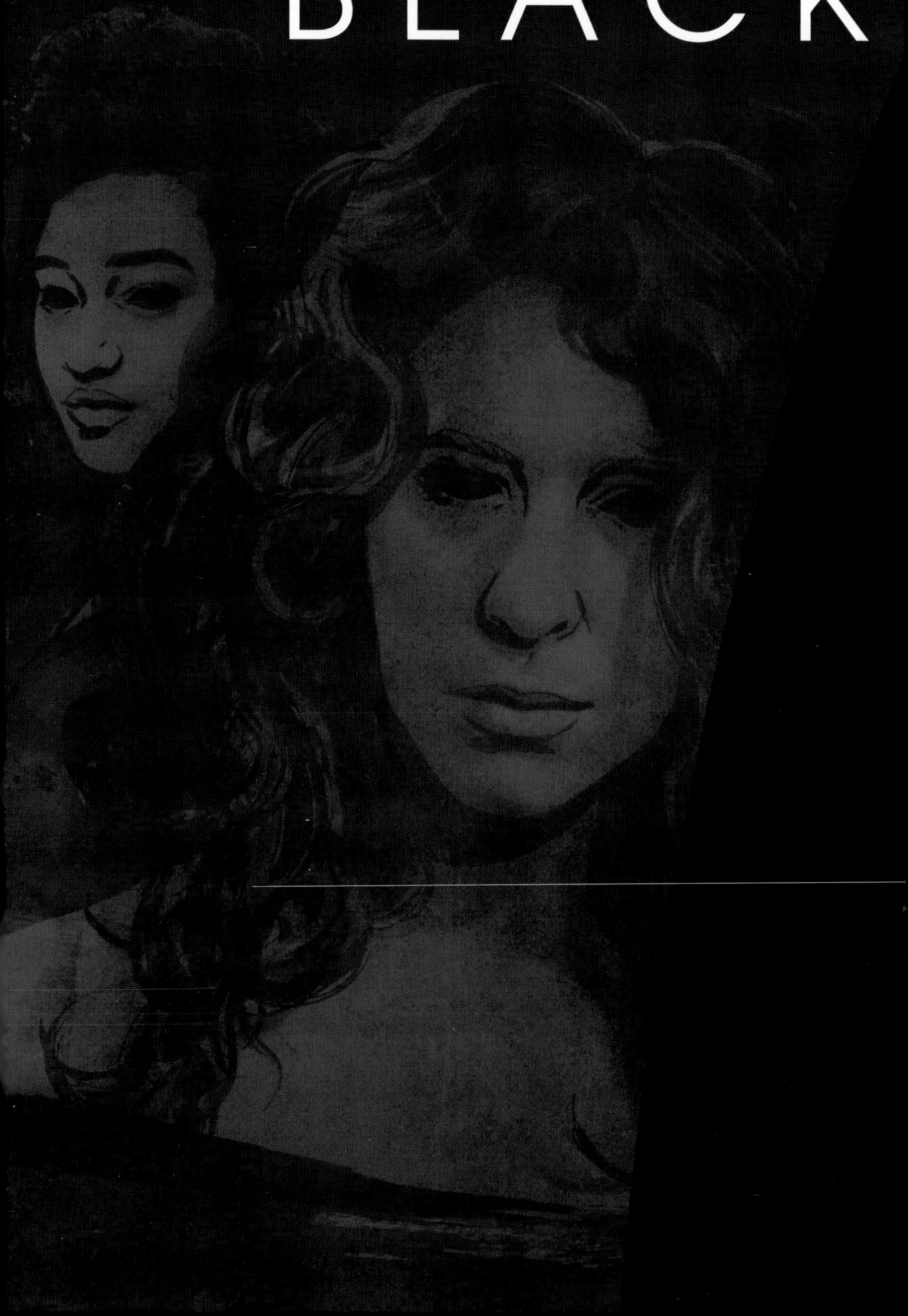

EYED KIDS
VOLUME 2
THE ADULTS

JOE PRUETT co-creator & writer

SZYMON KUDRANSKI co-creator & artist

GUY MAJOR colorist

MARSHALL DILLON letterer

FRANCESCO FRANCAVILLA front & original series covers

MICHAEL GAYDOS &
SZYMON KUDRANSKI variant covers

JOHN J. HILL book & logo designer

MIKE MARTS editor

AFTERSHOCK

MIKE MARTS - Editor-in-Chief • **JOE PRUETT** - Publisher/ Chief Creative Officer
LEE KRAMER - President • **JAWAD QURESHI** - SVP, Investor Relations • **JON KRAMER** - Chief Executive Officer
MIKE ZAGARI - SVP Digital/Creative • **JAY BEHLING** - Chief Financial Officer
STEPHAN NILSON - Publishing Operations Manager • **LISA Y. WU** - Retailer/Fan Relations Manager
ASHLEY WYATT - Publishing Assistant

AfterShock Trade Dress and Interior Design by **JOHN J. HILL** • AfterShock Logo Design by **COMICRAFT**
Original series production (issues 9-10) by **CHARLES PRITCHETT** • Proofreading by **J. HARBORE** & **DOCTOR Z.**
Publicity: contact **AARON MARION** (aaron@fifteenminutes.com) & **RYAN CROY** (ryan@fifteenminutes.com) at **15 MINUTES**

INTRODUCTION

Joe Pruett is a son-of-a-bitch! You heard me right, and here is why.

I had the pleasure to write and executive produce a TV show called *"Supernatural"*. My job was to create stories that both scared the bejesus out of people and explored the things that went "bump" in the night.

The first time I read about the *creepypasta* phenomenon known as BLACK-EYED KIDS, I knew I wanted to write a story about them. Mysterious kids with black eyes hitching and panhandling through America had all the makings of a great horror story. It was a no-brainer.

So, it took me a few weeks to craft my perfect opus. And I finally walked into my boss's office and pitched away...surprisingly, he didn't see the genius of my story, and I left empty handed. But I was not done, and I pitched BEK for the next three seasons, never landing but always hoping to.

Finally, when I left *Supernatural* and moved on to another show, I thought I'd finally write Black-Eyed Kids as a graphic novel — only to find out that Joe Pruett had beaten me to it!

Well, to say I was ready to crap all over BEK when I picked it up would be an understatement... but instead, Joe not only wrote a great horror story, it was also so much better than mine.

Grounding the story through a regular suburban family and using tension instead of jump-scares heightened both the material and the genre. Joe's deft and literary writing style never panders to its audience, but instead allows us to use our imagination — fear of the unknown is the scariest thing there is, and Joe's writing has it in spades.

Accompanied by great, creepy, weird art by Szymon Kudranski — whose linework is at one moment mysterious, then the next moment exciting with brutal action — BEK is all at once complimentary and challenging to the storyline. This series has the five elements of good horror: FEAR, SURPRISE, SUSPENSE, MYSTERY and SPOILERS. It's a great book, and because of that I will curse Joe Pruett's name for eternity! And I better never see him alone in an alley.

–ADAM GLASS

(Jealous Writer)

6

“DINE & DASH”

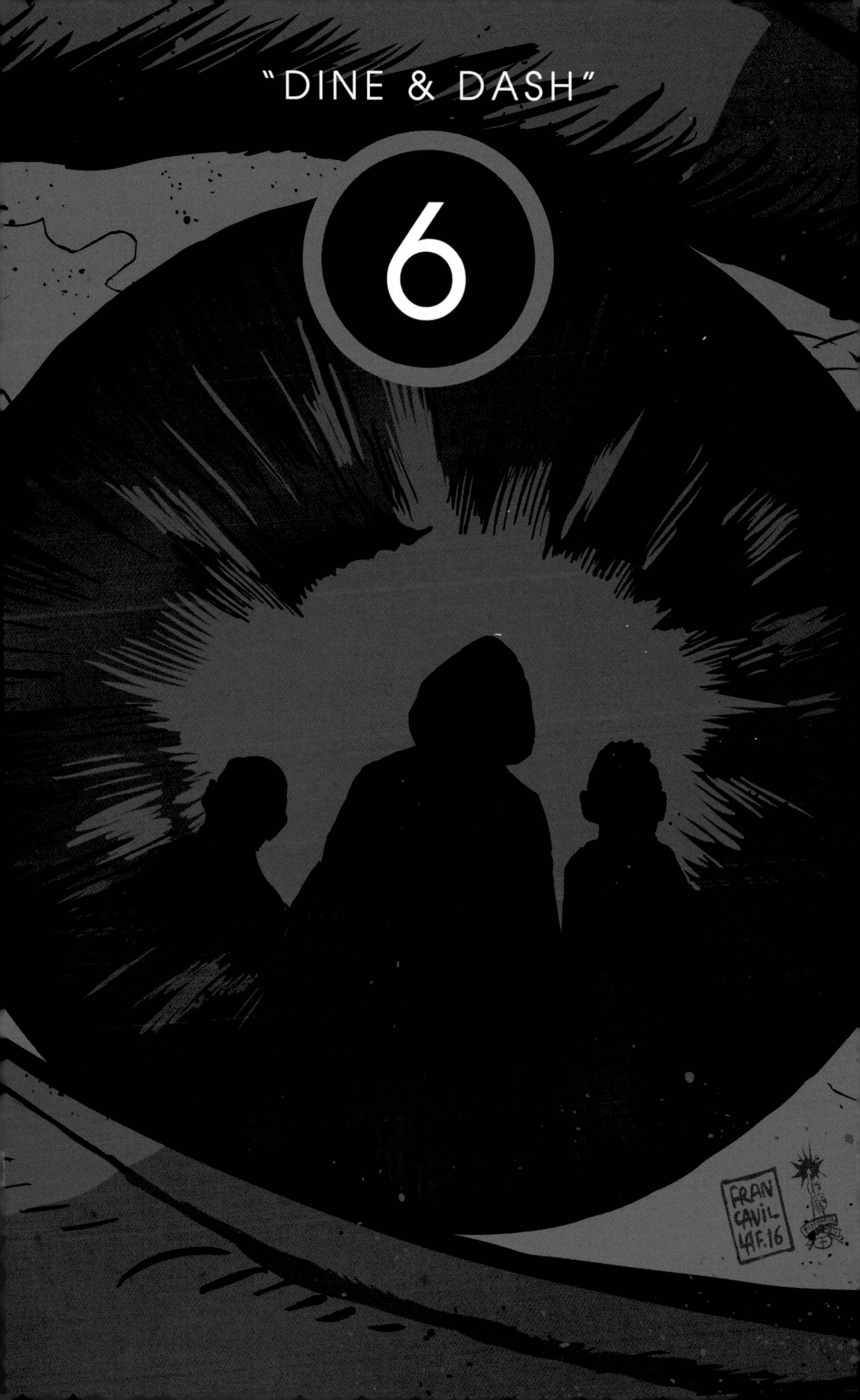

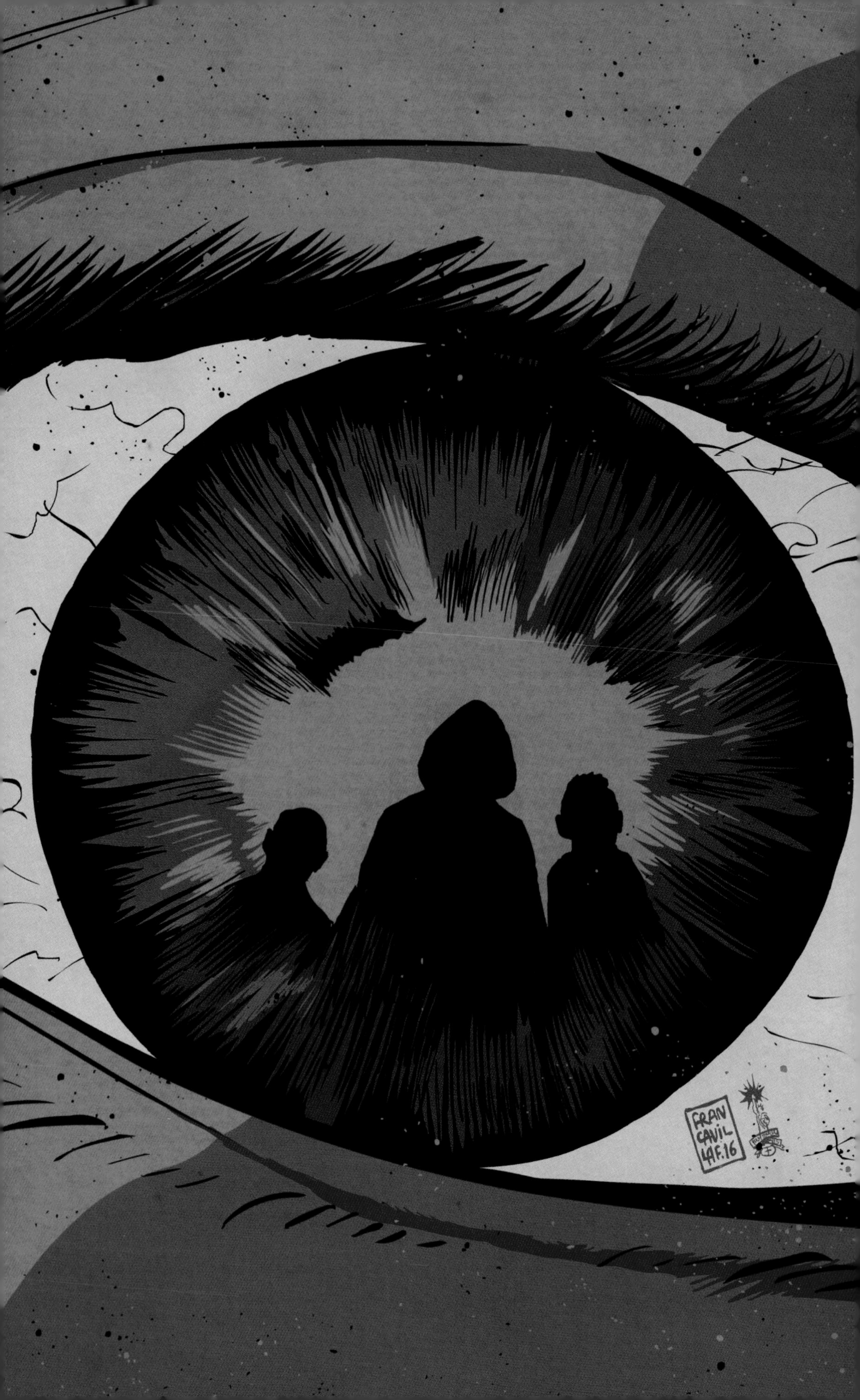

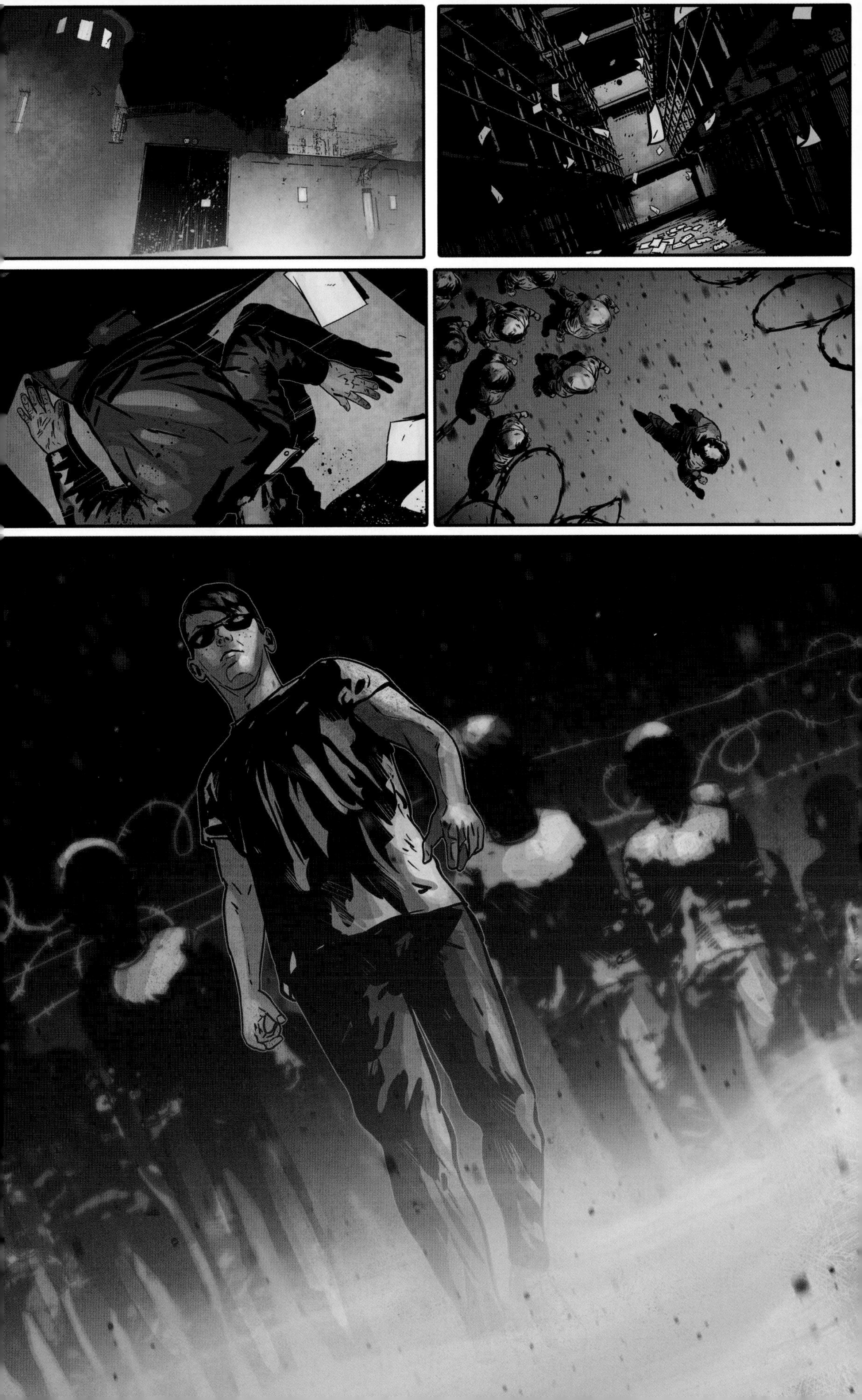

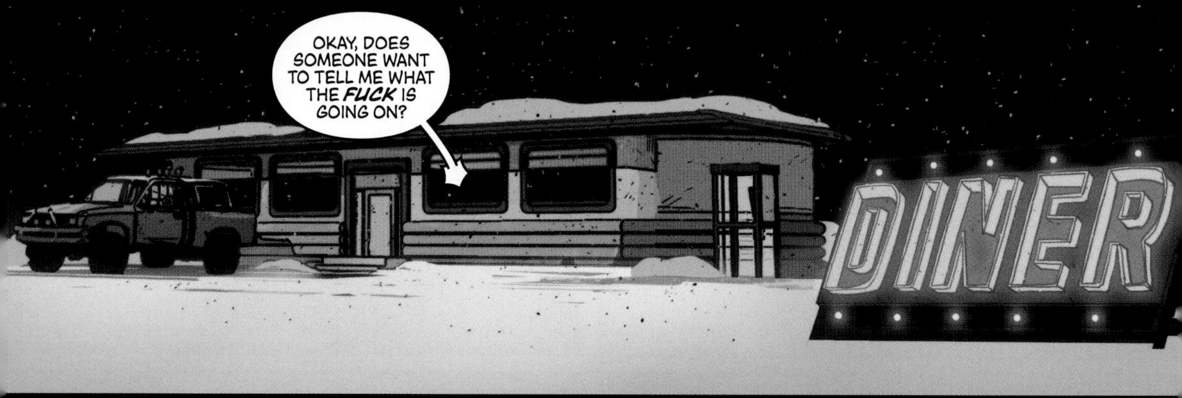
OKAY, DOES SOMEONE WANT TO TELL ME WHAT THE FUCK IS GOING ON?
DINER

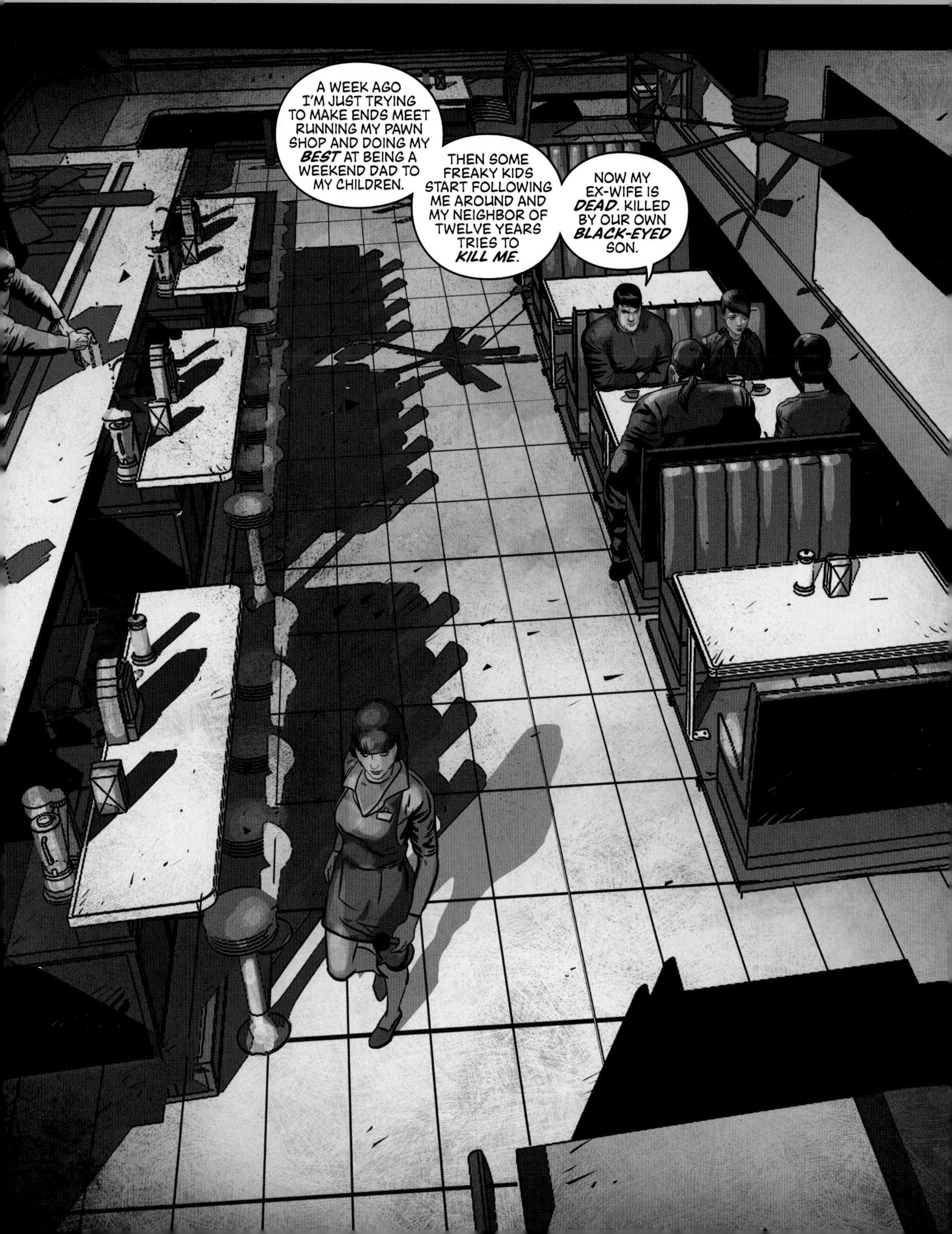
A WEEK AGO I'M JUST TRYING TO MAKE ENDS MEET RUNNING MY PAWN SHOP AND DOING MY BEST AT BEING A WEEKEND DAD TO MY CHILDREN.
THEN SOME FREAKY KIDS START FOLLOWING ME AROUND AND MY NEIGHBOR OF TWELVE YEARS TRIES TO KILL ME.
NOW MY EX-WIFE IS DEAD. KILLED BY OUR OWN BLACK-EYED SON.

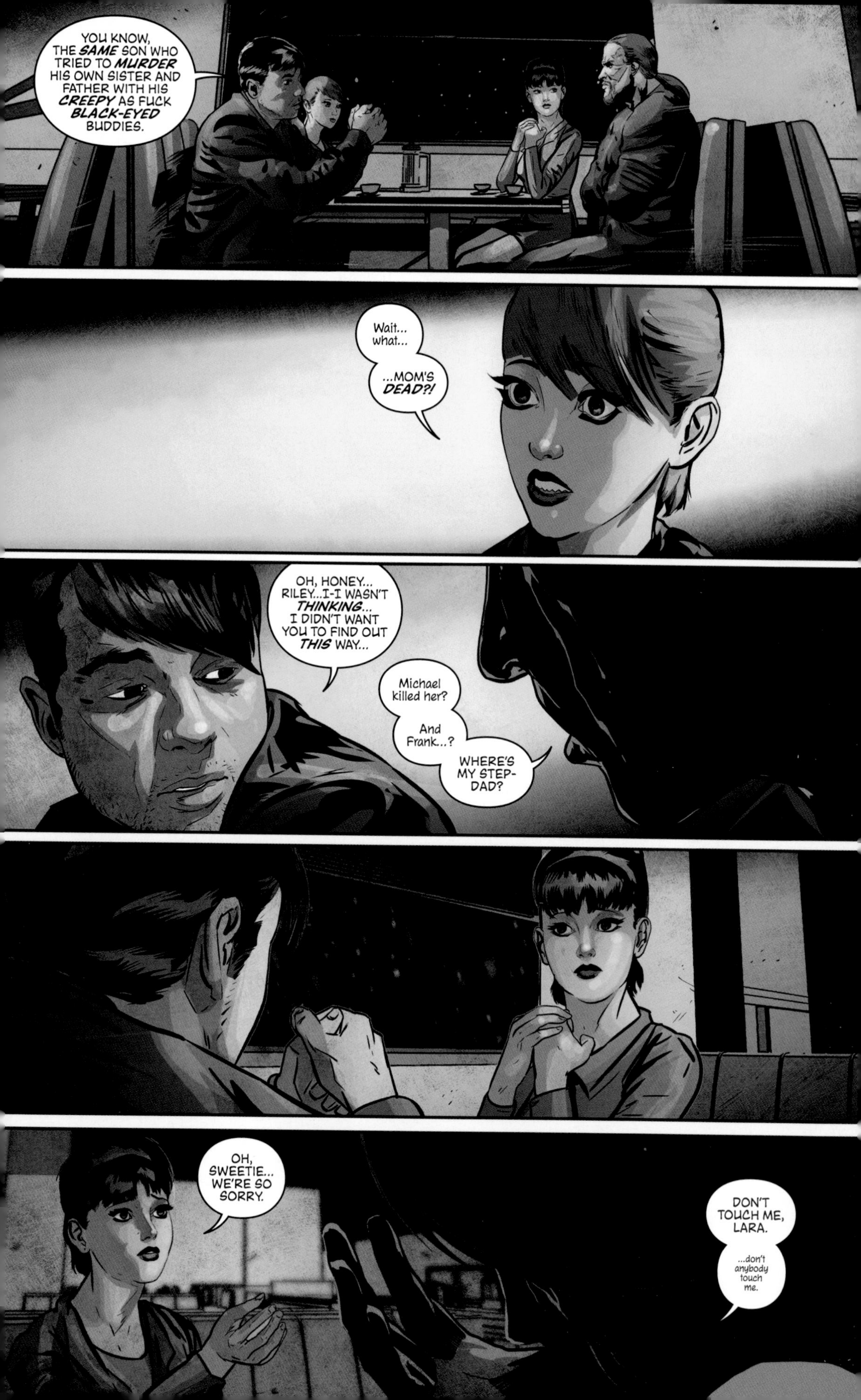
YOU KNOW, THE SAME SON WHO TRIED TO MURDER HIS OWN SISTER AND FATHER WITH HIS CREEPY AS FUCK BLACK-EYED BUDDIES.
Wait... what...
...MOM'S DEAD?!
OH, HONEY... RILEY...I-I WASN'T THINKING... I DIDN'T WANT YOU TO FIND OUT THIS WAY...
Michael killed her?
And Frank...?
WHERE'S MY STEP-DAD?
OH, SWEETIE... WE'RE SO SORRY.
DON'T TOUCH ME, LARA.
...don't anybody touch me.

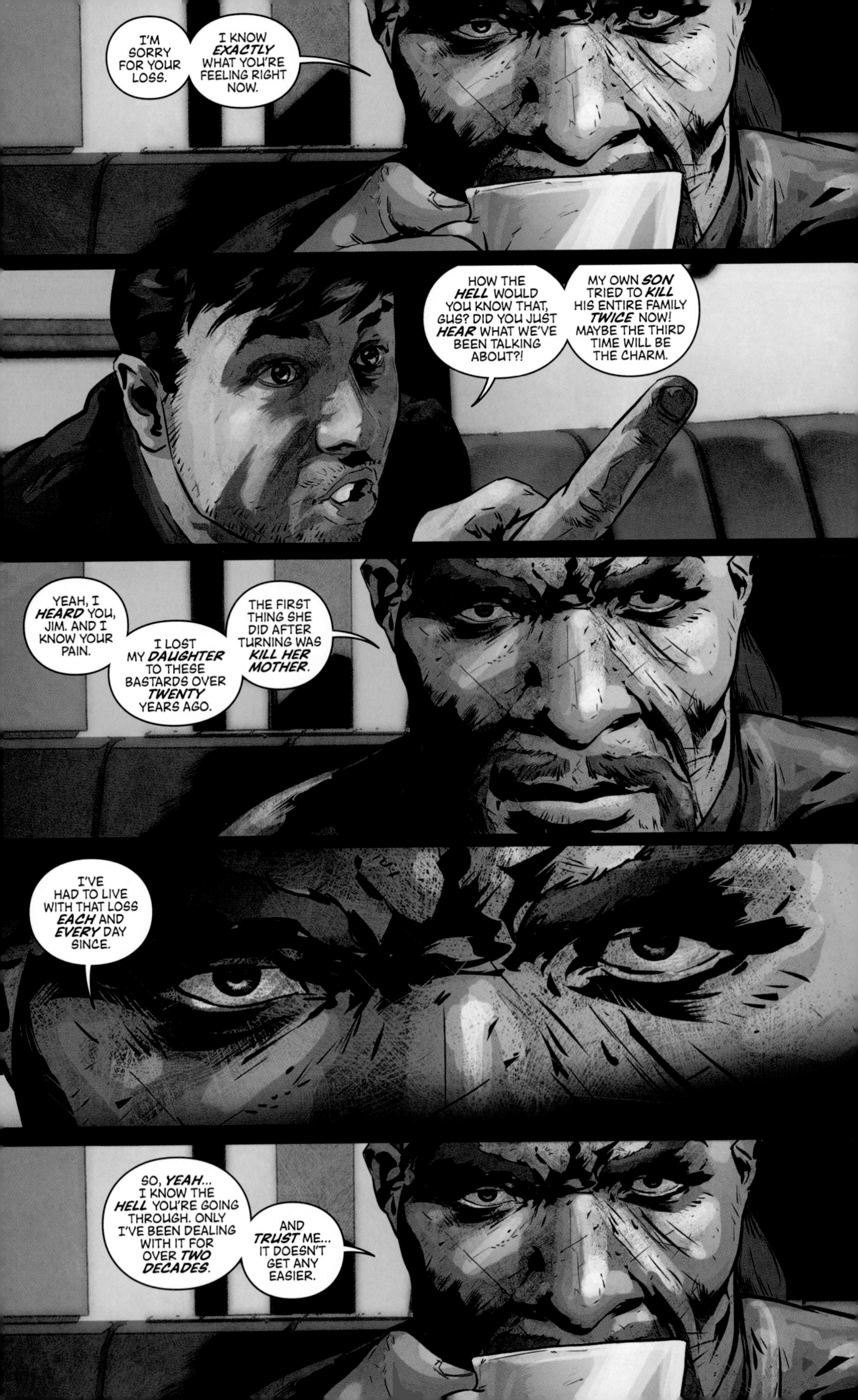
I'M SORRY FOR YOUR LOSS.
I KNOW EXACTLY WHAT YOU'RE FEELING RIGHT NOW.
HOW THE HELL WOULD YOU KNOW THAT, GUS? DID YOU JUST HEAR WHAT WE'VE BEEN TALKING ABOUT?!
MY OWN SON TRIED TO KILL HIS ENTIRE FAMILY TWICE NOW! MAYBE THE THIRD TIME WILL BE THE CHARM.
YEAH, I HEARD YOU, JIM. AND I KNOW YOUR PAIN.
I LOST MY DAUGHTER TO THESE BASTARDS OVER TWENTY YEARS AGO.
THE FIRST THING SHE DID AFTER TURNING WAS KILL HER MOTHER.
I'VE HAD TO LIVE WITH THAT LOSS EACH AND EVERY DAY SINCE.
SO, YEAH... I KNOW THE HELL YOU'RE GOING THROUGH. ONLY I'VE BEEN DEALING WITH IT FOR OVER TWO DECADES.
AND TRUST ME... IT DOESN'T GET ANY EASIER.

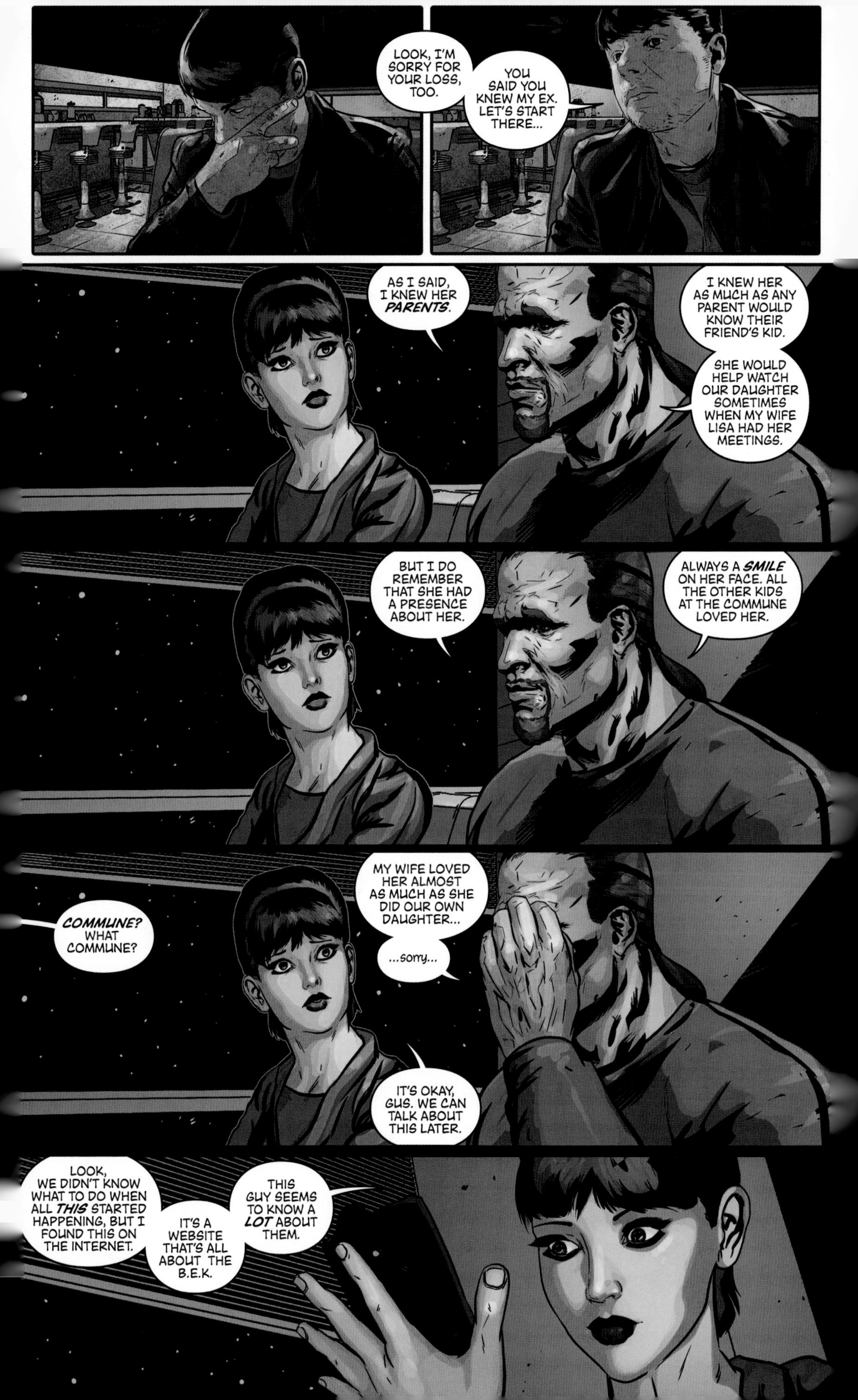

LOOK, I'M SORRY FOR YOUR LOSS, TOO.
YOU SAID YOU KNEW MY EX. LET'S START THERE...
AS I SAID, I KNEW HER *PARENTS*.
I KNEW HER AS MUCH AS ANY PARENT WOULD KNOW THEIR FRIEND'S KID.
SHE WOULD HELP WATCH OUR DAUGHTER SOMETIMES WHEN MY WIFE LISA HAD HER MEETINGS.
BUT I DO REMEMBER THAT SHE HAD A PRESENCE ABOUT HER.
ALWAYS A *SMILE* ON HER FACE. ALL THE OTHER KIDS AT THE COMMUNE LOVED HER.
MY WIFE LOVED HER ALMOST AS MUCH AS SHE DID OUR OWN DAUGHTER...
...sorry...
COMMUNE? WHAT COMMUNE?
IT'S OKAY, GUS. WE CAN TALK ABOUT THIS LATER.
LOOK, WE DIDN'T KNOW WHAT TO DO WHEN ALL *THIS* STARTED HAPPENING, BUT I FOUND THIS ON THE INTERNET.
IT'S A WEBSITE THAT'S ALL ABOUT THE B.E.K.
THIS GUY SEEMS TO KNOW A *LOT* ABOUT THEM.

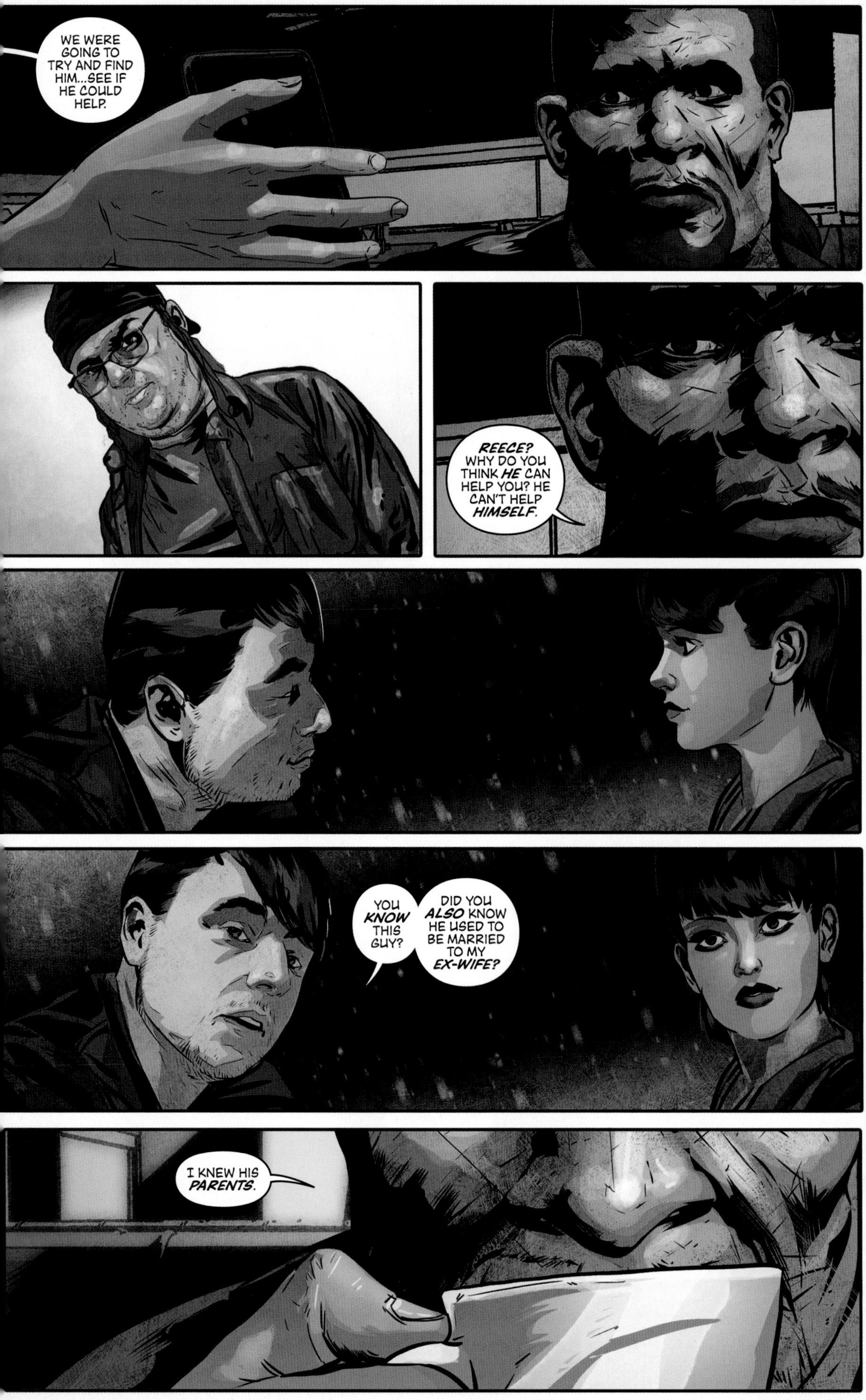
WE WERE GOING TO TRY AND FIND HIM...SEE IF HE COULD HELP.
REECE? WHY DO YOU THINK HE CAN HELP YOU? HE CAN'T HELP HIMSELF.
YOU KNOW THIS GUY?
DID YOU ALSO KNOW HE USED TO BE MARRIED TO MY EX-WIFE?
I KNEW HIS PARENTS.

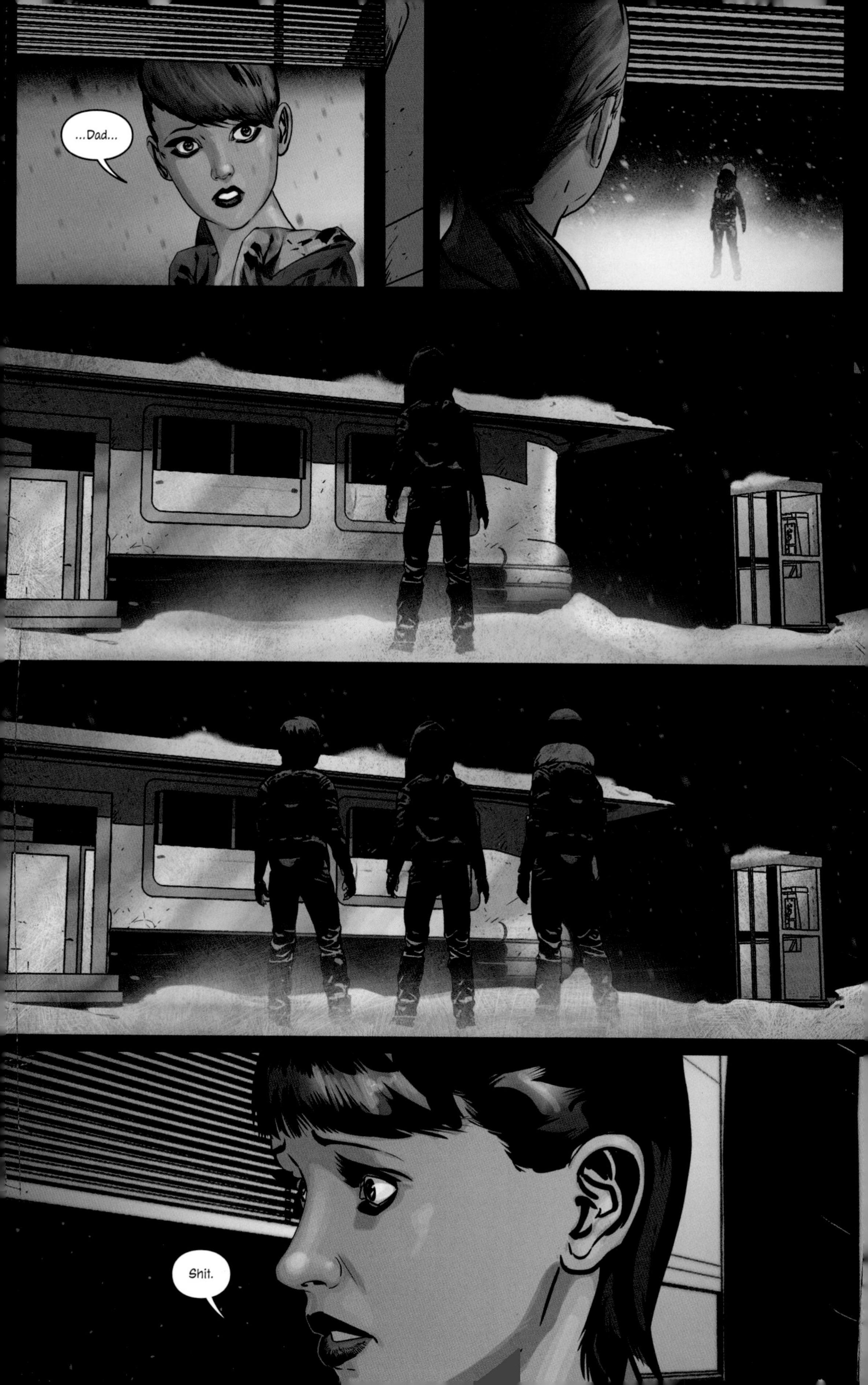
...Dad...
Shit.

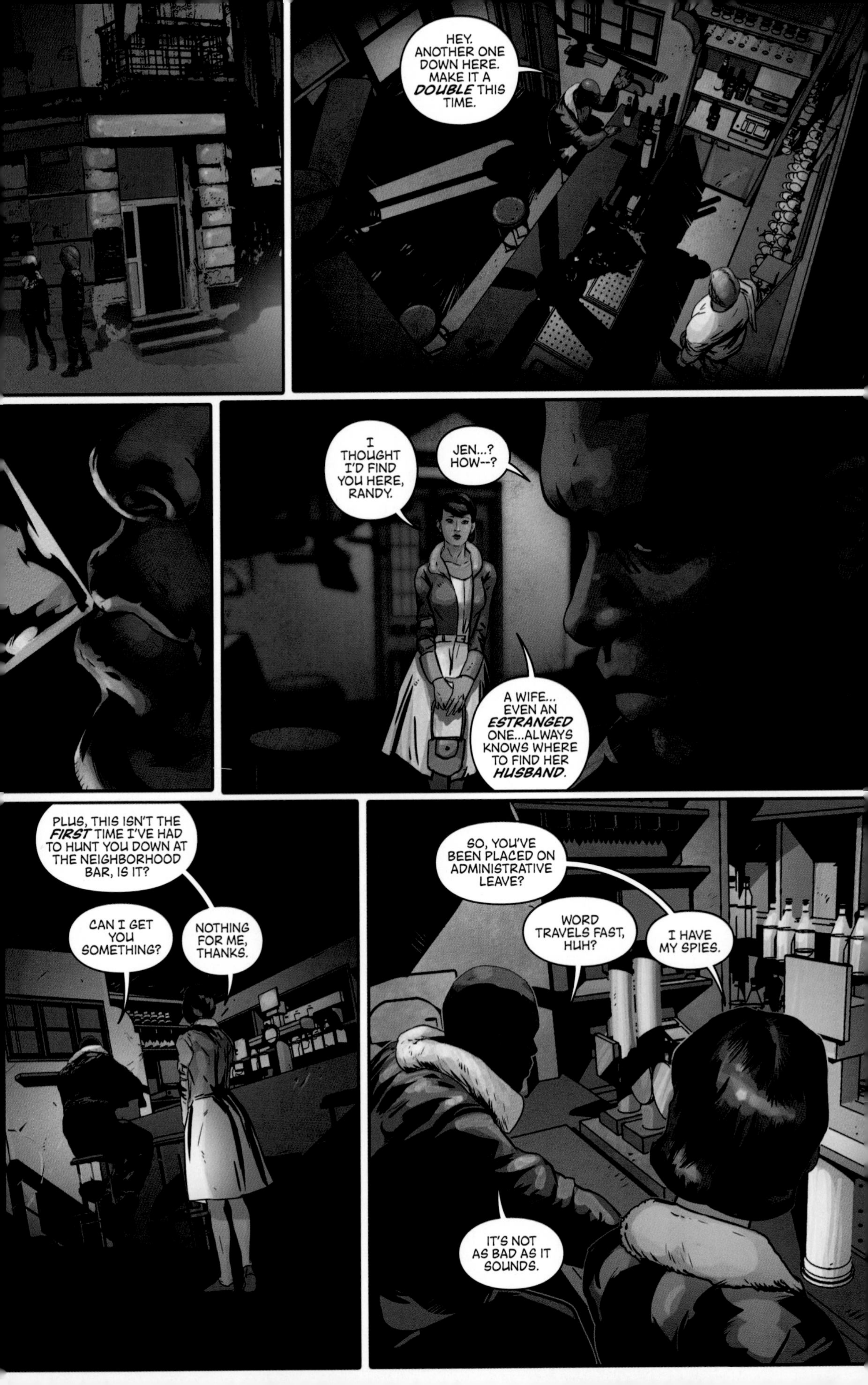
HEY. ANOTHER ONE DOWN HERE. MAKE IT A DOUBLE THIS TIME.
I THOUGHT I'D FIND YOU HERE, RANDY.
JEN...? HOW--?
A WIFE... EVEN AN ESTRANGED ONE...ALWAYS KNOWS WHERE TO FIND HER HUSBAND.
PLUS, THIS ISN'T THE FIRST TIME I'VE HAD TO HUNT YOU DOWN AT THE NEIGHBORHOOD BAR, IS IT?
CAN I GET YOU SOMETHING?
NOTHING FOR ME, THANKS.
SO, YOU'VE BEEN PLACED ON ADMINISTRATIVE LEAVE?
WORD TRAVELS FAST, HUH?
I HAVE MY SPIES.
IT'S NOT AS BAD AS IT SOUNDS.

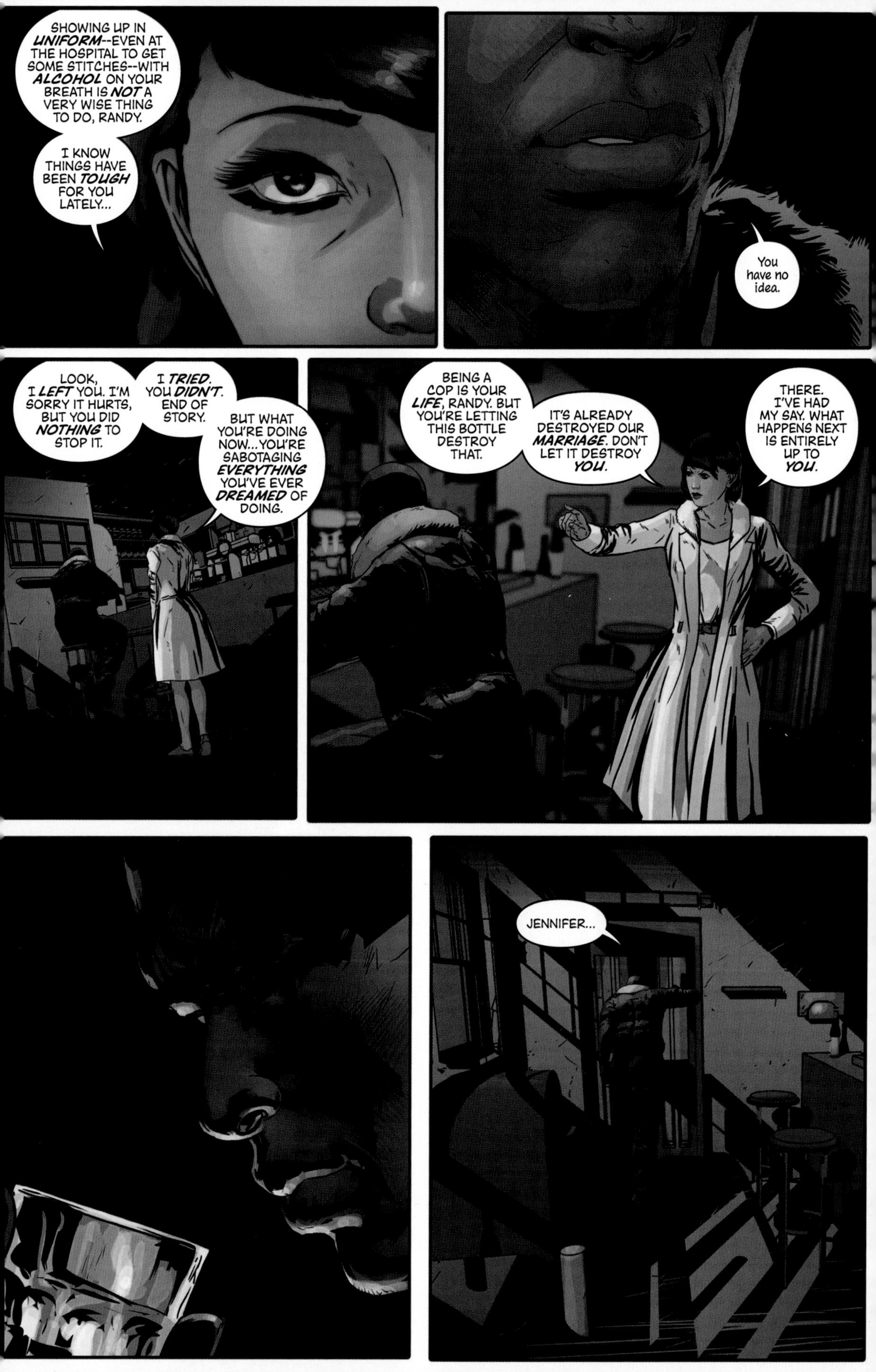
SHOWING UP IN UNIFORM--EVEN AT THE HOSPITAL TO GET SOME STITCHES--WITH ALCOHOL ON YOUR BREATH IS NOT A VERY WISE THING TO DO, RANDY.
I KNOW THINGS HAVE BEEN TOUGH FOR YOU LATELY...
You have no idea.
LOOK, I LEFT YOU. I'M SORRY IT HURTS, BUT YOU DID NOTHING TO STOP IT.
I TRIED. YOU DIDN'T. END OF STORY.
BUT WHAT YOU'RE DOING NOW...YOU'RE SABOTAGING EVERYTHING YOU'VE EVER DREAMED OF DOING.
BEING A COP IS YOUR LIFE, RANDY. BUT YOU'RE LETTING THIS BOTTLE DESTROY THAT.
IT'S ALREADY DESTROYED OUR MARRIAGE. DON'T LET IT DESTROY YOU.
THERE. I'VE HAD MY SAY. WHAT HAPPENS NEXT IS ENTIRELY UP TO YOU.
JENNIFER...

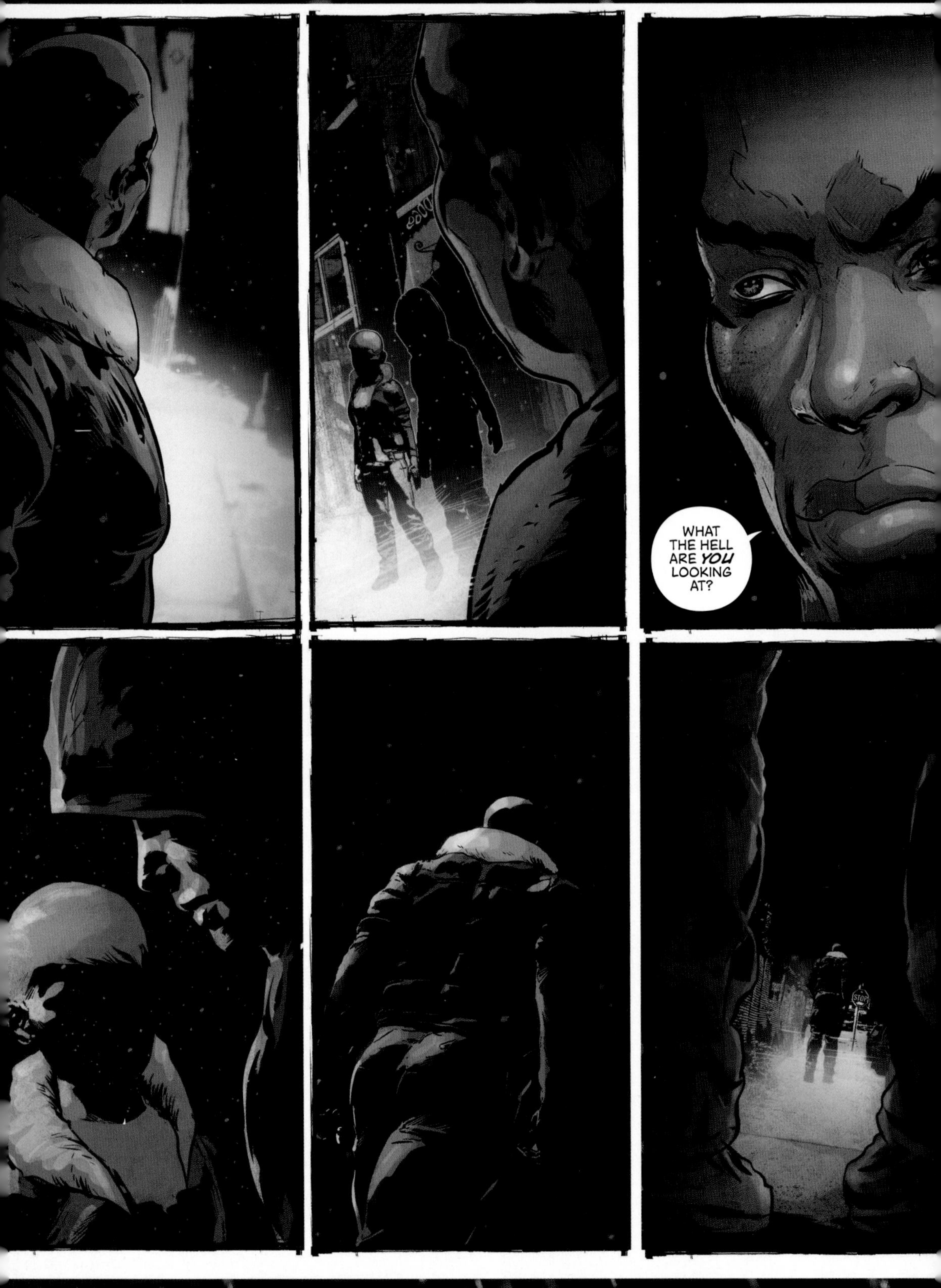
WHAT THE HELL ARE YOU LOOKING AT?

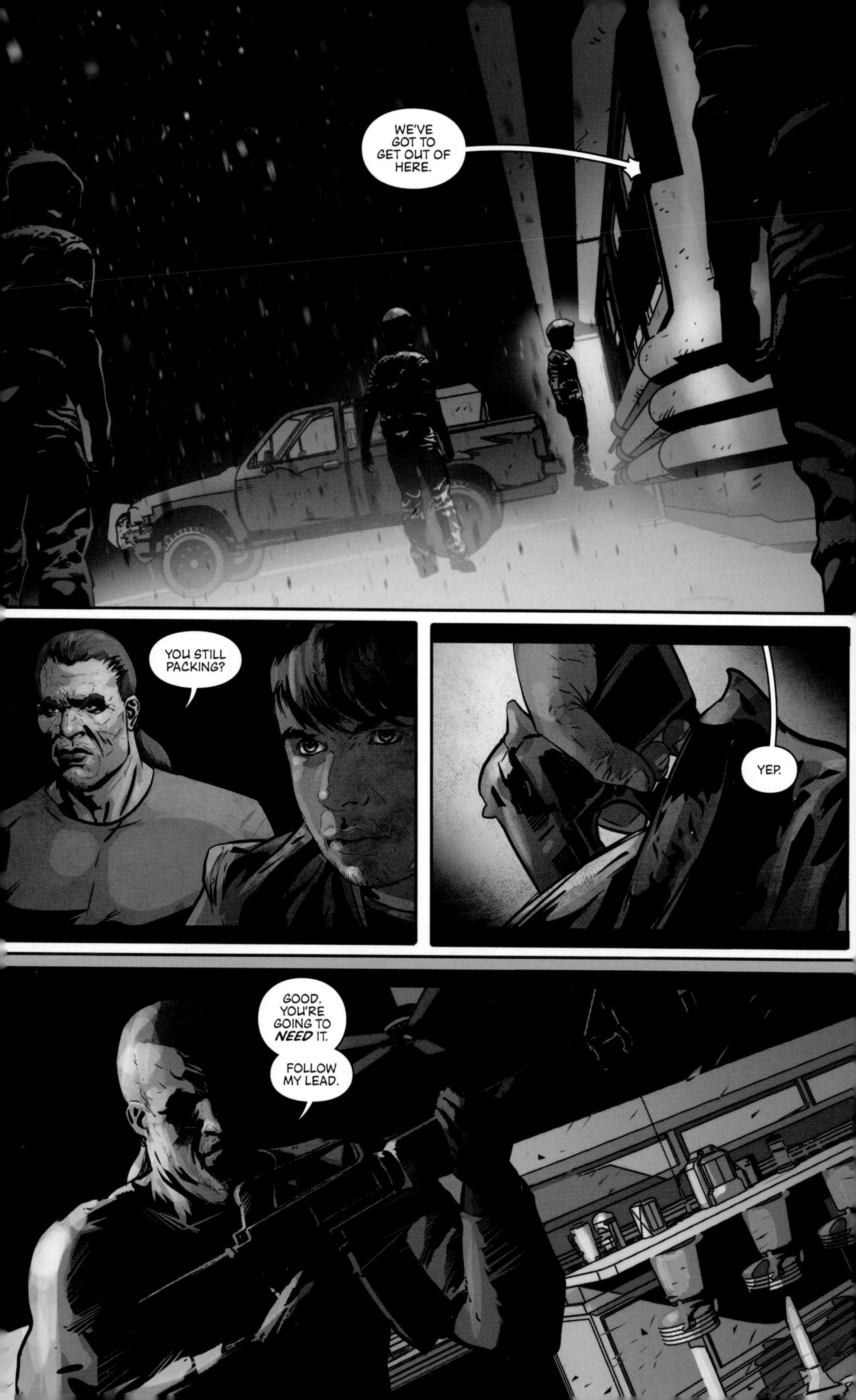
WE'VE GOT TO GET OUT OF HERE.
YOU STILL PACKING?
YEP.
GOOD. YOU'RE GOING TO *NEED* IT.
FOLLOW MY LEAD.

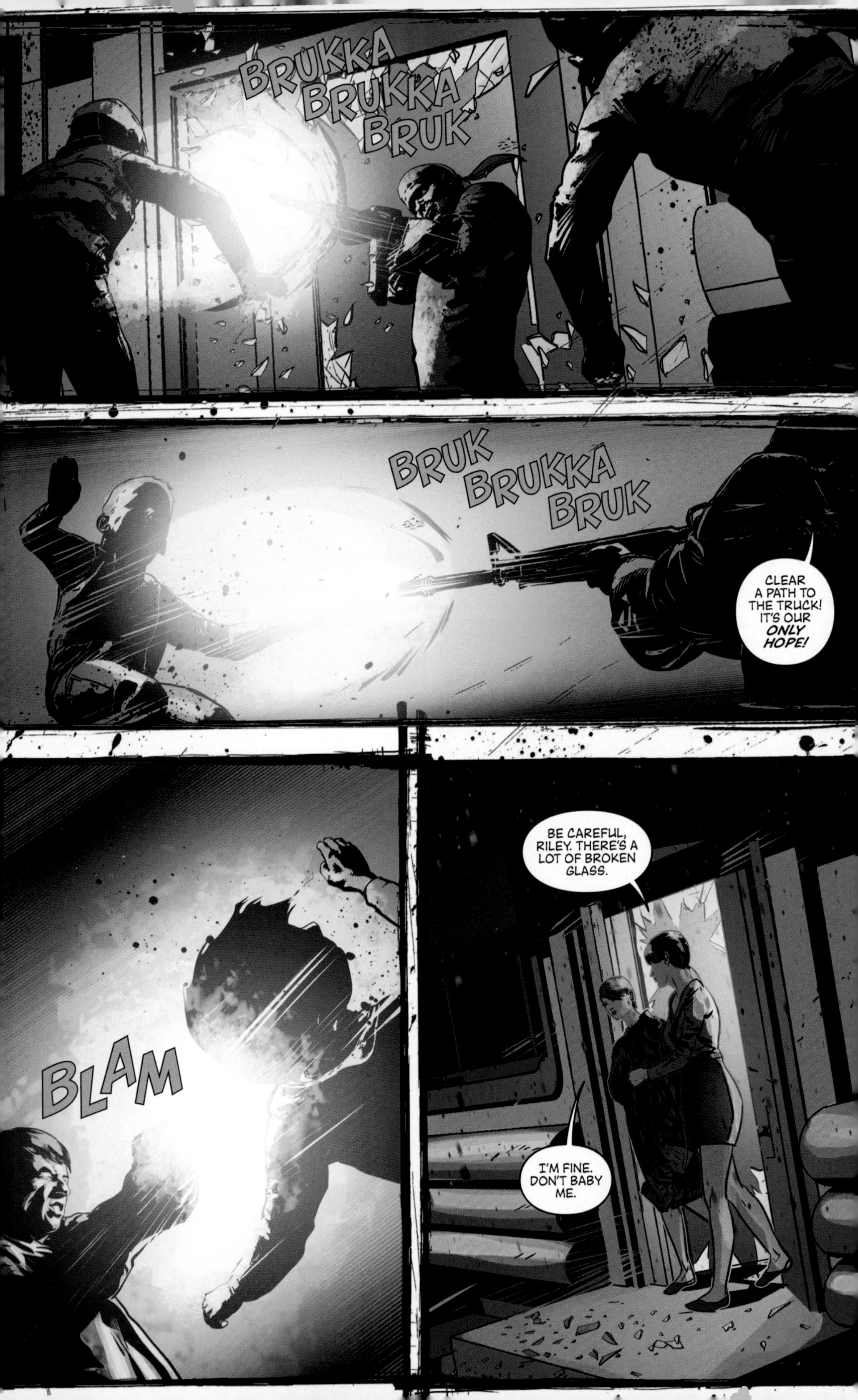
BRUKKA
BRUKKA
BRUK
BRUK
BRUKKA
BRUK
CLEAR A PATH TO THE TRUCK! IT'S OUR *ONLY HOPE!*
BLAM
BE CAREFUL, RILEY. THERE'S A LOT OF BROKEN GLASS.
I'M FINE. DON'T BABY ME.

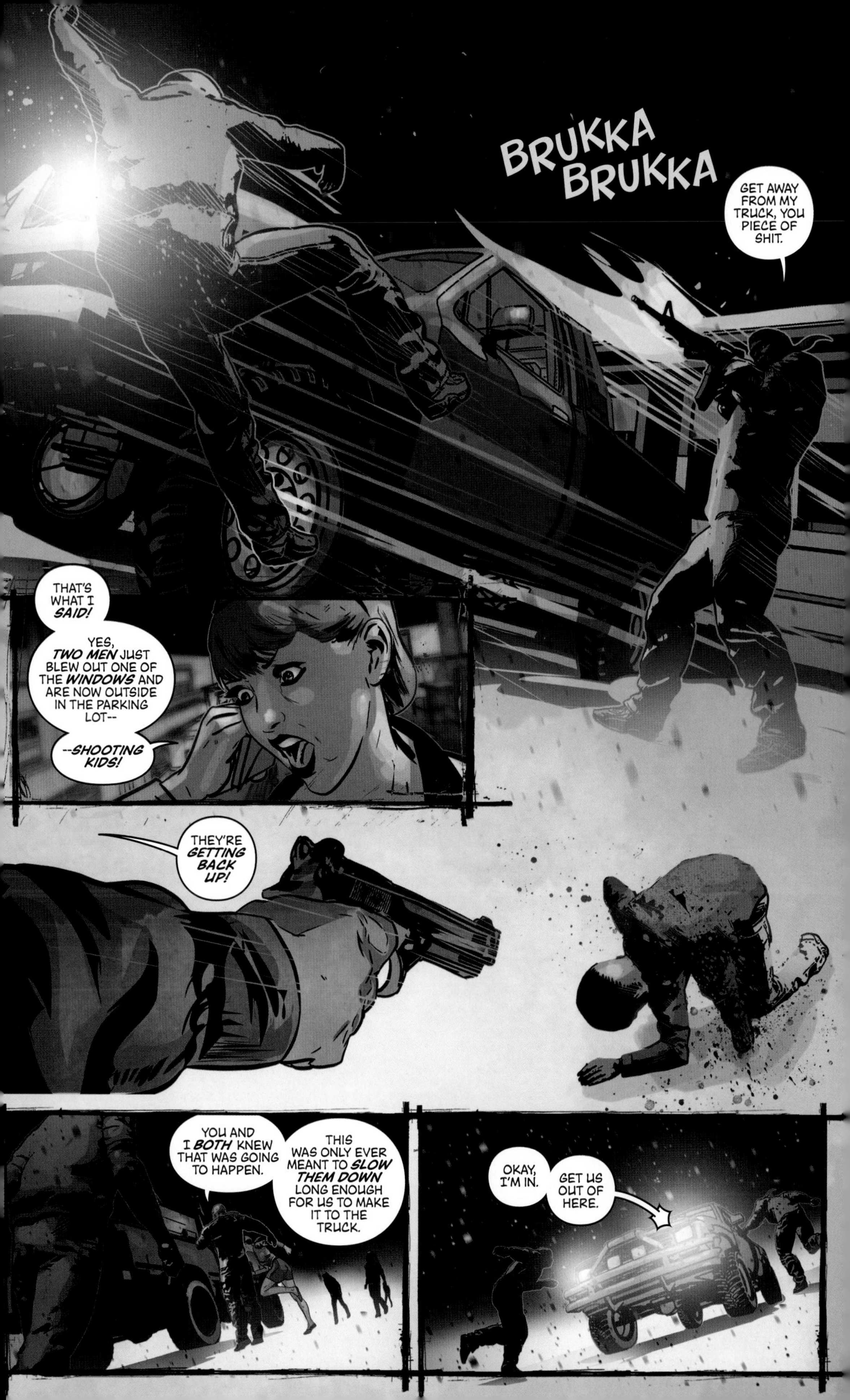
BRUKKA BRUKKA
GET AWAY FROM MY TRUCK, YOU PIECE OF SHIT.
THAT'S WHAT I *SAID!*
YES, ***TWO MEN*** JUST BLEW OUT ONE OF THE ***WINDOWS*** AND ARE NOW OUTSIDE IN THE PARKING LOT--
--***SHOOTING KIDS!***
THEY'RE ***GETTING BACK UP!***
YOU AND I ***BOTH*** KNEW THAT WAS GOING TO HAPPEN.
THIS WAS ONLY EVER MEANT TO ***SLOW THEM DOWN*** LONG ENOUGH FOR US TO MAKE IT TO THE TRUCK.
OKAY, I'M IN.
GET US OUT OF HERE.

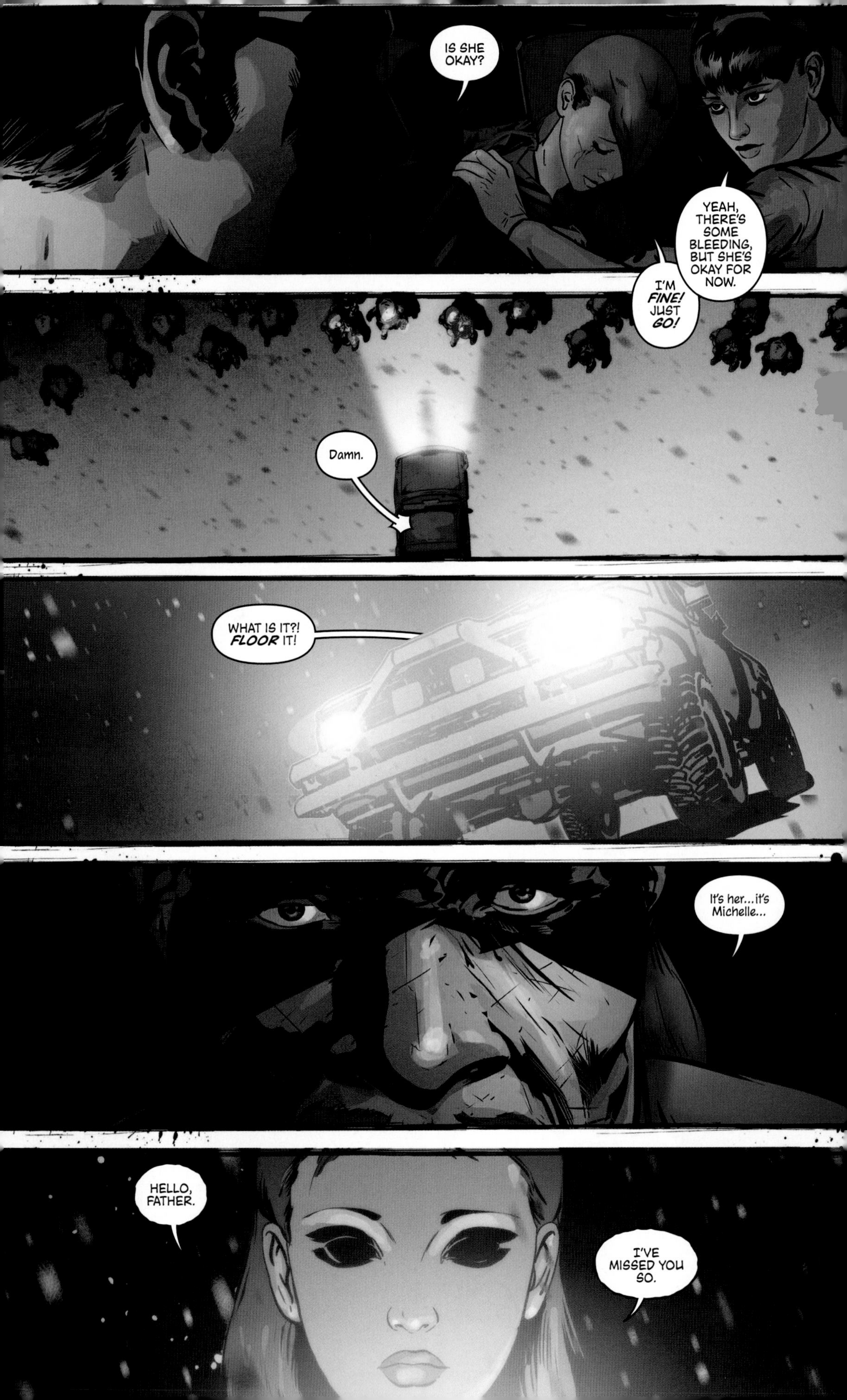
IS SHE OKAY?
YEAH, THERE'S SOME BLEEDING, BUT SHE'S OKAY FOR NOW.
I'M FINE! JUST GO!
Damn.
WHAT IS IT?! FLOOR IT!
It's her...it's Michelle...
HELLO, FATHER.
I'VE MISSED YOU SO.

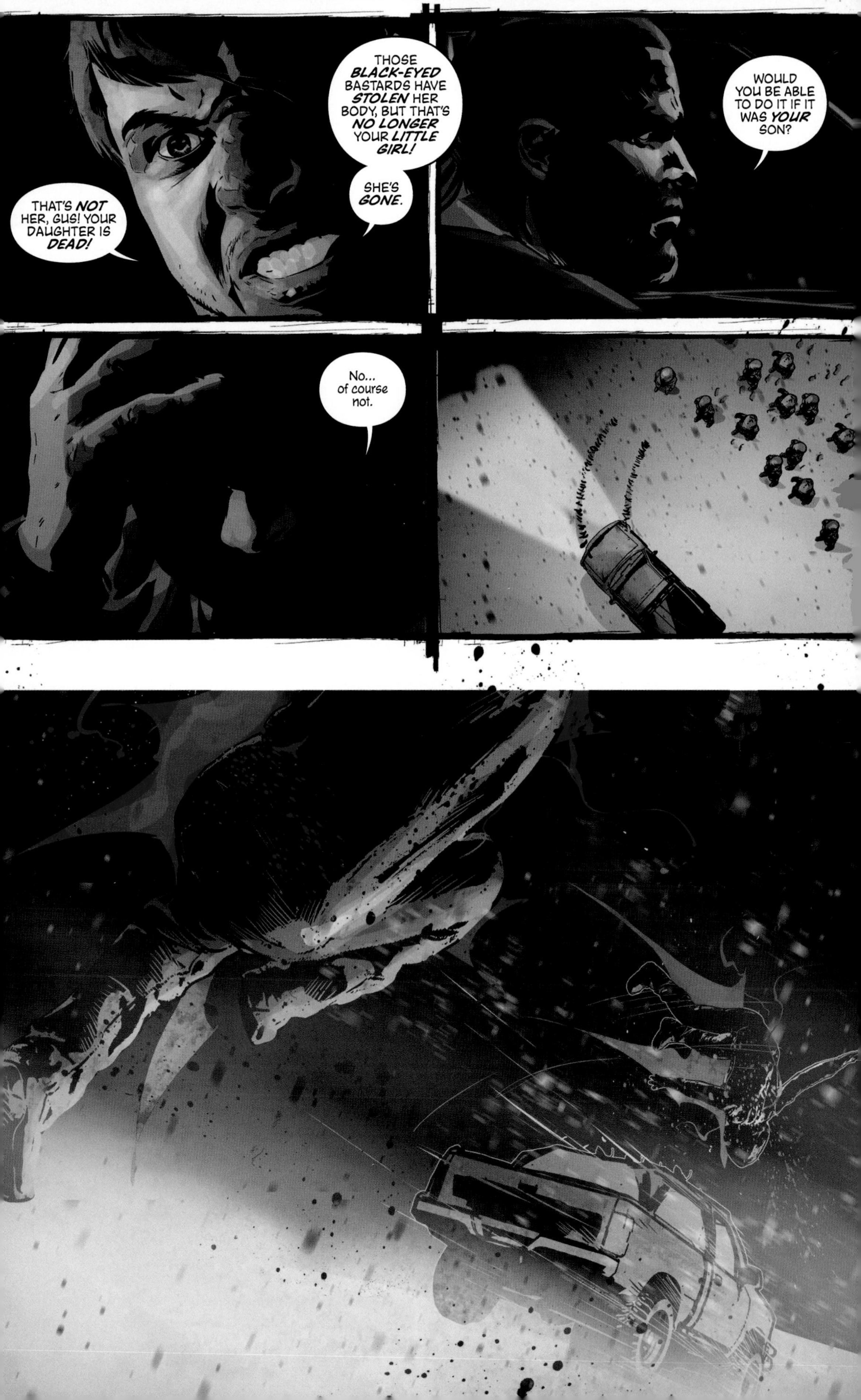
THAT'S NOT HER, GUS! YOUR DAUGHTER IS DEAD!
THOSE BLACK-EYED BASTARDS HAVE STOLEN HER BODY, BUT THAT'S NO LONGER YOUR LITTLE GIRL!
SHE'S GONE.
WOULD YOU BE ABLE TO DO IT IF IT WAS YOUR SON?
No... of course not.

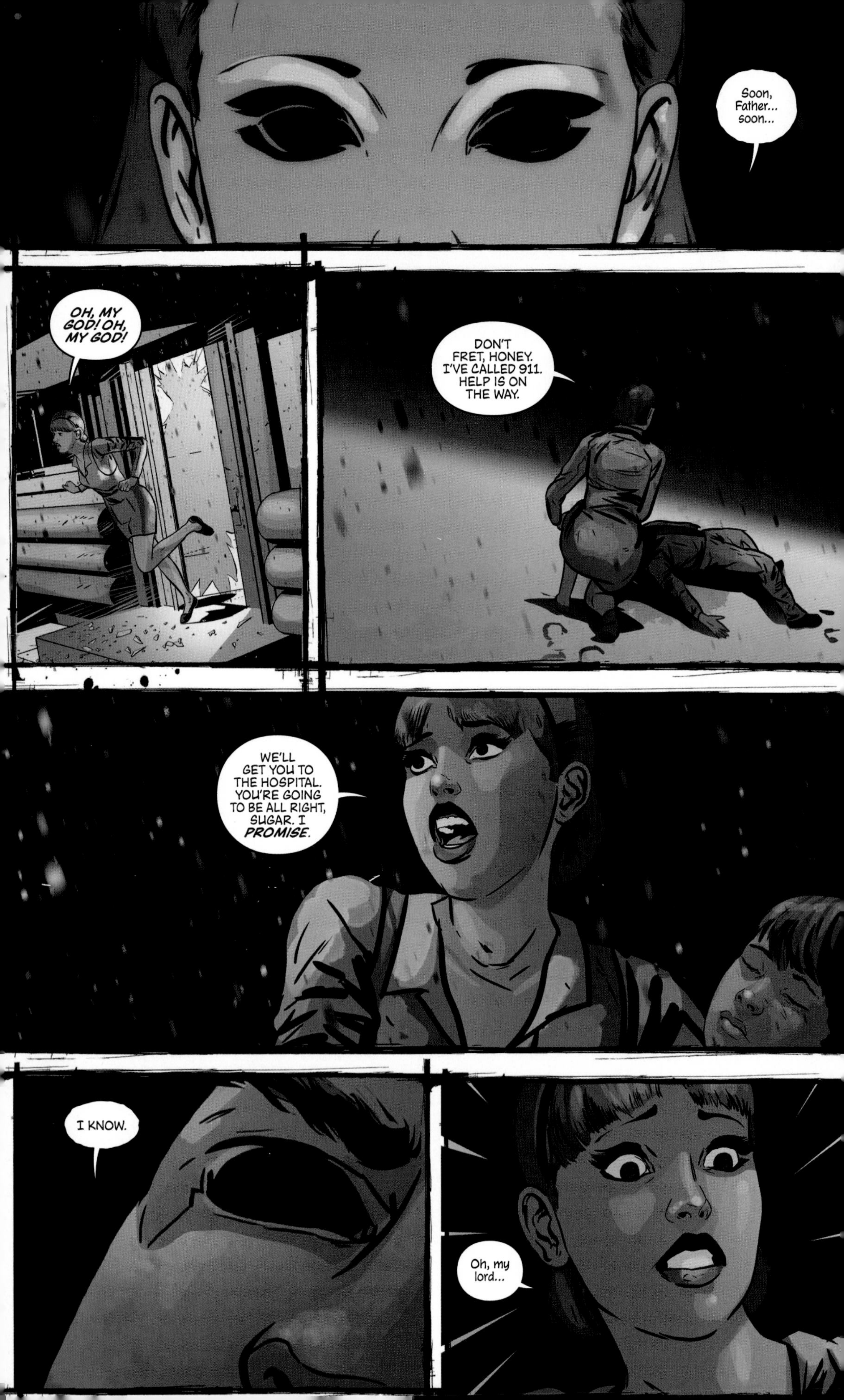
Soon, Father... soon...
OH, MY GOD! OH, MY GOD!
DON'T FRET, HONEY. I'VE CALLED 911. HELP IS ON THE WAY.
WE'LL GET YOU TO THE HOSPITAL. YOU'RE GOING TO BE ALL RIGHT, SUGAR. I PROMISE.
I KNOW.
Oh, my lord...

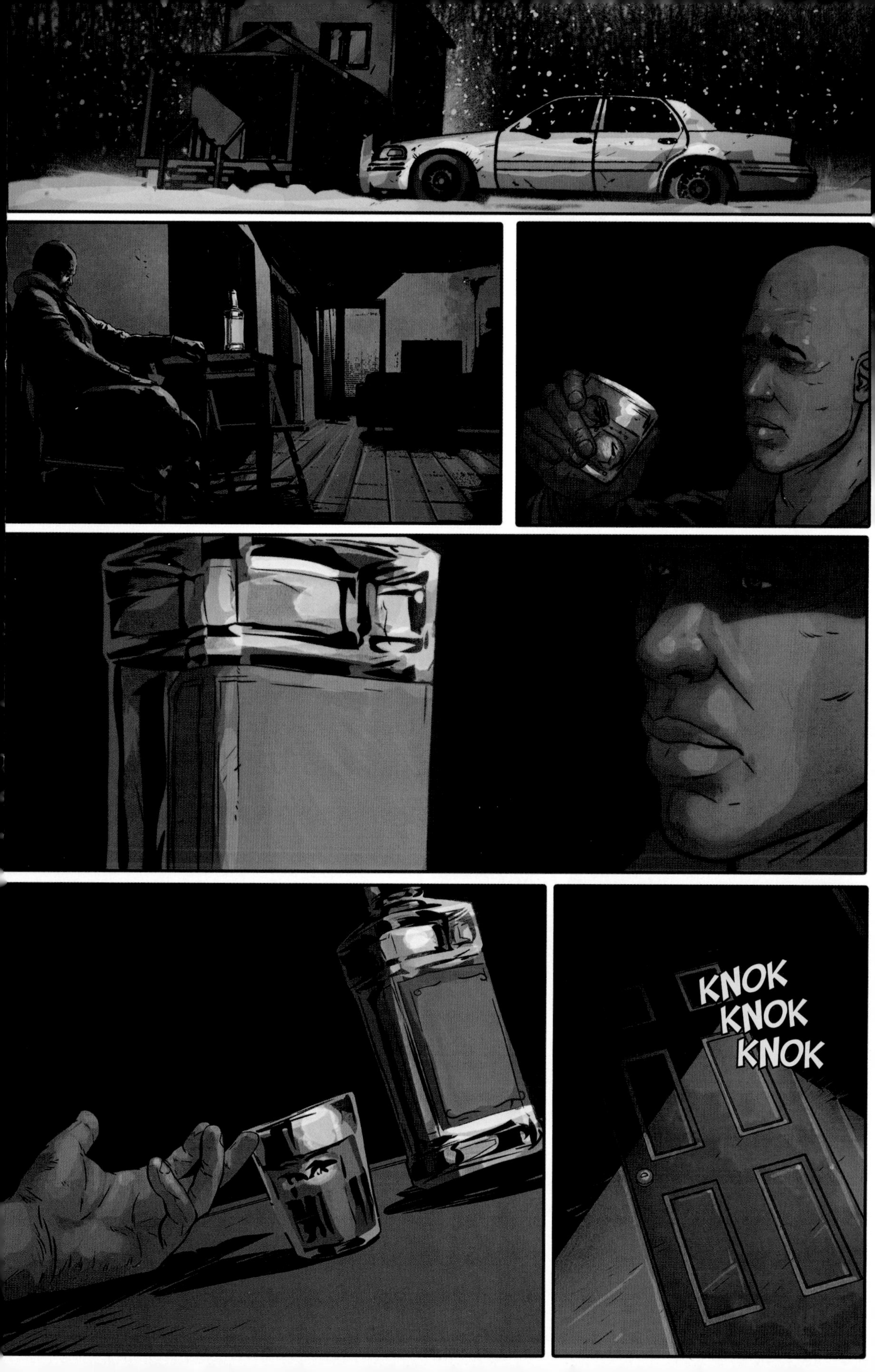
KNOK
KNOK
KNOK

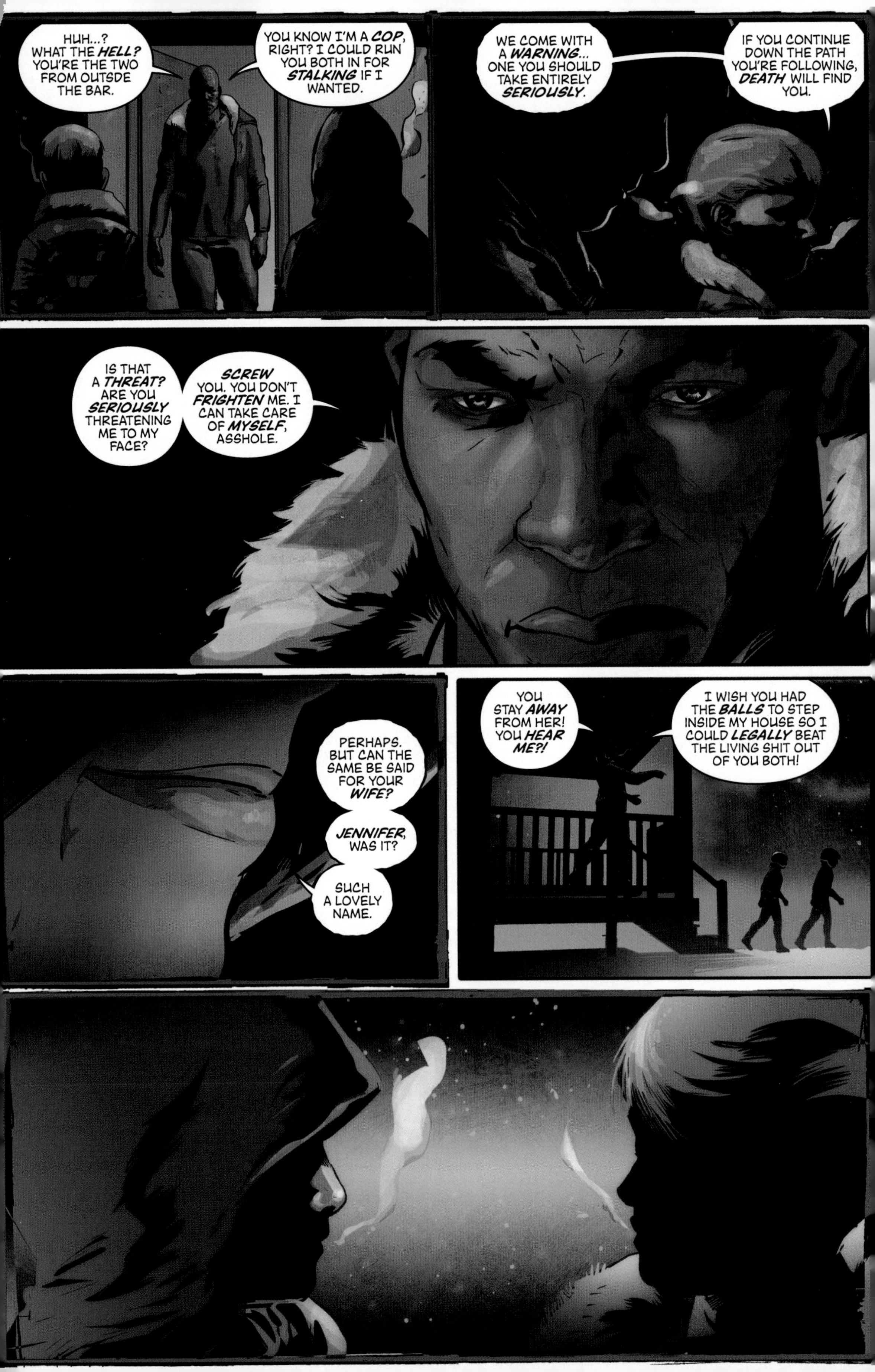
HUH...? WHAT THE HELL? YOU'RE THE TWO FROM OUTSDE THE BAR.
YOU KNOW I'M A COP, RIGHT? I COULD RUN YOU BOTH IN FOR STALKING IF I WANTED.
WE COME WITH A WARNING... ONE YOU SHOULD TAKE ENTIRELY SERIOUSLY.
IF YOU CONTINUE DOWN THE PATH YOU'RE FOLLOWING, DEATH WILL FIND YOU.
IS THAT A THREAT? ARE YOU SERIOUSLY THREATENING ME TO MY FACE?
SCREW YOU. YOU DON'T FRIGHTEN ME. I CAN TAKE CARE OF MYSELF, ASSHOLE.
PERHAPS. BUT CAN THE SAME BE SAID FOR YOUR WIFE?
JENNIFER, WAS IT?
SUCH A LOVELY NAME.
YOU STAY AWAY FROM HER! YOU HEAR ME?!
I WISH YOU HAD THE BALLS TO STEP INSIDE MY HOUSE SO I COULD LEGALLY BEAT THE LIVING SHIT OUT OF YOU BOTH!

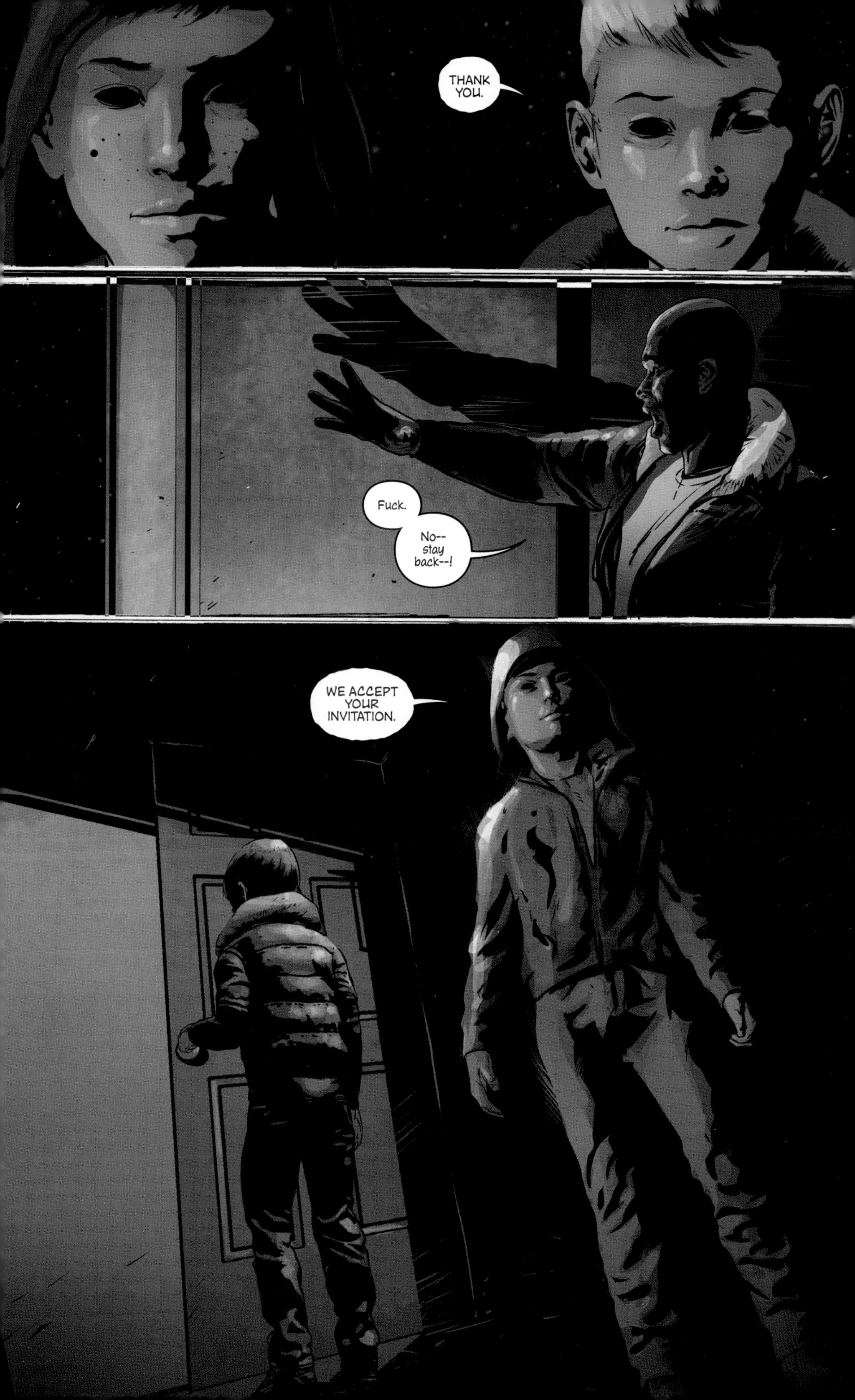
THANK YOU.
Fuck.
No-- stay back--!
WE ACCEPT YOUR INVITATION.

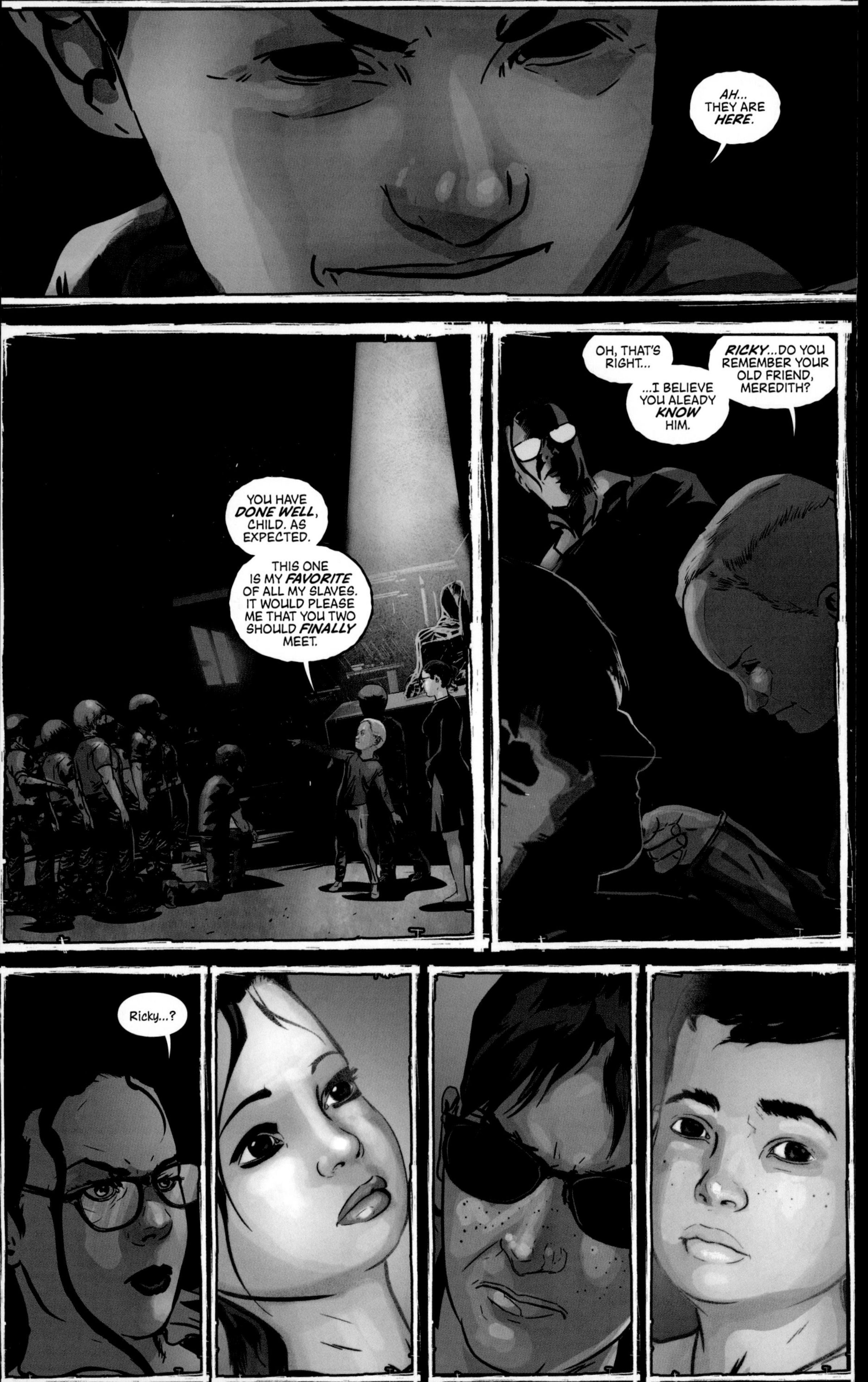
AH... THEY ARE HERE.
YOU HAVE DONE WELL, CHILD. AS EXPECTED.
THIS ONE IS MY FAVORITE OF ALL MY SLAVES. IT WOULD PLEASE ME THAT YOU TWO SHOULD FINALLY MEET.
OH, THAT'S RIGHT...
...I BELIEVE YOU ALEADY KNOW HIM.
RICKY...DO YOU REMEMBER YOUR OLD FRIEND, MEREDITH?
Ricky...?

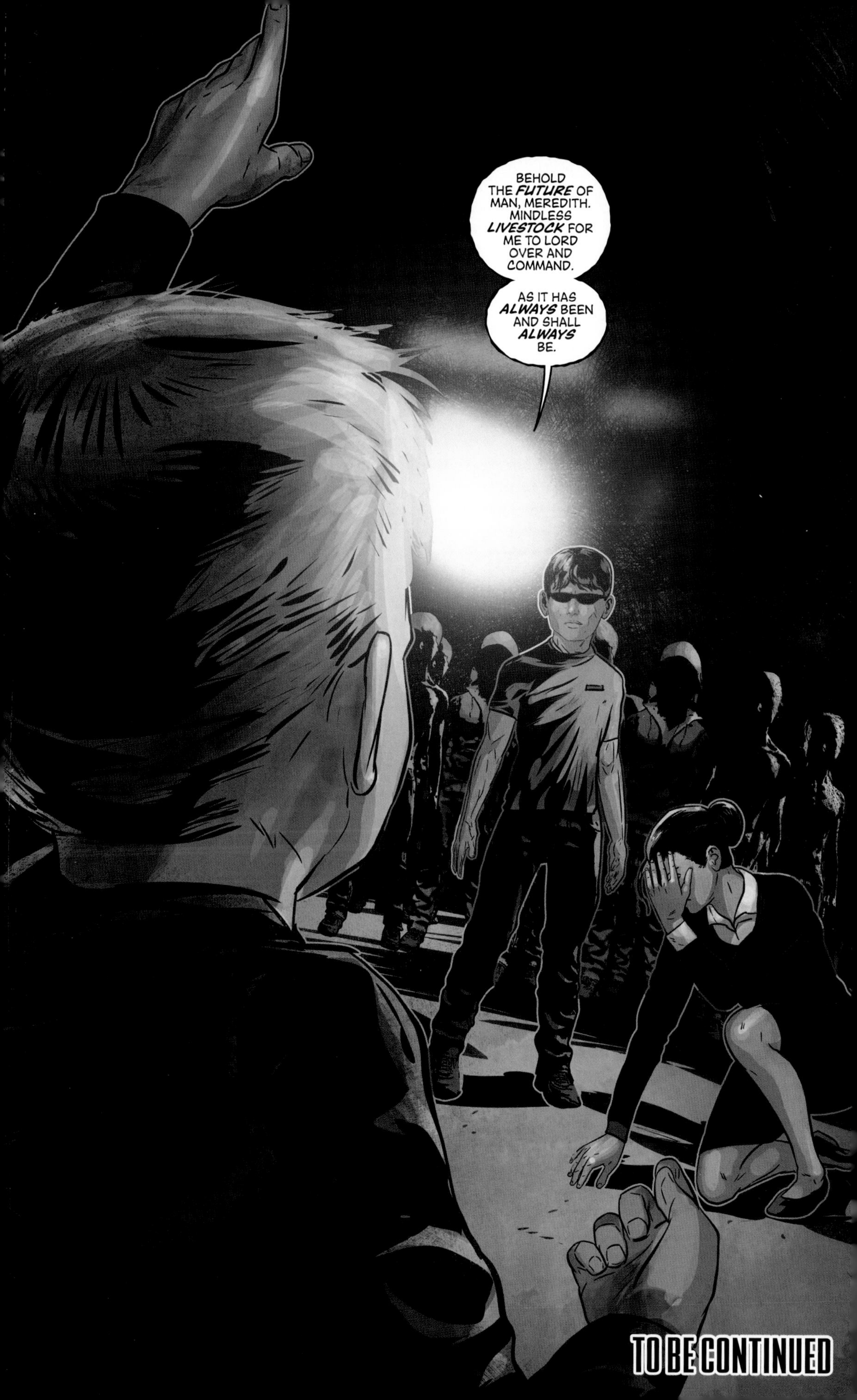
BEHOLD THE FUTURE OF MAN, MEREDITH. MINDLESS LIVESTOCK FOR ME TO LORD OVER AND COMMAND.
AS IT HAS ALWAYS BEEN AND SHALL ALWAYS BE.
TO BE CONTINUED

issue 6
NYCC variant cover
SZYMON KUDRANSKI

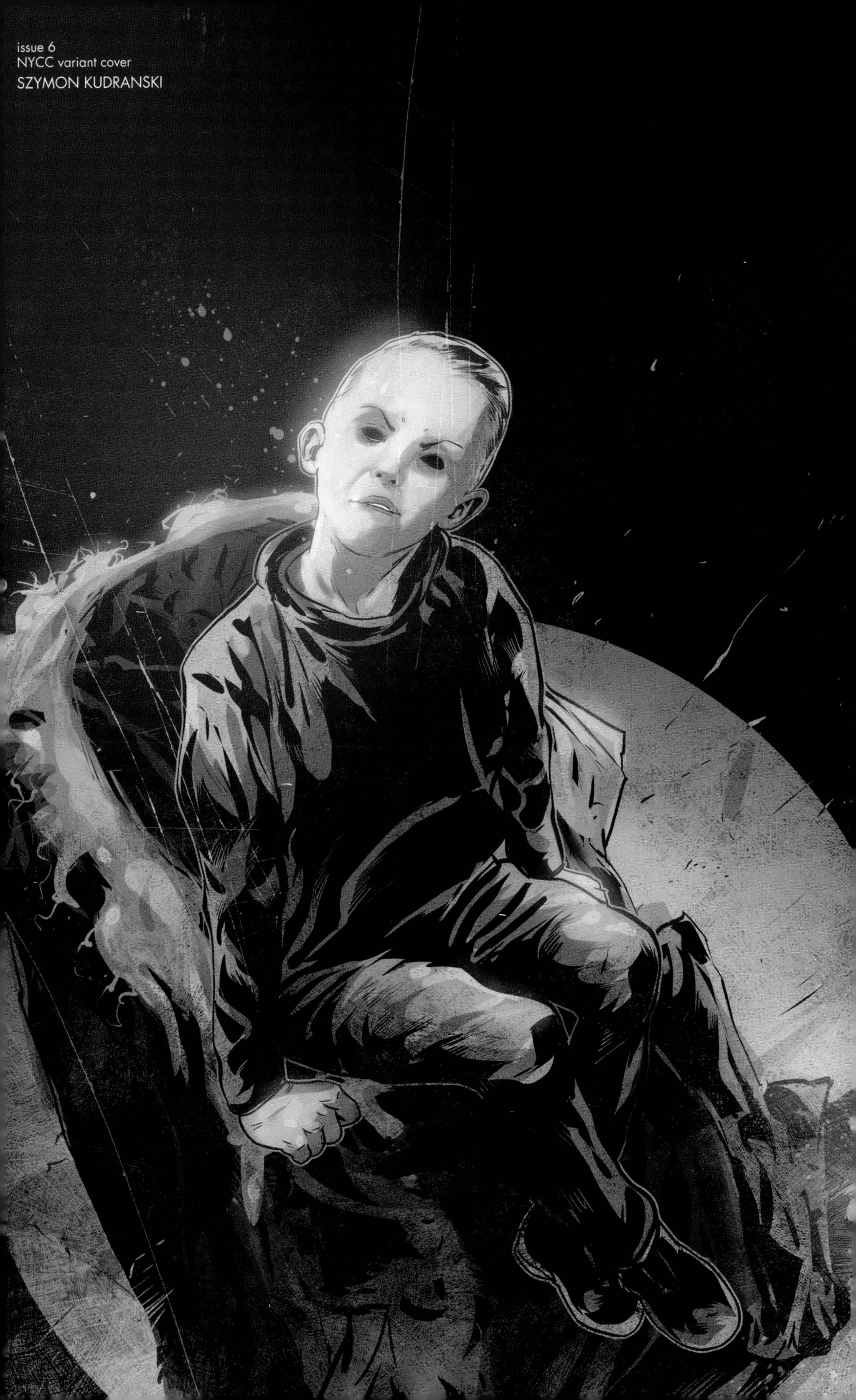

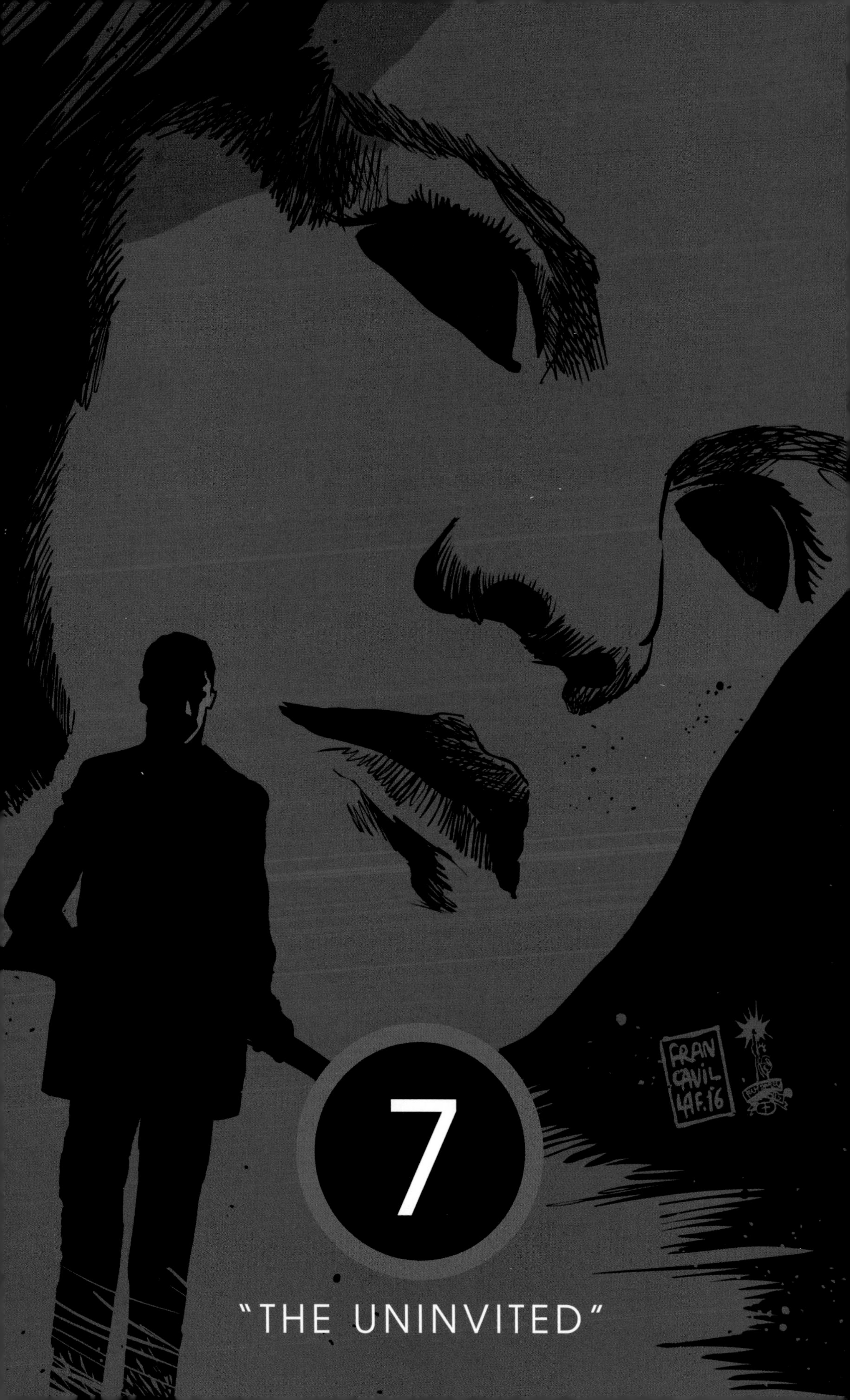
7
"THE UNINVITED"

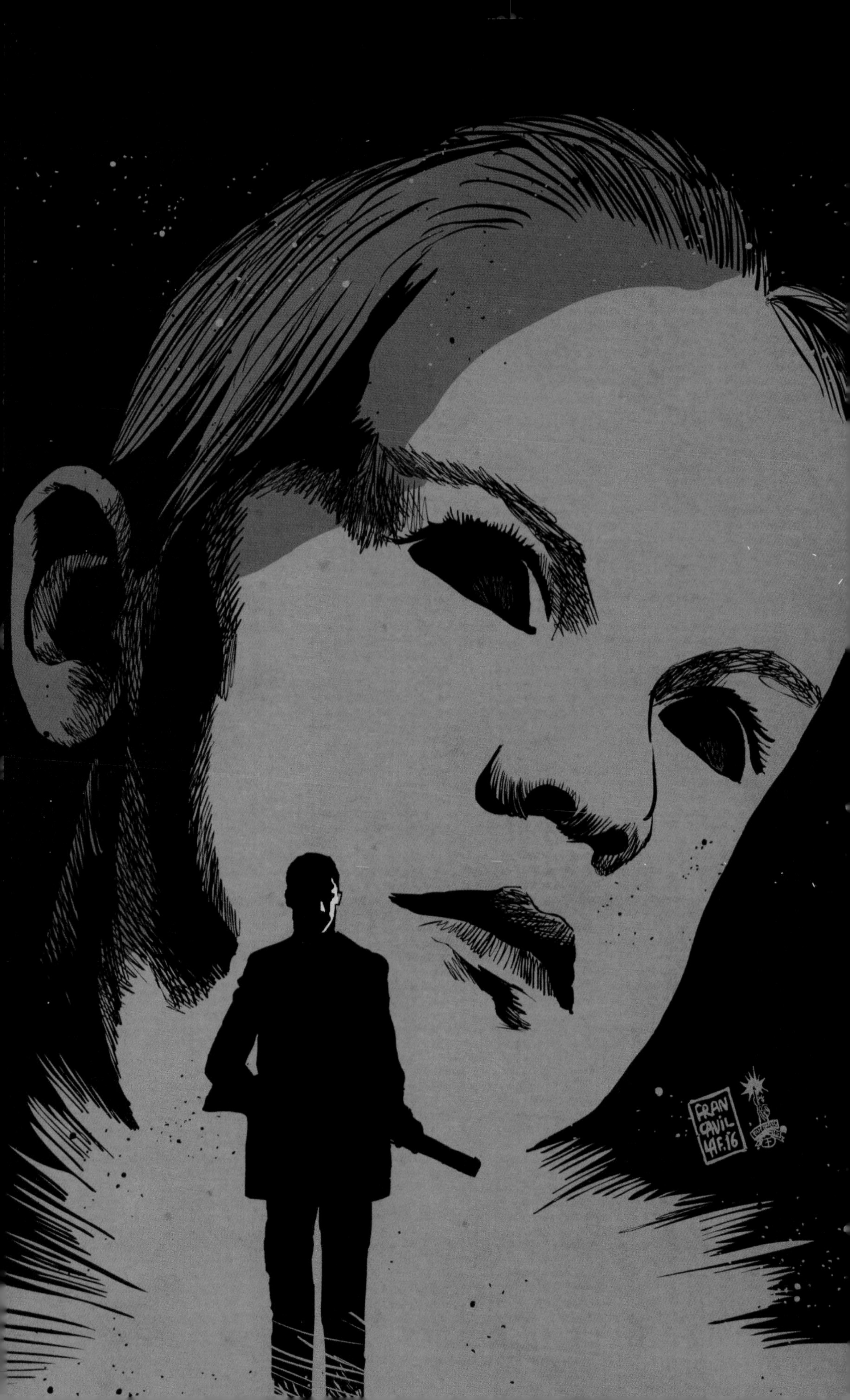
FRAN GAVIL 14F.16

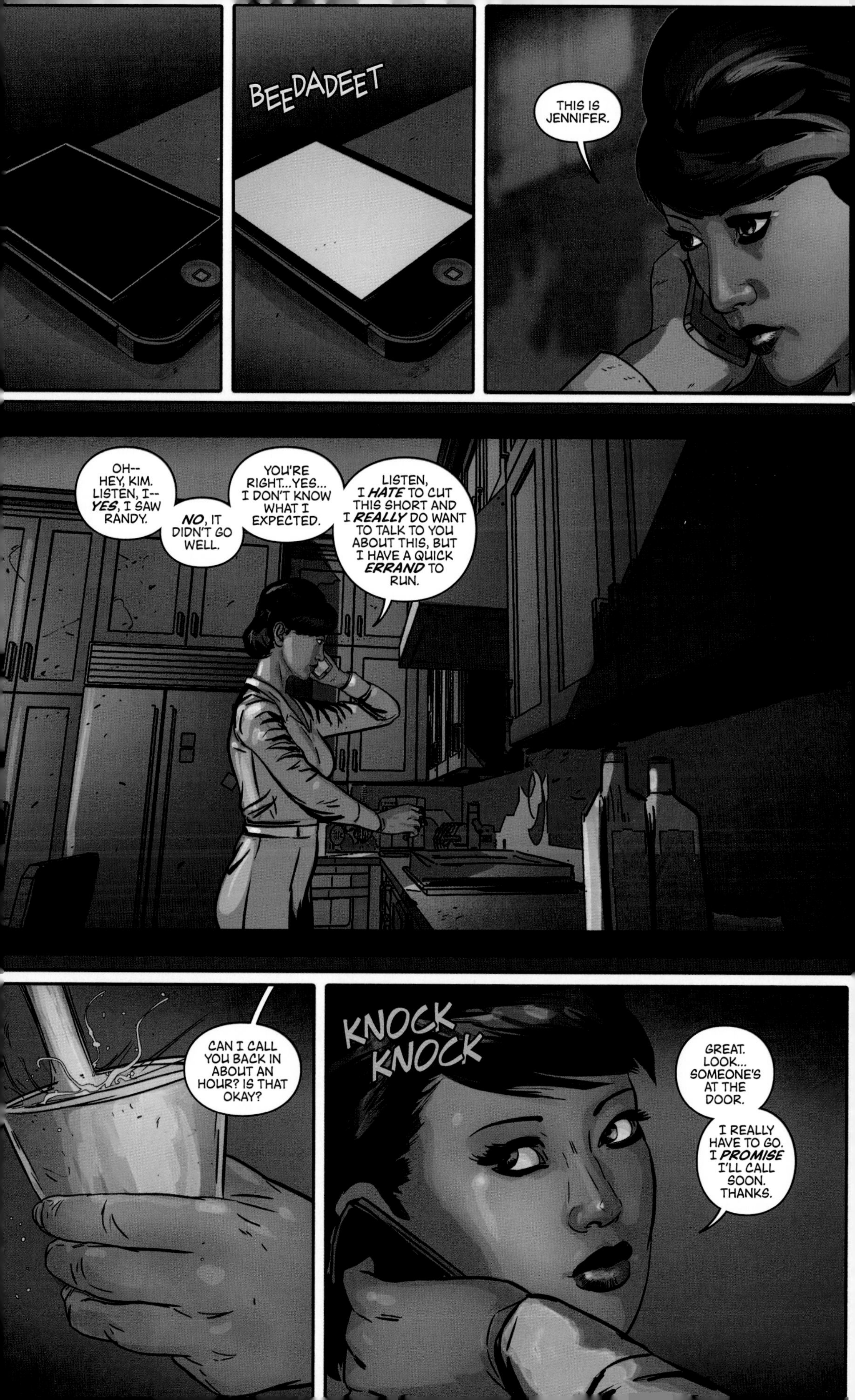
BEEDADEET
THIS IS JENNIFER.
OH-- HEY, KIM. LISTEN, I-- YES, I SAW RANDY.
NO, IT DIDN'T GO WELL.
YOU'RE RIGHT...YES... I DON'T KNOW WHAT I EXPECTED.
LISTEN, I HATE TO CUT THIS SHORT AND I REALLY DO WANT TO TALK TO YOU ABOUT THIS, BUT I HAVE A QUICK ERRAND TO RUN.
CAN I CALL YOU BACK IN ABOUT AN HOUR? IS THAT OKAY?
KNOCK KNOCK
GREAT. LOOK... SOMEONE'S AT THE DOOR.
I REALLY HAVE TO GO. I PROMISE I'LL CALL SOON. THANKS.

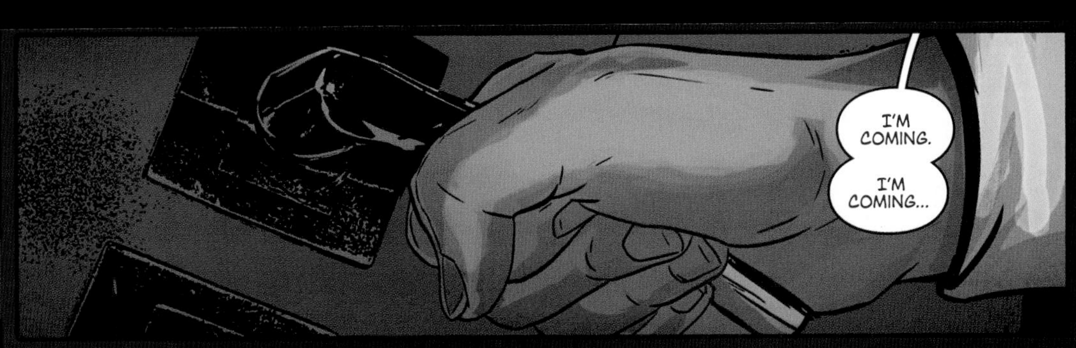
I'M COMING.
I'M COMING...
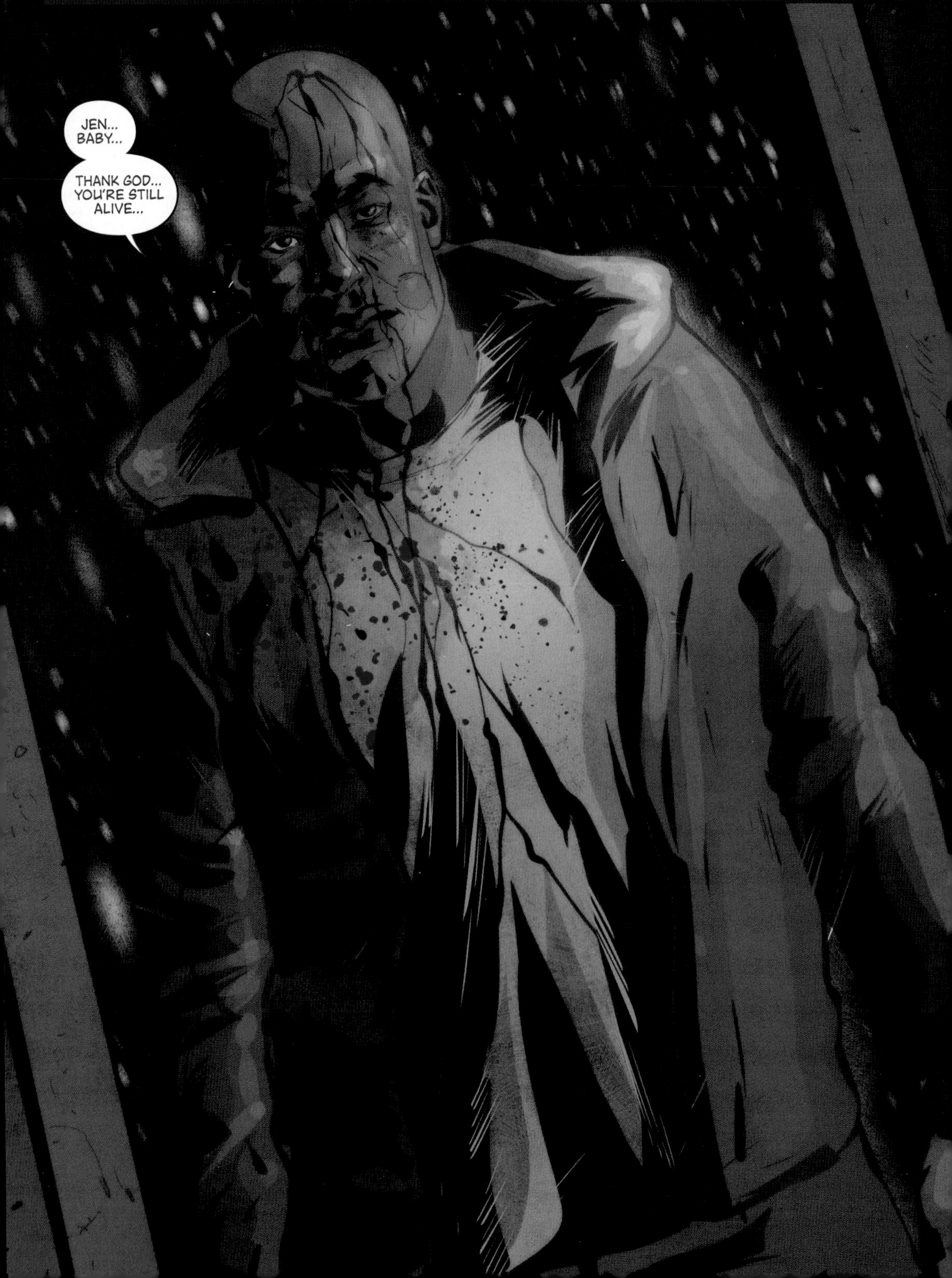
JEN... BABY...
THANK GOD... YOU'RE STILL ALIVE...

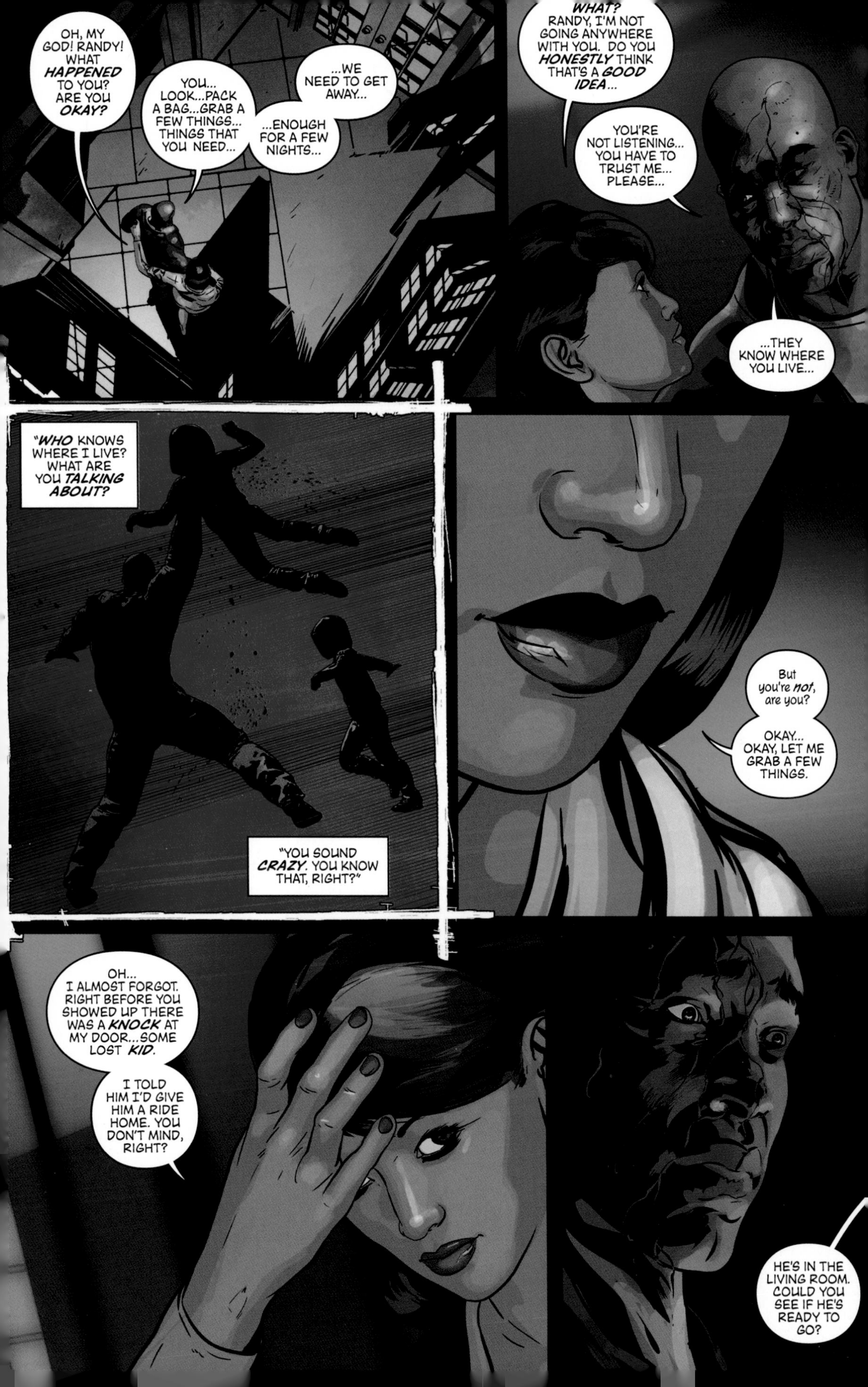
OH, MY GOD! RANDY! WHAT HAPPENED TO YOU? ARE YOU OKAY?
YOU... LOOK...PACK A BAG...GRAB A FEW THINGS... THINGS THAT YOU NEED...
...ENOUGH FOR A FEW NIGHTS...
...WE NEED TO GET AWAY...
WHAT? RANDY, I'M NOT GOING ANYWHERE WITH YOU. DO YOU HONESTLY THINK THAT'S A GOOD IDEA...
YOU'RE NOT LISTENING... YOU HAVE TO TRUST ME... PLEASE...
...THEY KNOW WHERE YOU LIVE...
"WHO KNOWS WHERE I LIVE? WHAT ARE YOU TALKING ABOUT?
"YOU SOUND CRAZY. YOU KNOW THAT, RIGHT?"
But you're not, are you?
OKAY... OKAY, LET ME GRAB A FEW THINGS.
OH... I ALMOST FORGOT. RIGHT BEFORE YOU SHOWED UP THERE WAS A KNOCK AT MY DOOR...SOME LOST KID.
I TOLD HIM I'D GIVE HIM A RIDE HOME. YOU DON'T MIND, RIGHT?
HE'S IN THE LIVING ROOM. COULD YOU SEE IF HE'S READY TO GO?

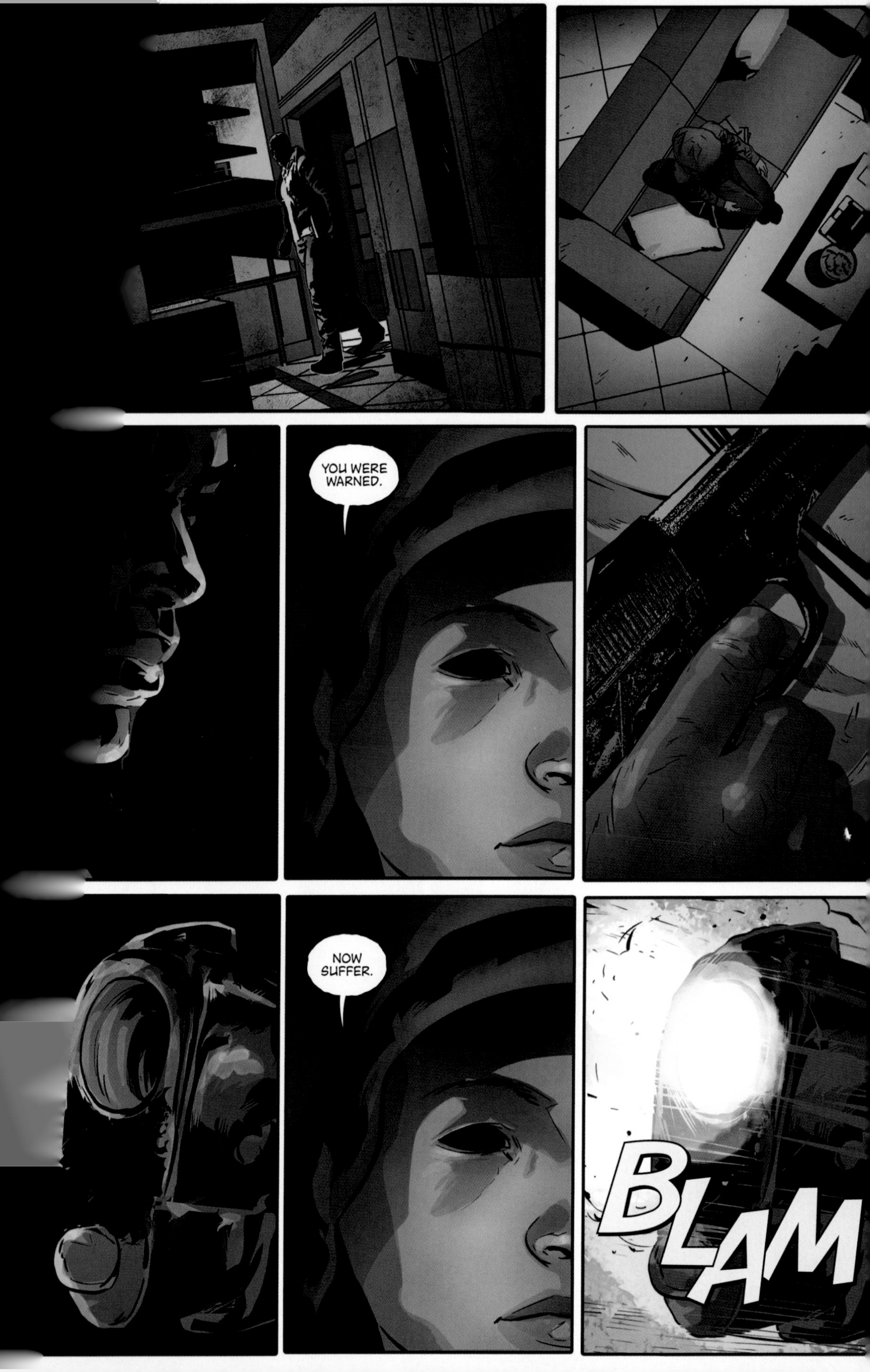
YOU WERE WARNED.
NOW SUFFER.
BLAM

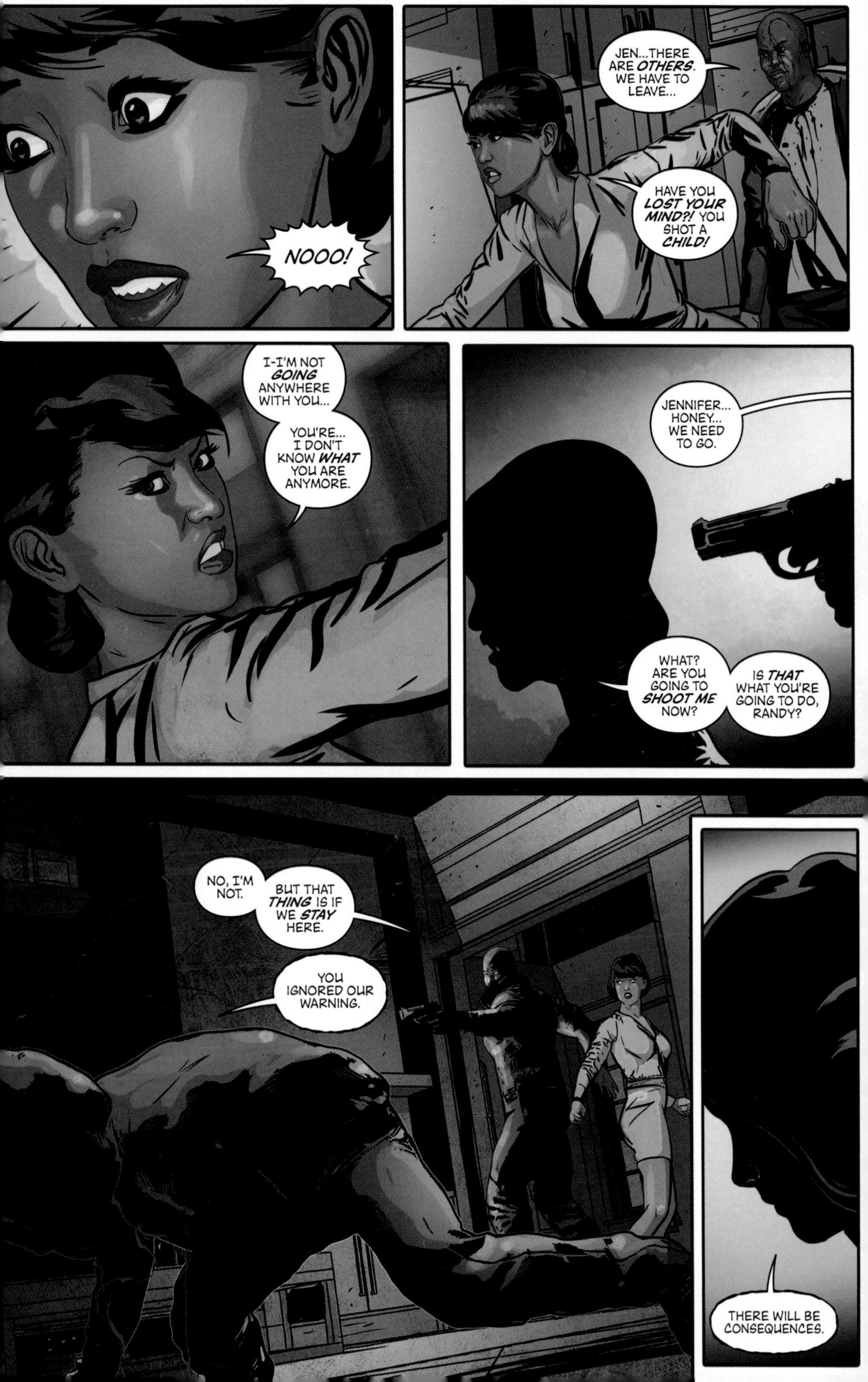
NOOO!
JEN...THERE ARE OTHERS. WE HAVE TO LEAVE...
HAVE YOU LOST YOUR MIND?! YOU SHOT A CHILD!
I-I'M NOT GOING ANYWHERE WITH YOU...
YOU'RE... I DON'T KNOW WHAT YOU ARE ANYMORE.
JENNIFER... HONEY... WE NEED TO GO.
WHAT? ARE YOU GOING TO SHOOT ME NOW?
IS THAT WHAT YOU'RE GOING TO DO, RANDY?
NO, I'M NOT.
BUT THAT THING IS IF WE STAY HERE.
YOU IGNORED OUR WARNING.
THERE WILL BE CONSEQUENCES.

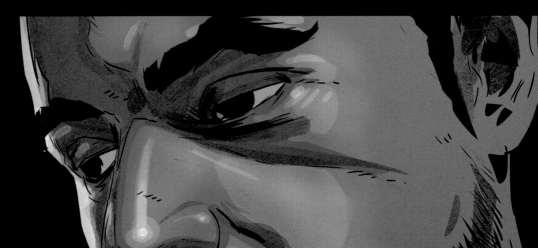

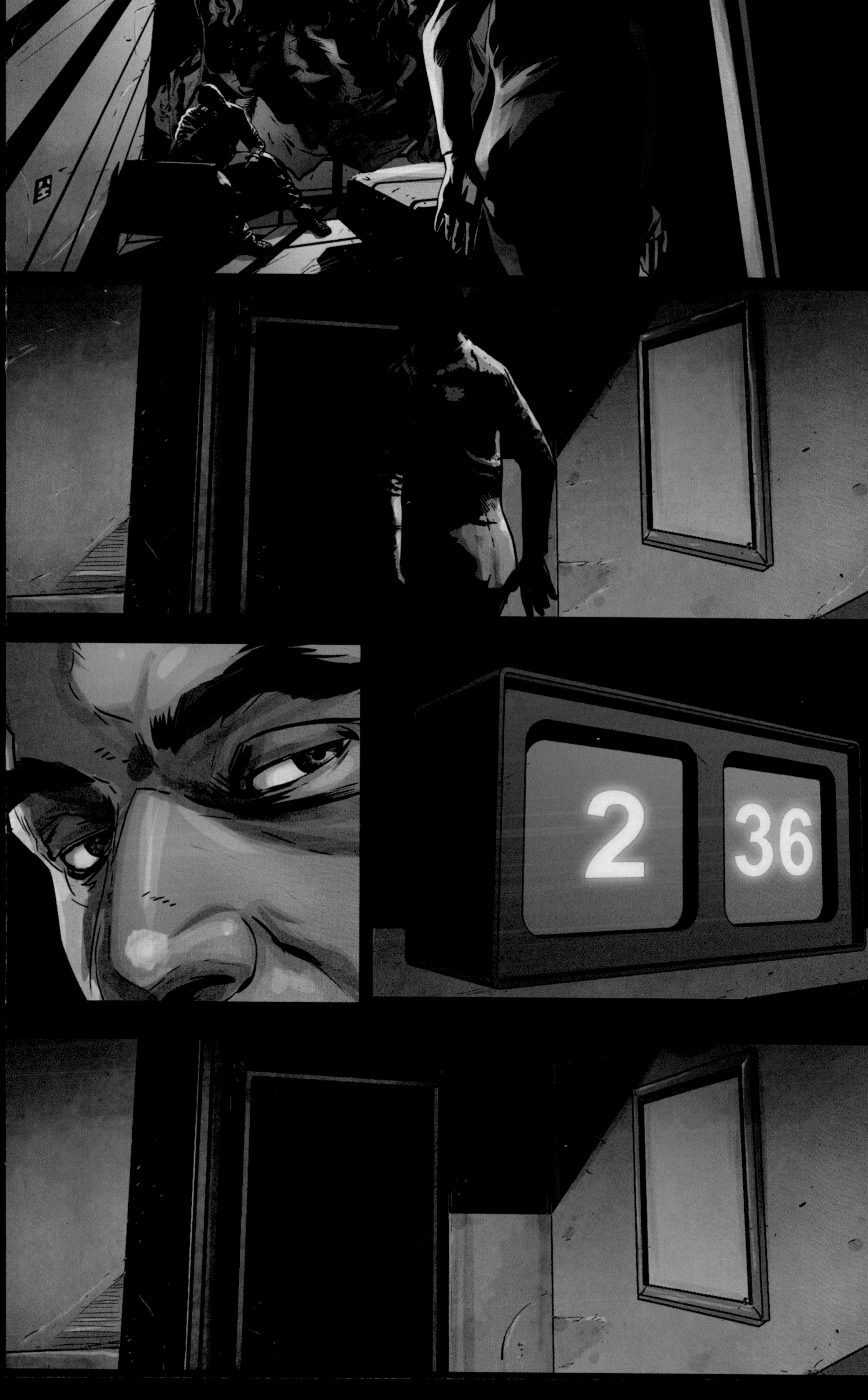
2 36

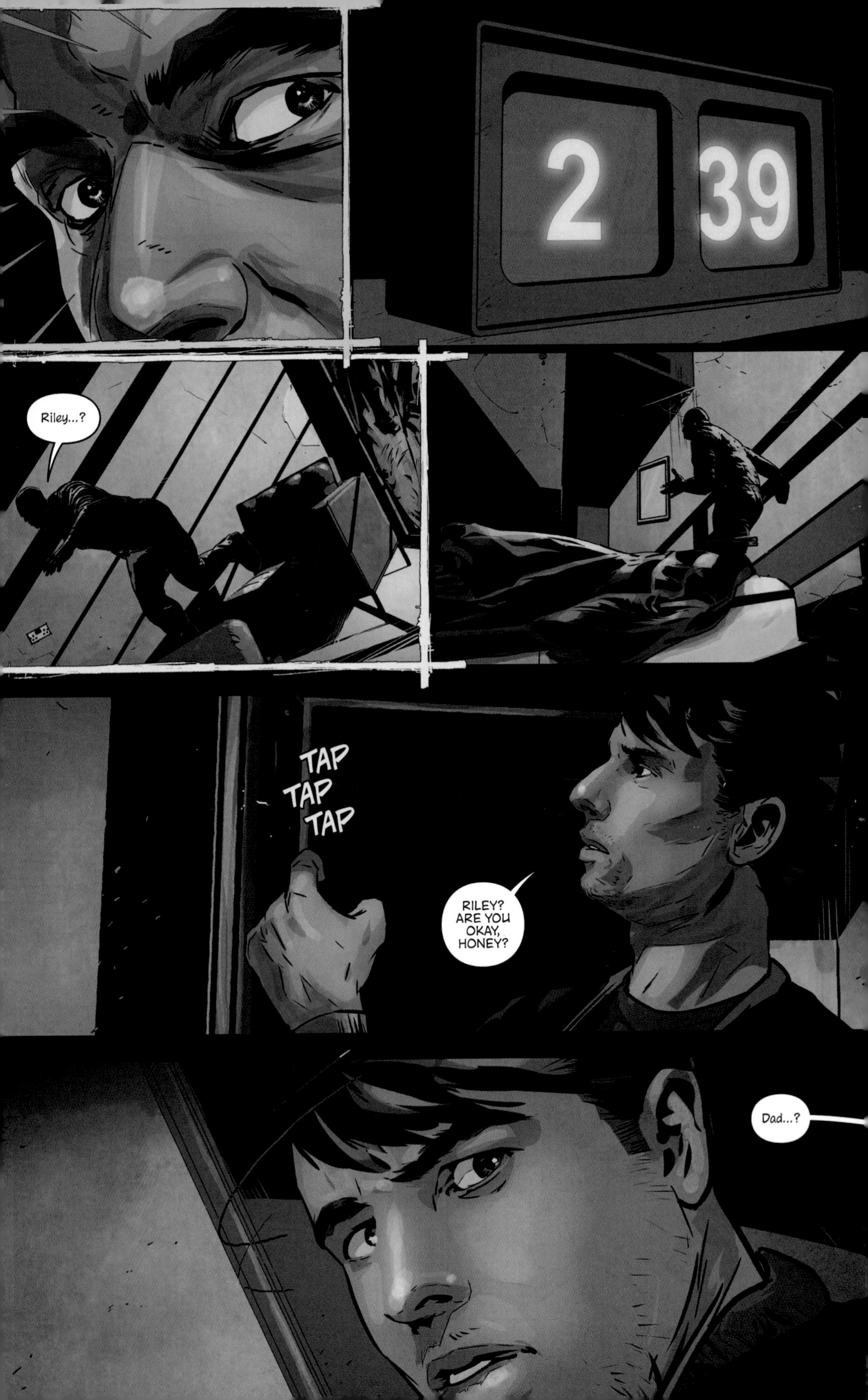
2 39
Riley...?
TAP
TAP
TAP
RILEY? ARE YOU OKAY, HONEY?
Dad...?

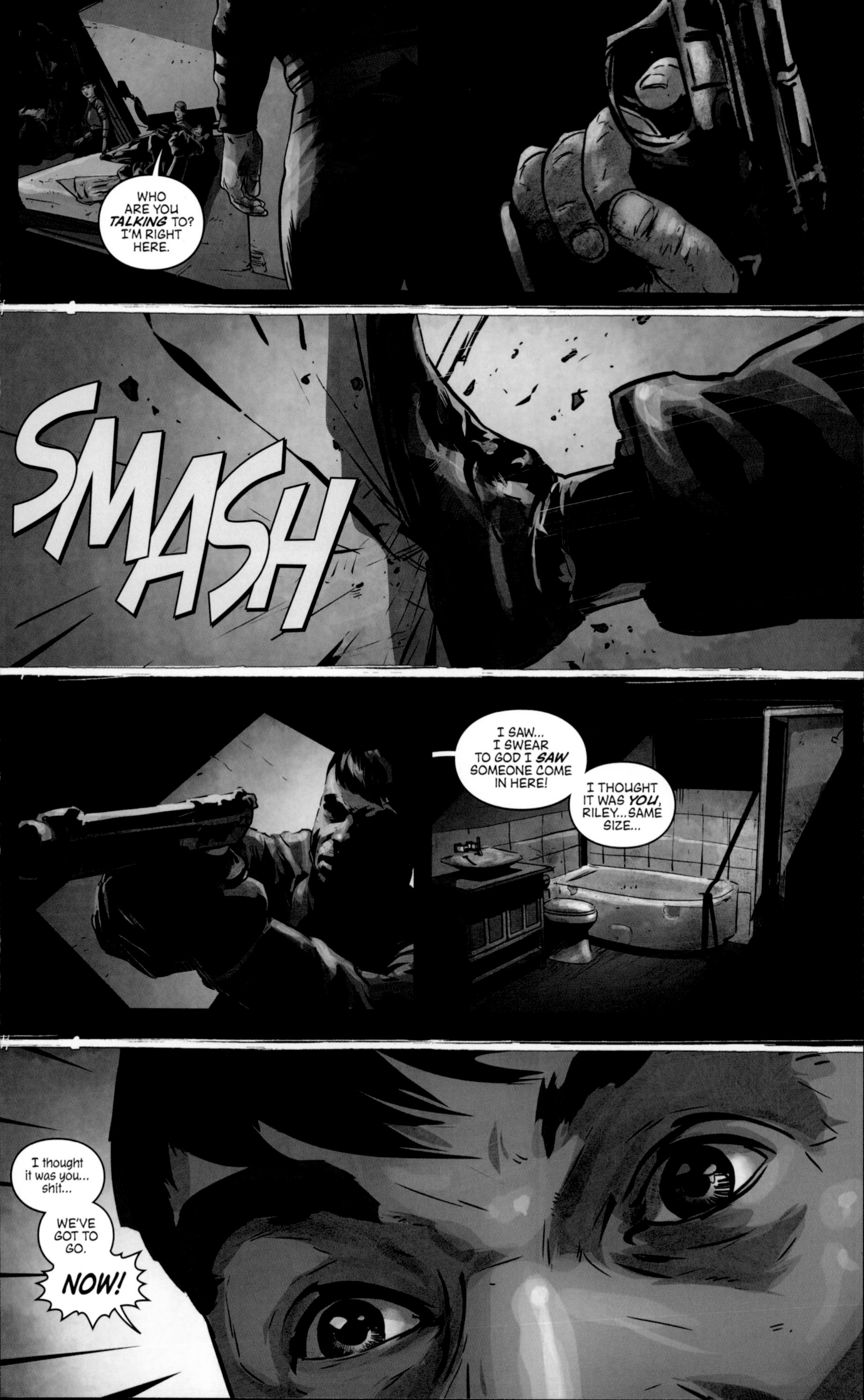
WHO ARE YOU *TALKING* TO? I'M RIGHT HERE.
SMASH
I SAW... I SWEAR TO GOD I *SAW* SOMEONE COME IN HERE!
I THOUGHT IT WAS *YOU*, RILEY...SAME SIZE...
I thought it was you... shit...
WE'VE GOT TO GO.
NOW!

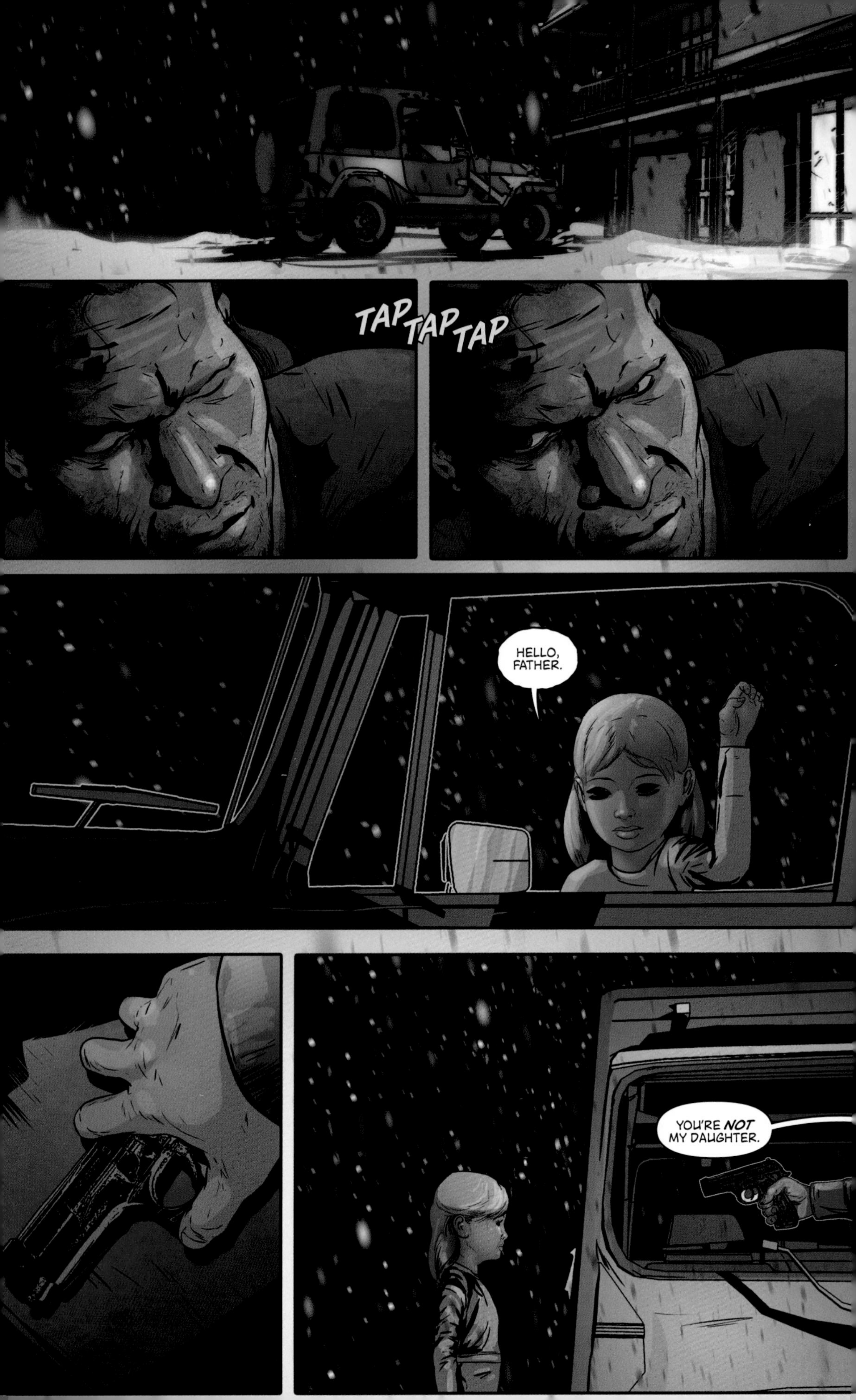
TAP TAP TAP
HELLO, FATHER.
YOU'RE NOT MY DAUGHTER.

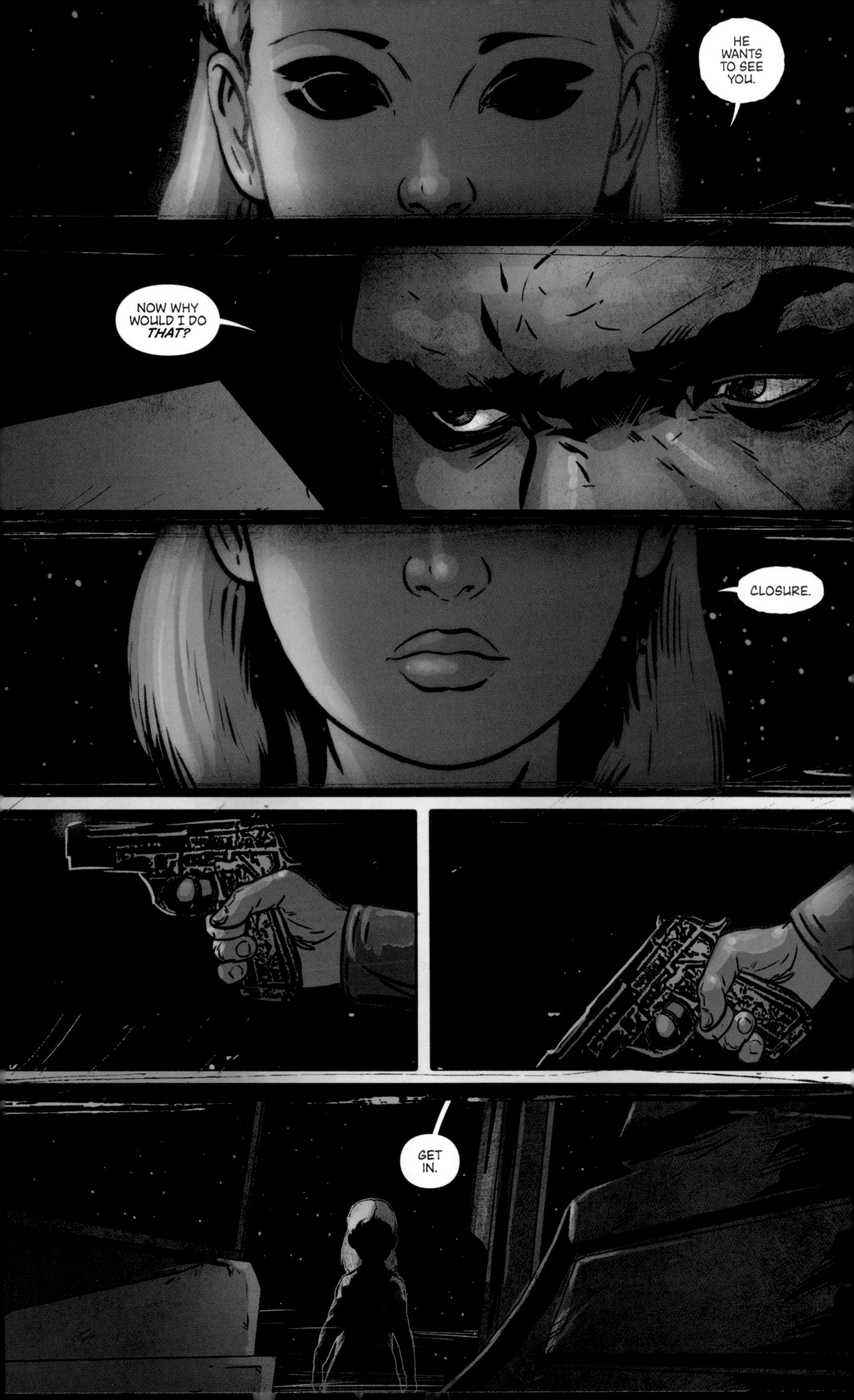
HE WANTS TO SEE YOU.
NOW WHY WOULD I DO *THAT?*
CLOSURE.
GET IN.

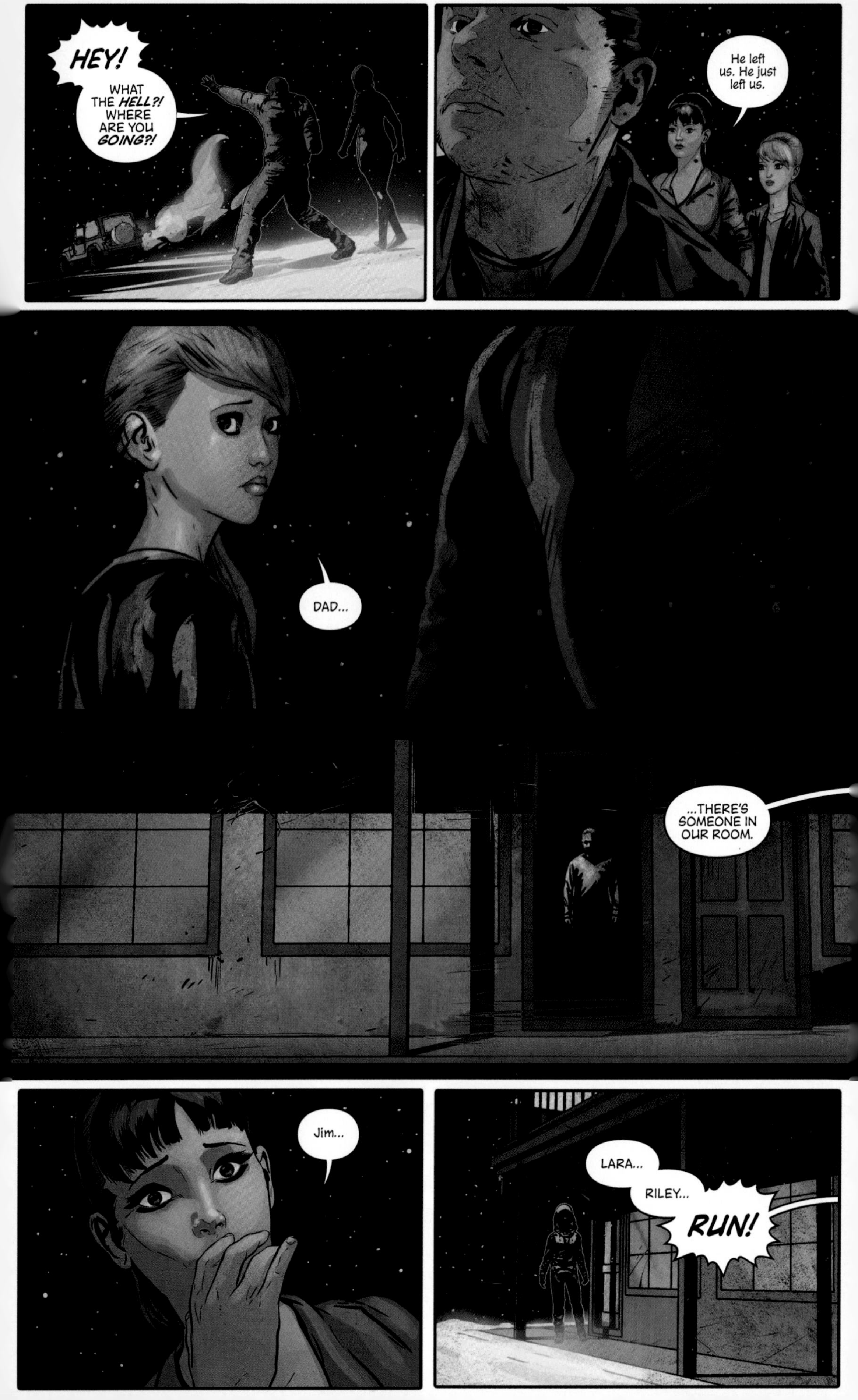
HEY!
WHAT THE HELL?! WHERE ARE YOU GOING?!
He left us. He just left us.
DAD...
...THERE'S SOMEONE IN OUR ROOM.
Jim...
LARA...
RILEY...
RUN!

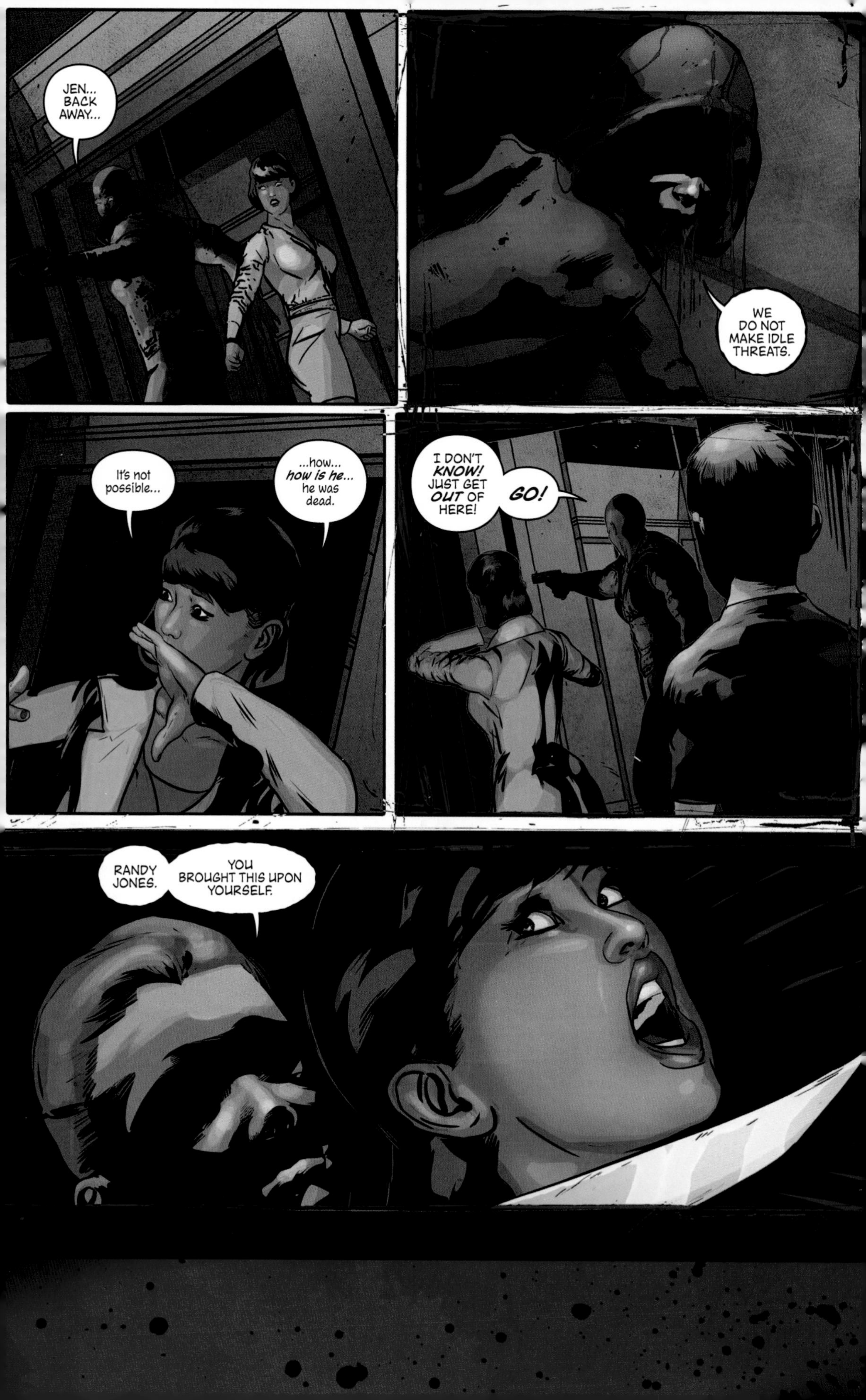
JEN... BACK AWAY...
WE DO NOT MAKE IDLE THREATS.
It's not possible...
...how... *how is he...* he was dead.
I DON'T *KNOW!* JUST GET *OUT* OF HERE!
GO!
RANDY JONES.
YOU BROUGHT THIS UPON YOURSELF.

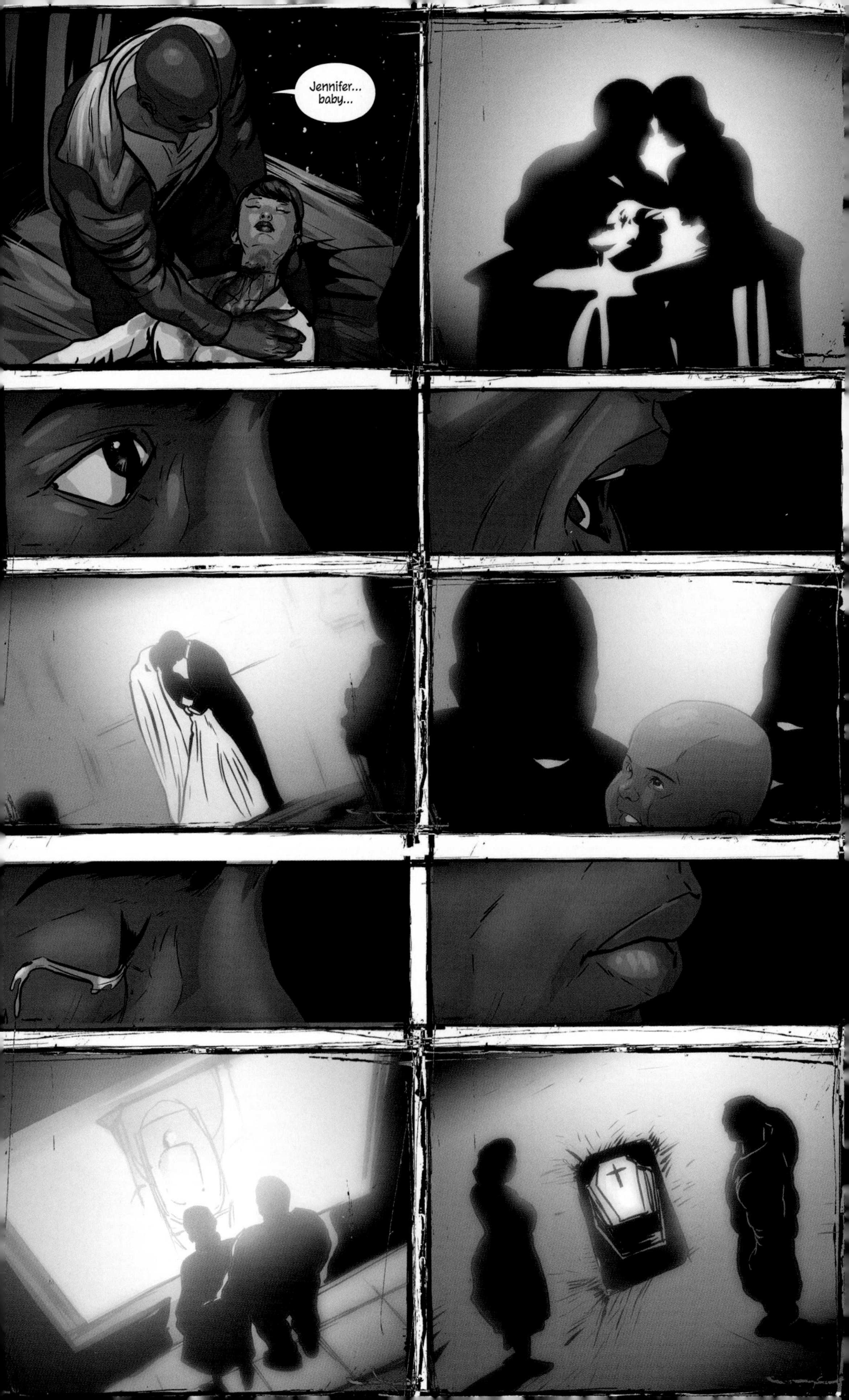
Jennifer... baby...

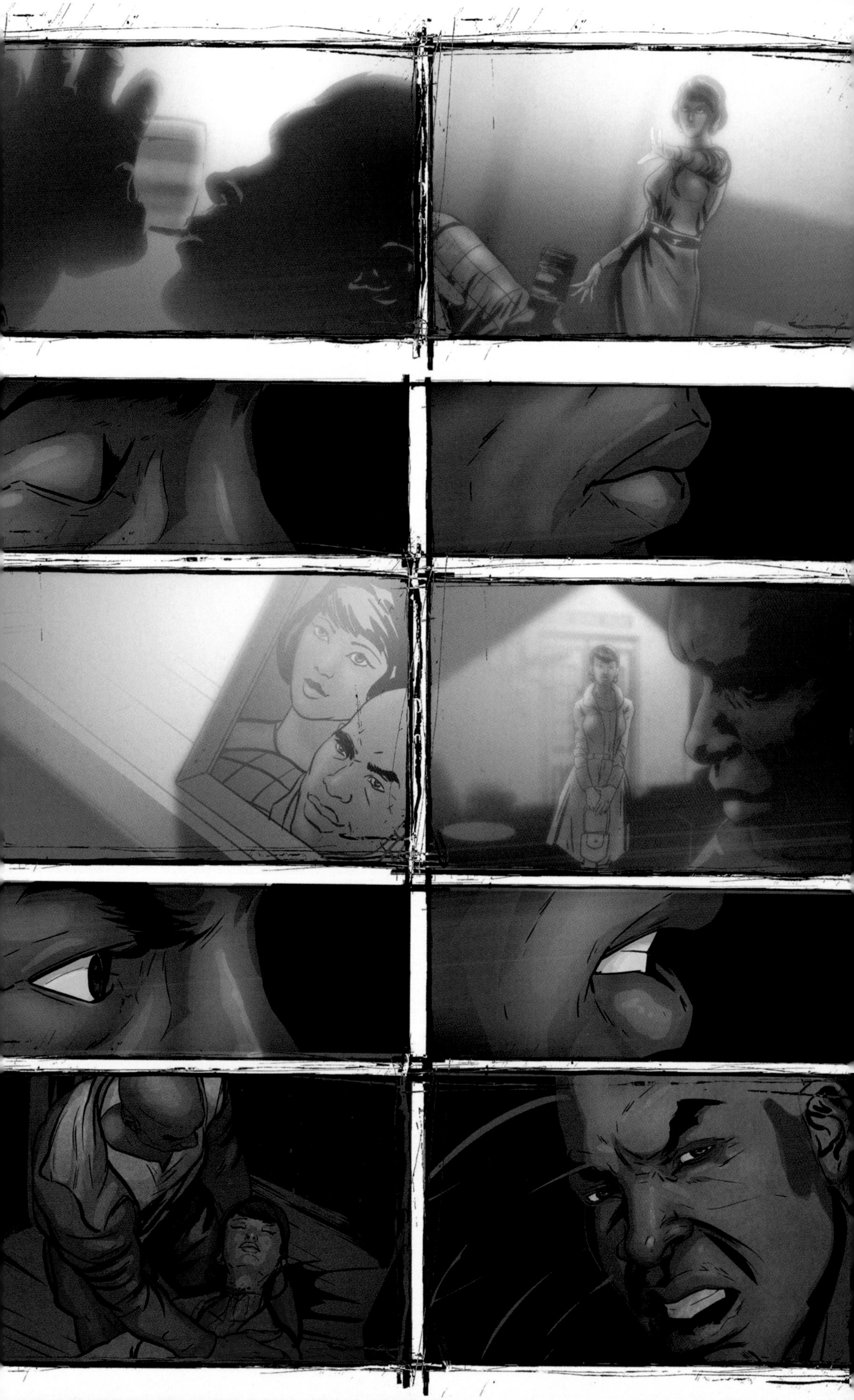

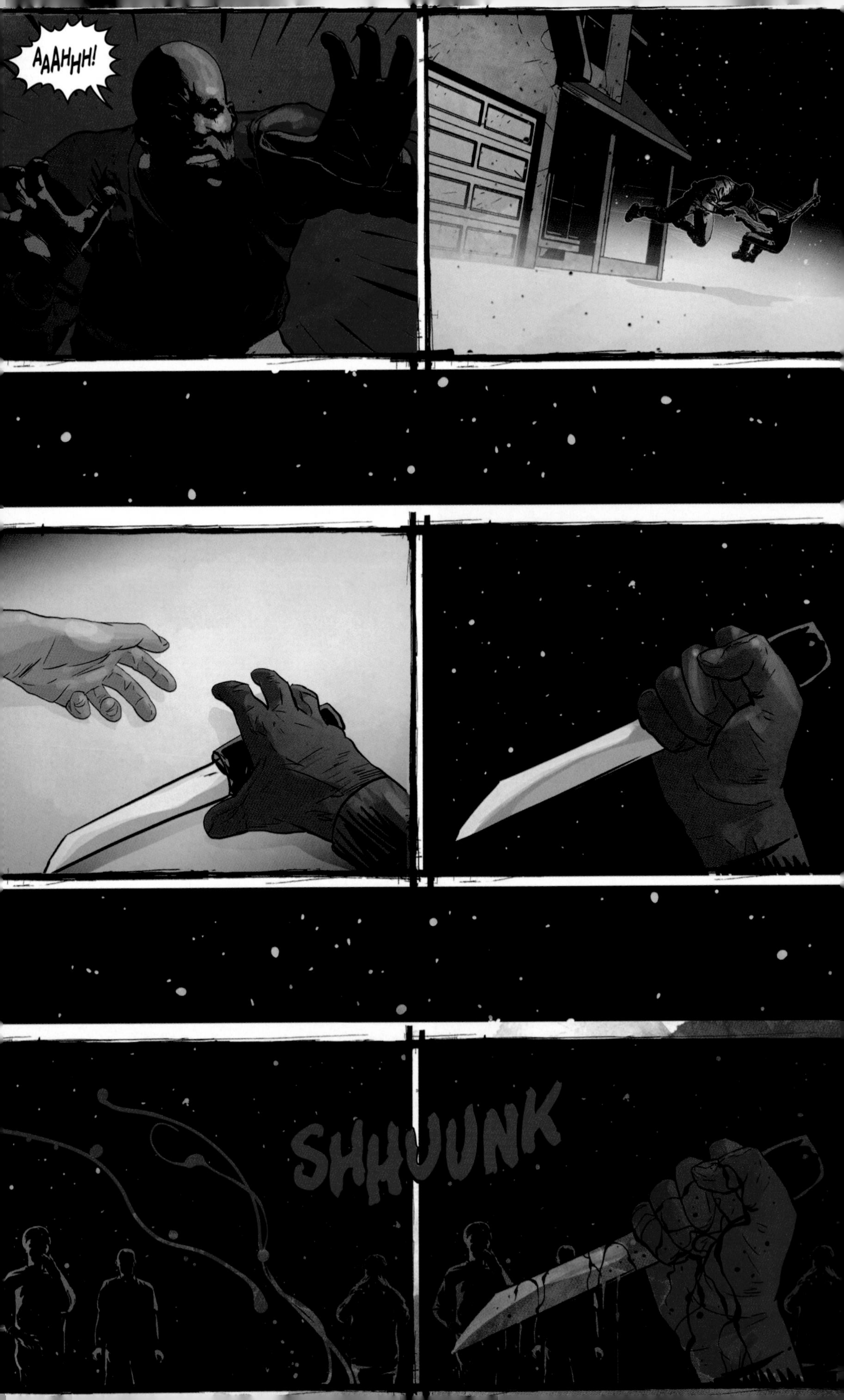
AAAHHH!
SHHUUNK

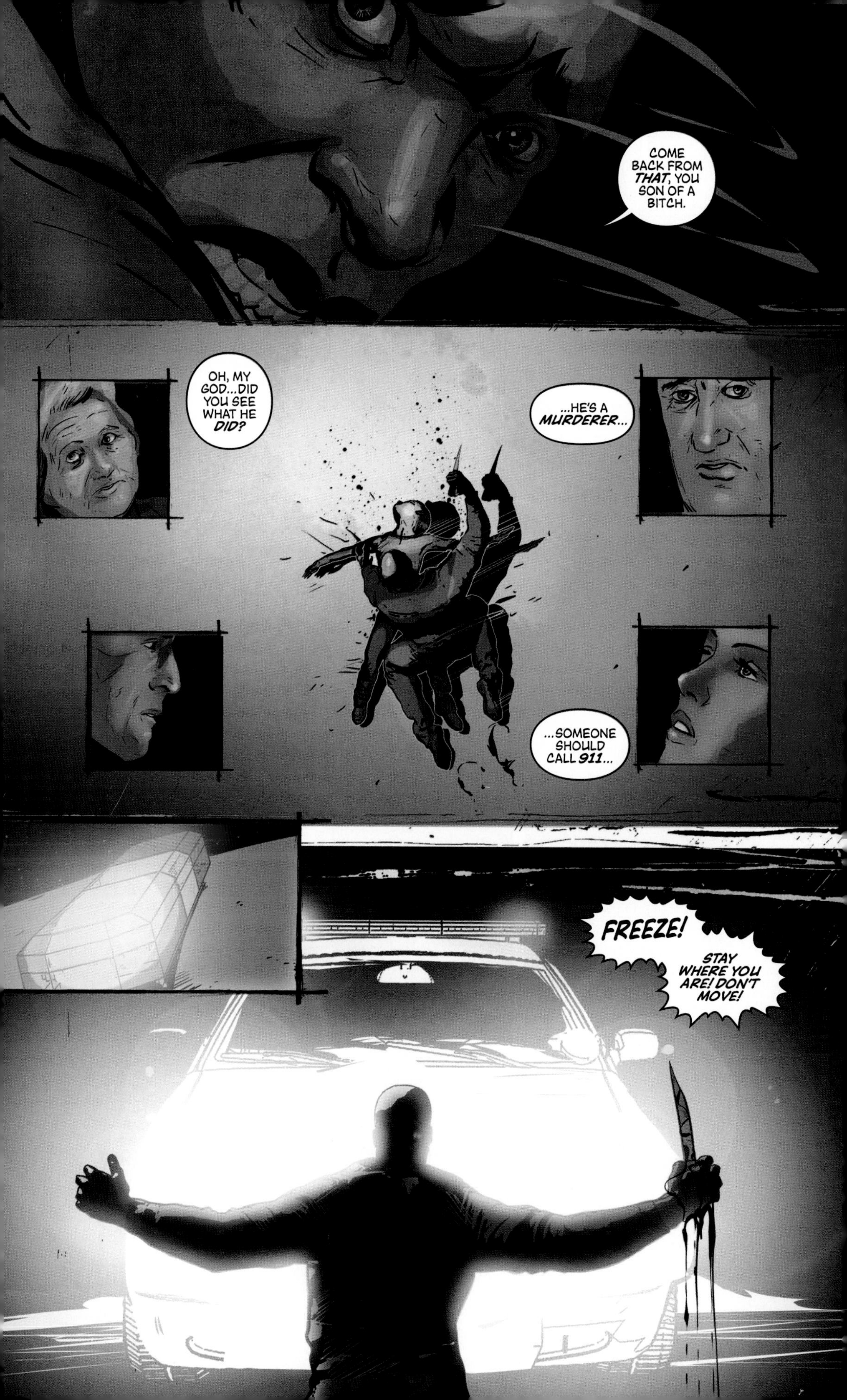
COME BACK FROM THAT, YOU SON OF A BITCH.
OH, MY GOD...DID YOU SEE WHAT HE DID?
...HE'S A MURDERER...
...SOMEONE SHOULD CALL 911...
FREEZE!
STAY WHERE YOU ARE! DON'T MOVE!

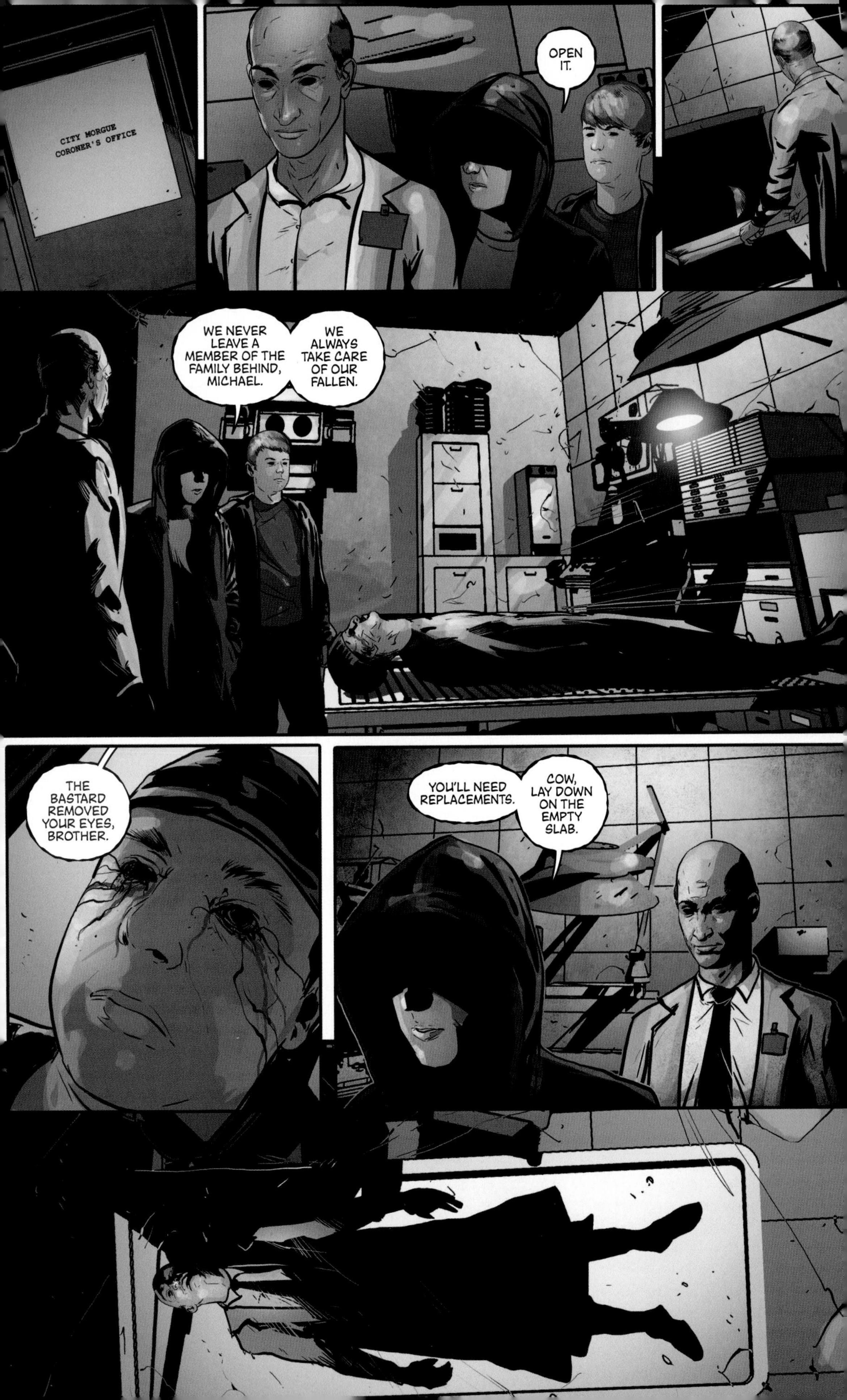
CITY MORGUE
CORONER'S OFFICE
OPEN IT.
WE NEVER LEAVE A MEMBER OF THE FAMILY BEHIND, MICHAEL.
WE ALWAYS TAKE CARE OF OUR FALLEN.
THE BASTARD REMOVED YOUR EYES, BROTHER.
YOU'LL NEED REPLACEMENTS.
COW, LAY DOWN ON THE EMPTY SLAB.

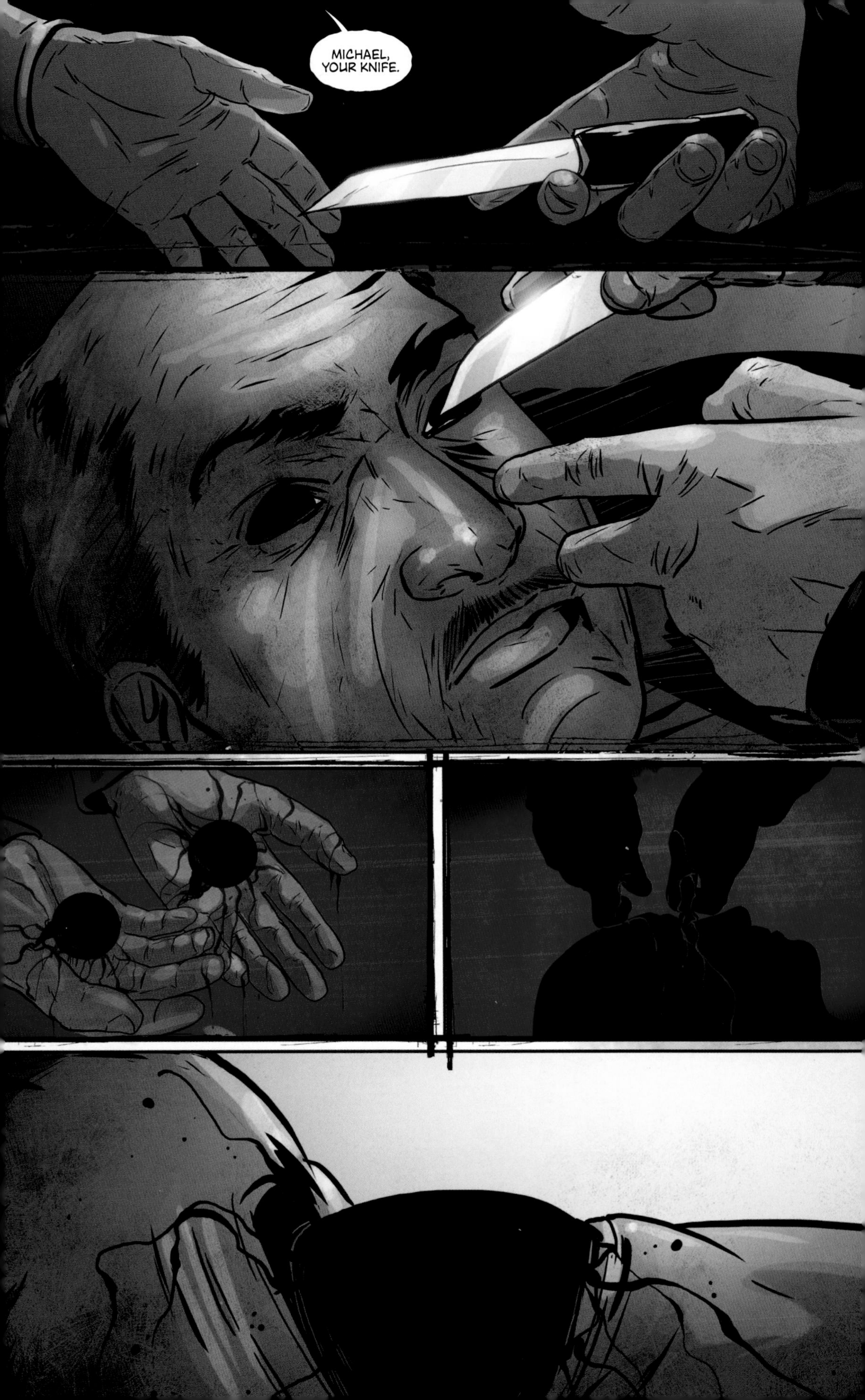
MICHAEL,
YOUR KNIFE.

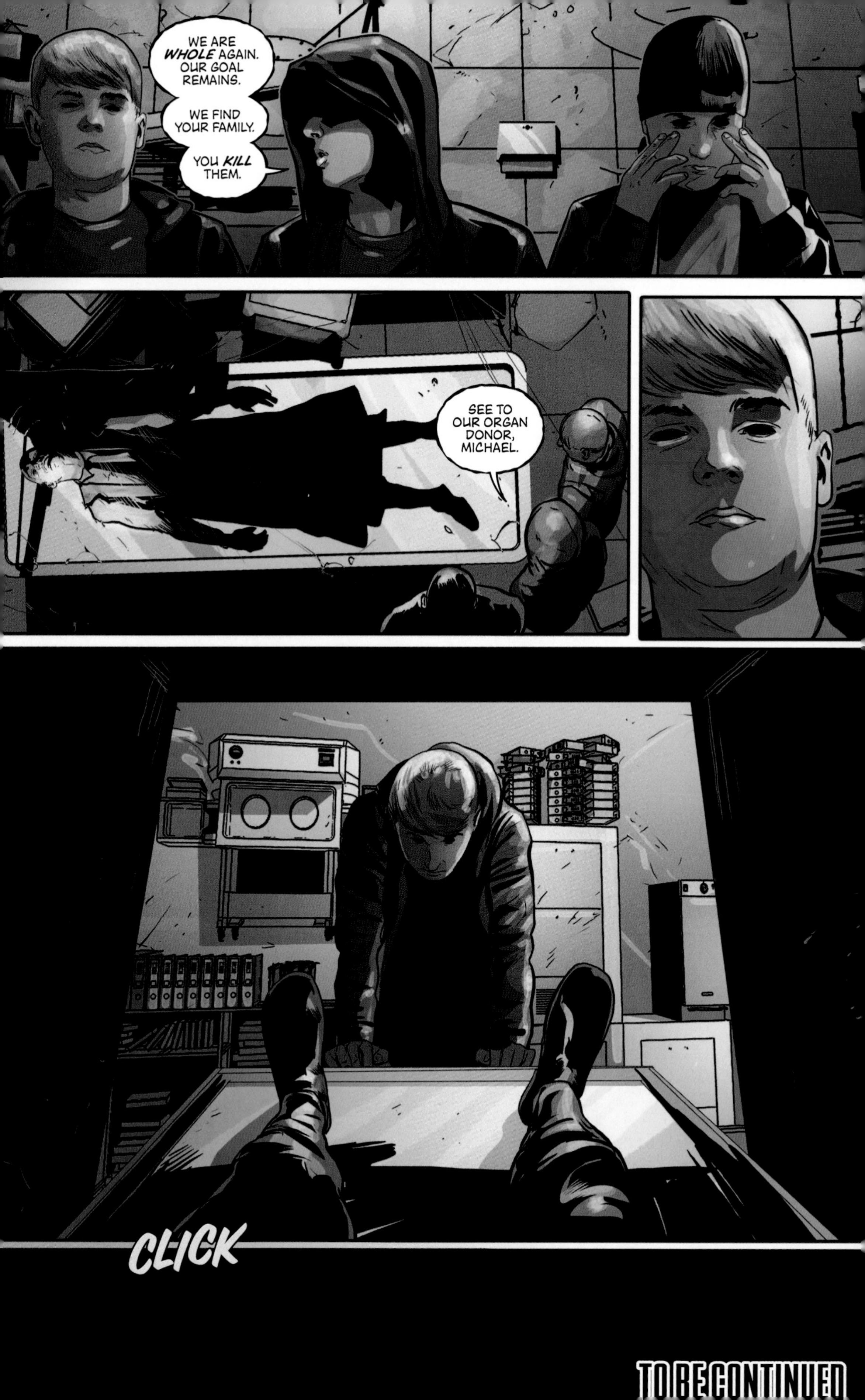
WE ARE WHOLE AGAIN. OUR GOAL REMAINS.
WE FIND YOUR FAMILY.
YOU KILL THEM.
SEE TO OUR ORGAN DONOR, MICHAEL.
CLICK
TO BE CONTINUED

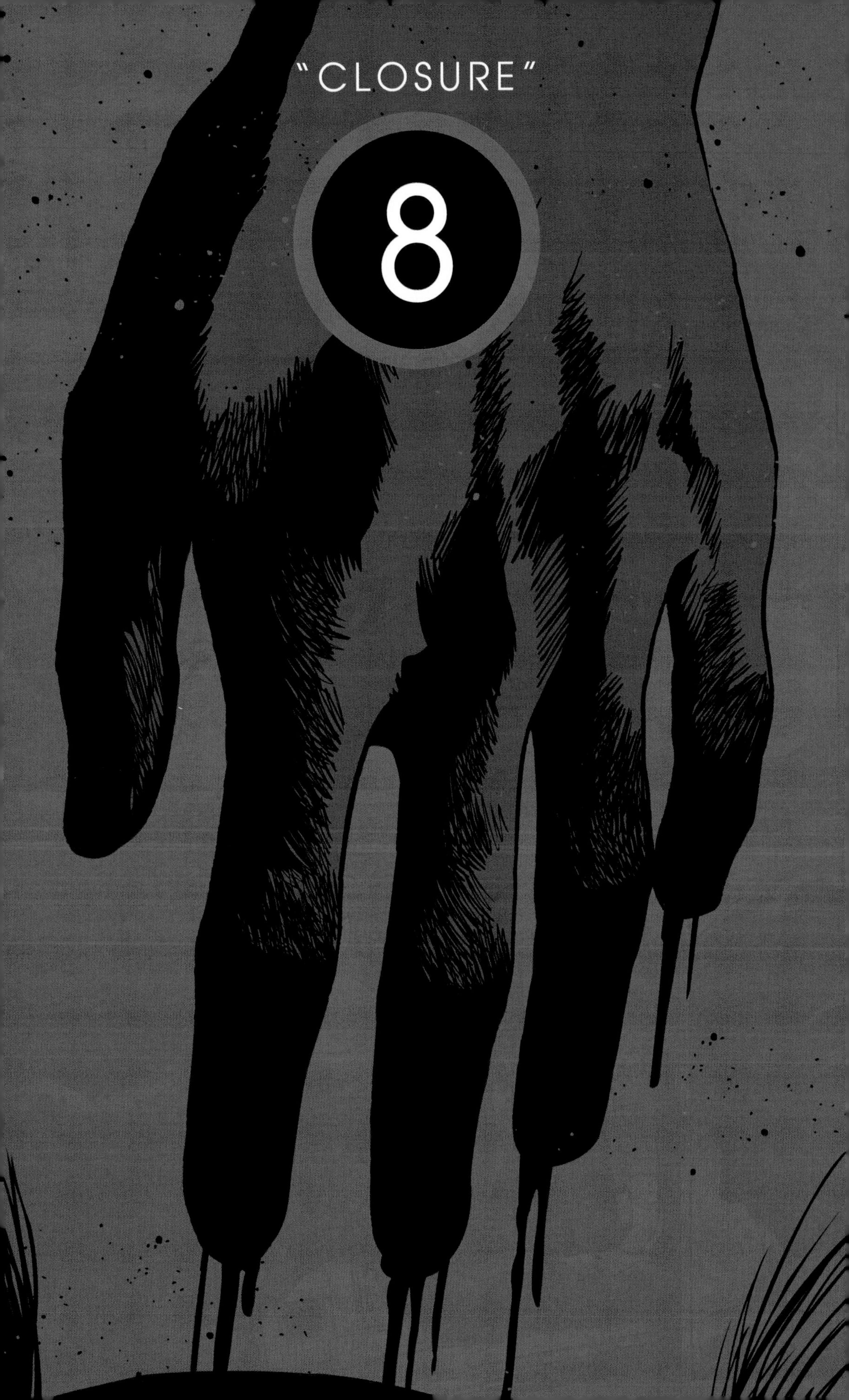
"CLOSURE"
8

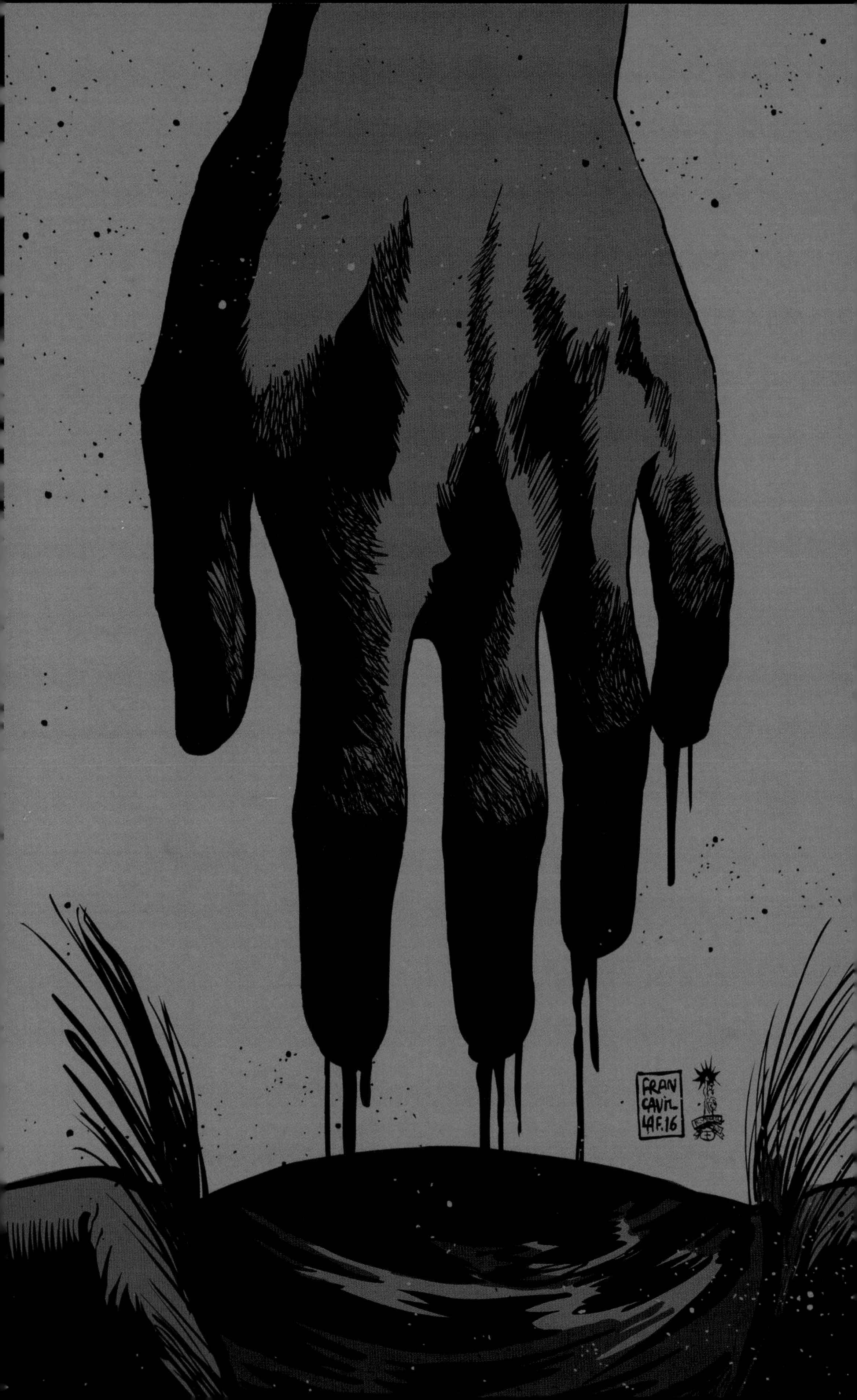
FRAN CAVIL LA F.16

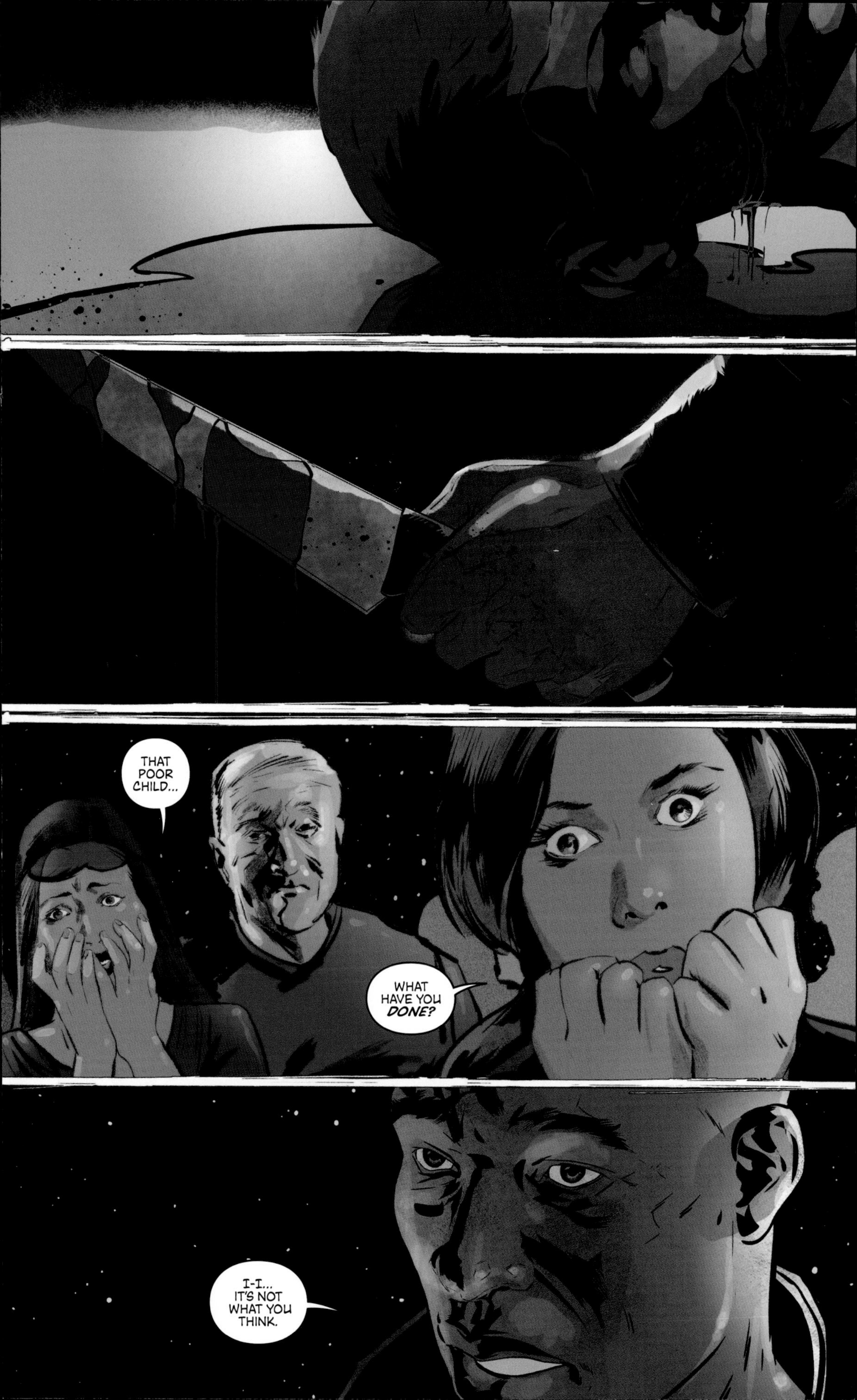
THAT POOR CHILD...
WHAT HAVE YOU DONE?
I-I... IT'S NOT WHAT YOU THINK.

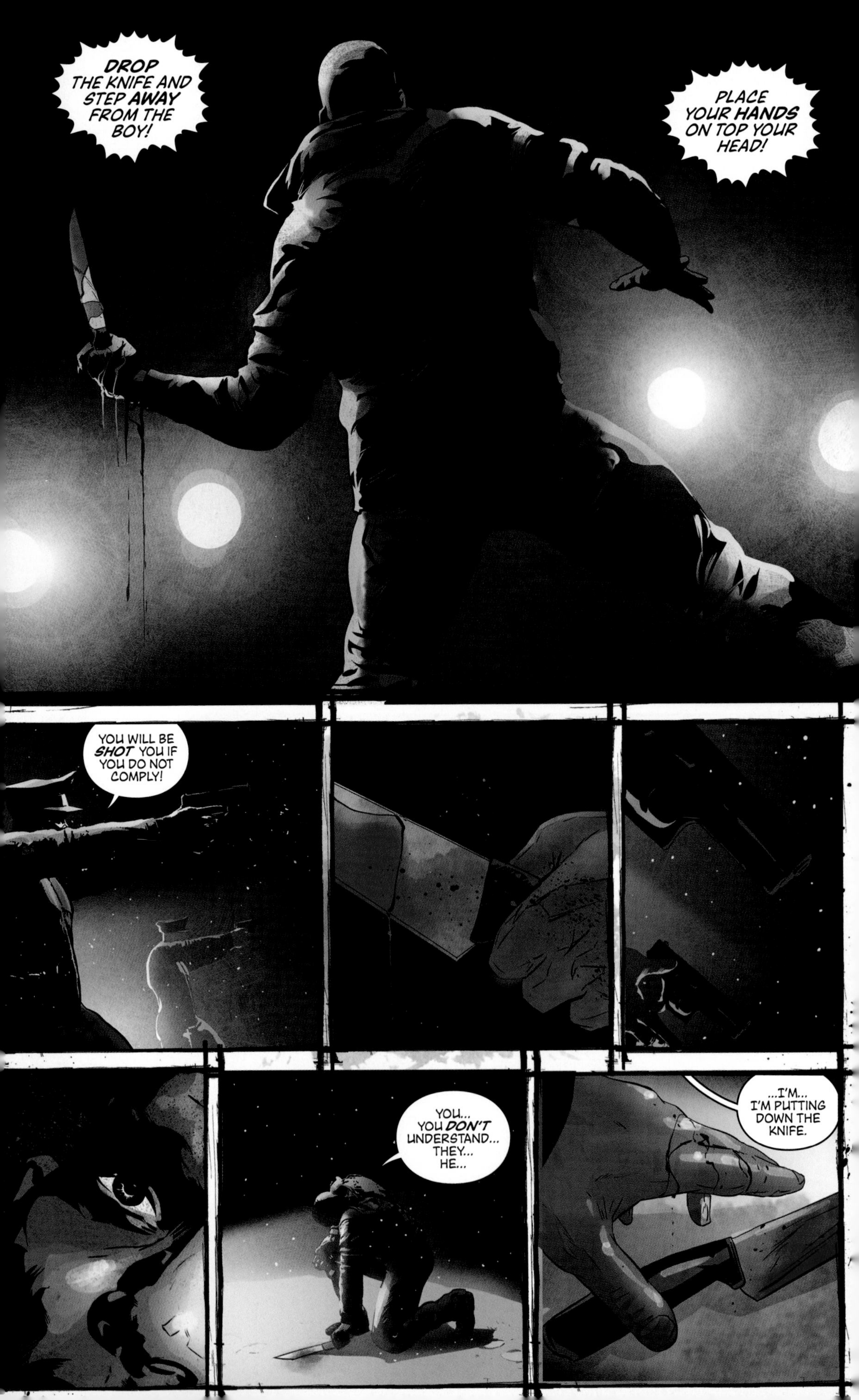
DROP THE KNIFE AND STEP AWAY FROM THE BOY!
PLACE YOUR HANDS ON TOP YOUR HEAD!
YOU WILL BE SHOT YOU IF YOU DO NOT COMPLY!
YOU... YOU DON'T UNDERSTAND... THEY... HE...
...I'M... I'M PUTTING DOWN THE KNIFE.

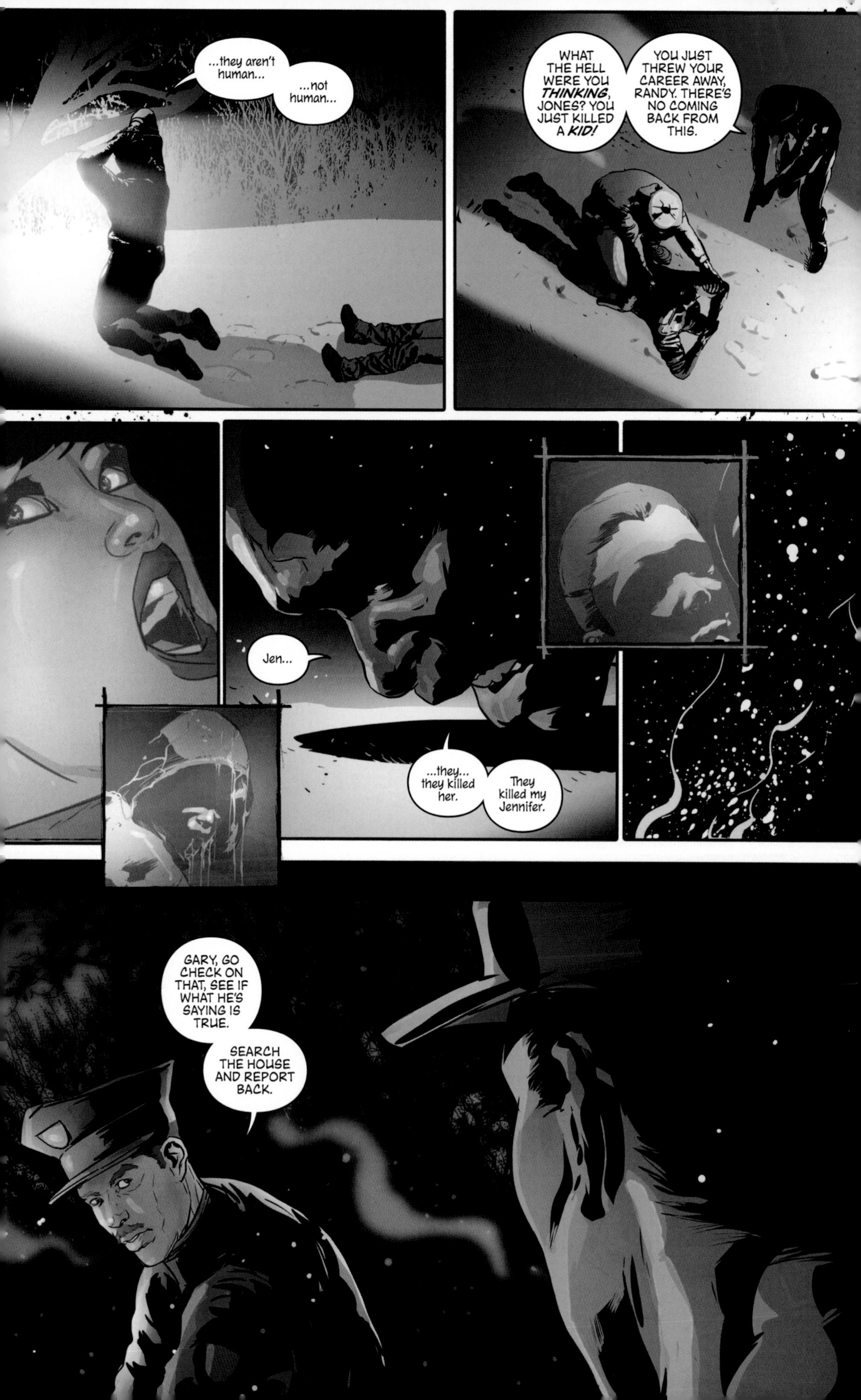
...they aren't human...
...not human...
WHAT THE HELL WERE YOU THINKING, JONES? YOU JUST KILLED A KID!
YOU JUST THREW YOUR CAREER AWAY, RANDY. THERE'S NO COMING BACK FROM THIS.
Jen...
...they... they killed her.
They killed my Jennifer.
GARY, GO CHECK ON THAT, SEE IF WHAT HE'S SAYING IS TRUE.
SEARCH THE HOUSE AND REPORT BACK.

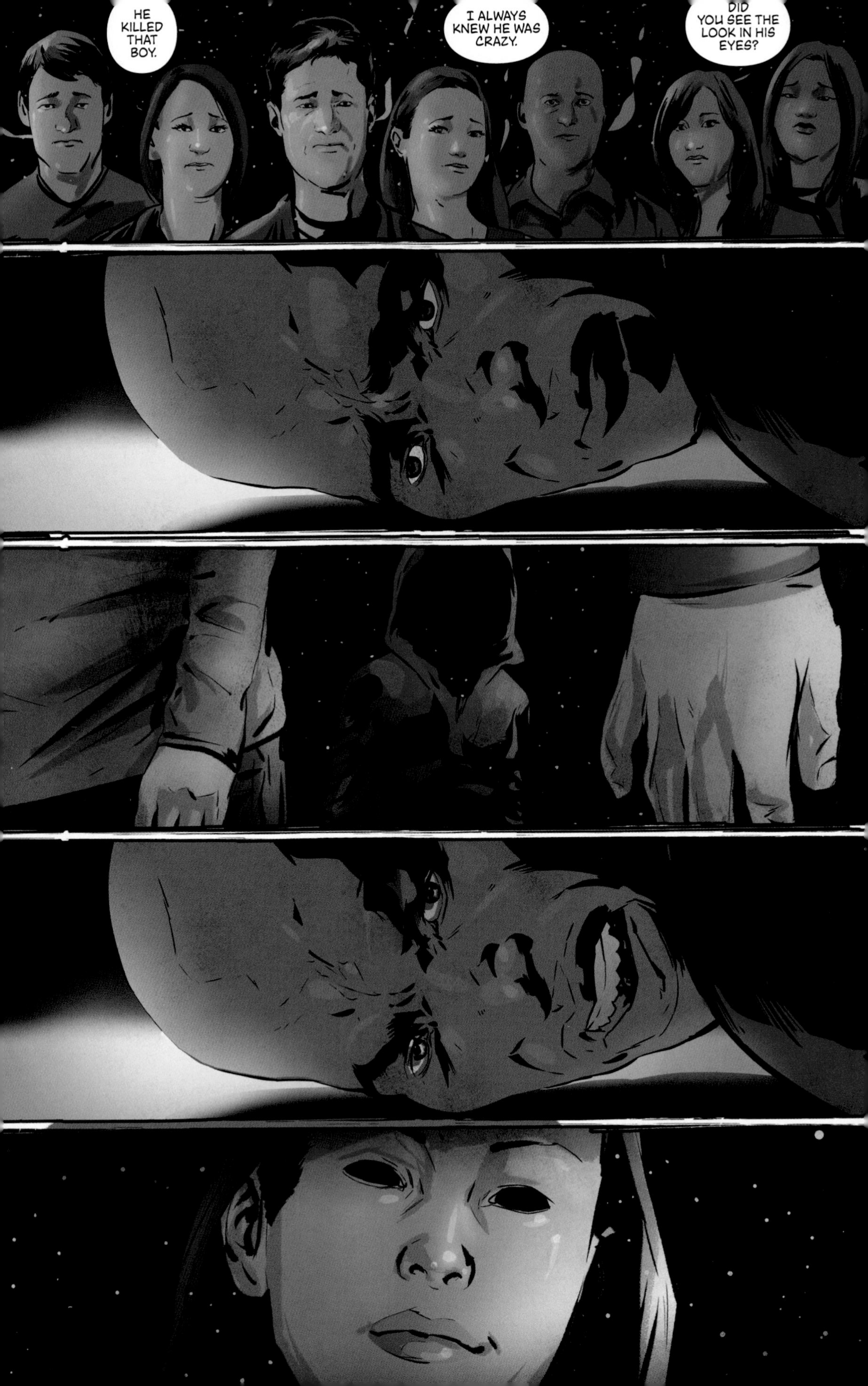
HE KILLED THAT BOY.
I ALWAYS KNEW HE WAS CRAZY.
DID YOU SEE THE LOOK IN HIS EYES?

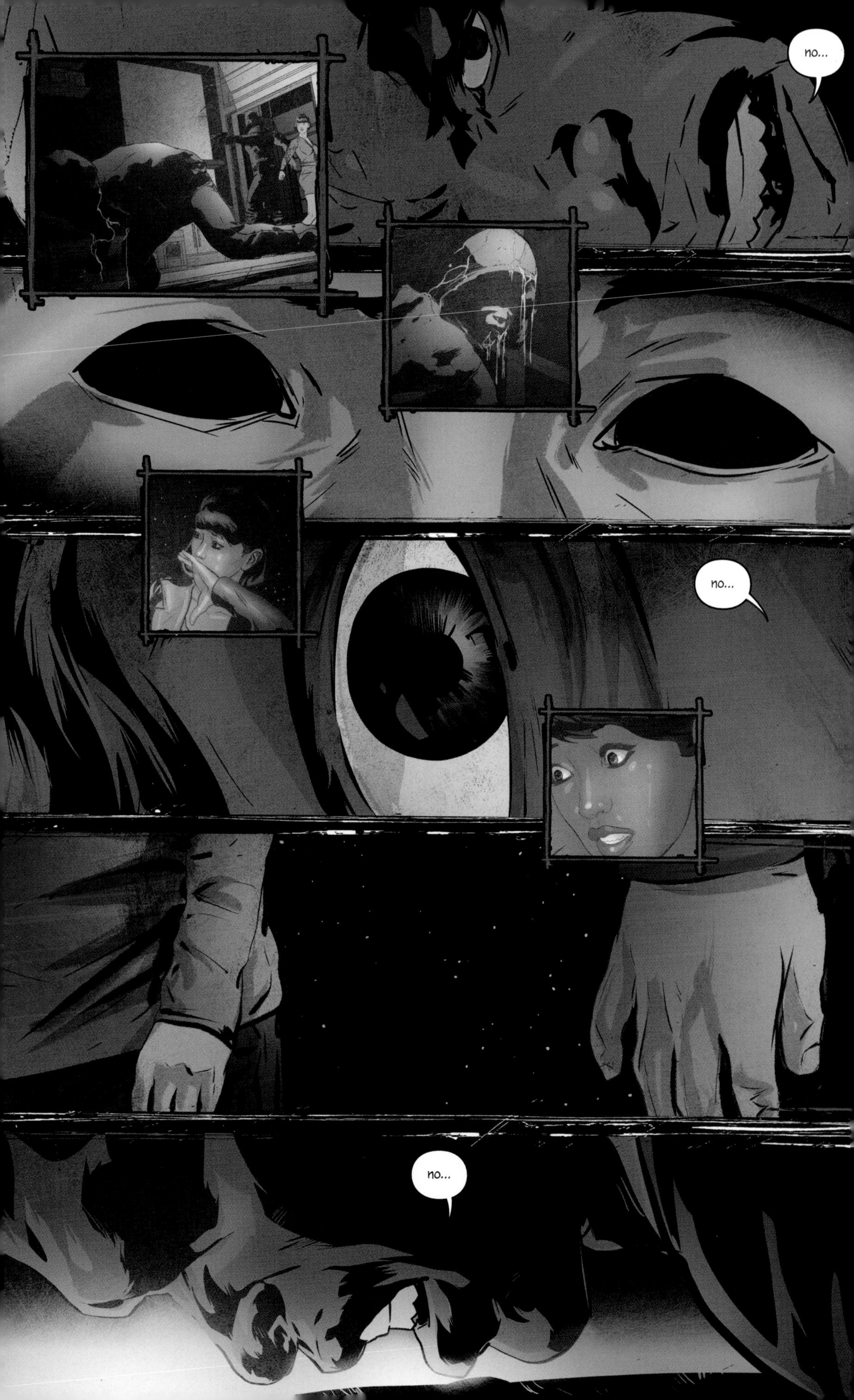
no...
no...
no...

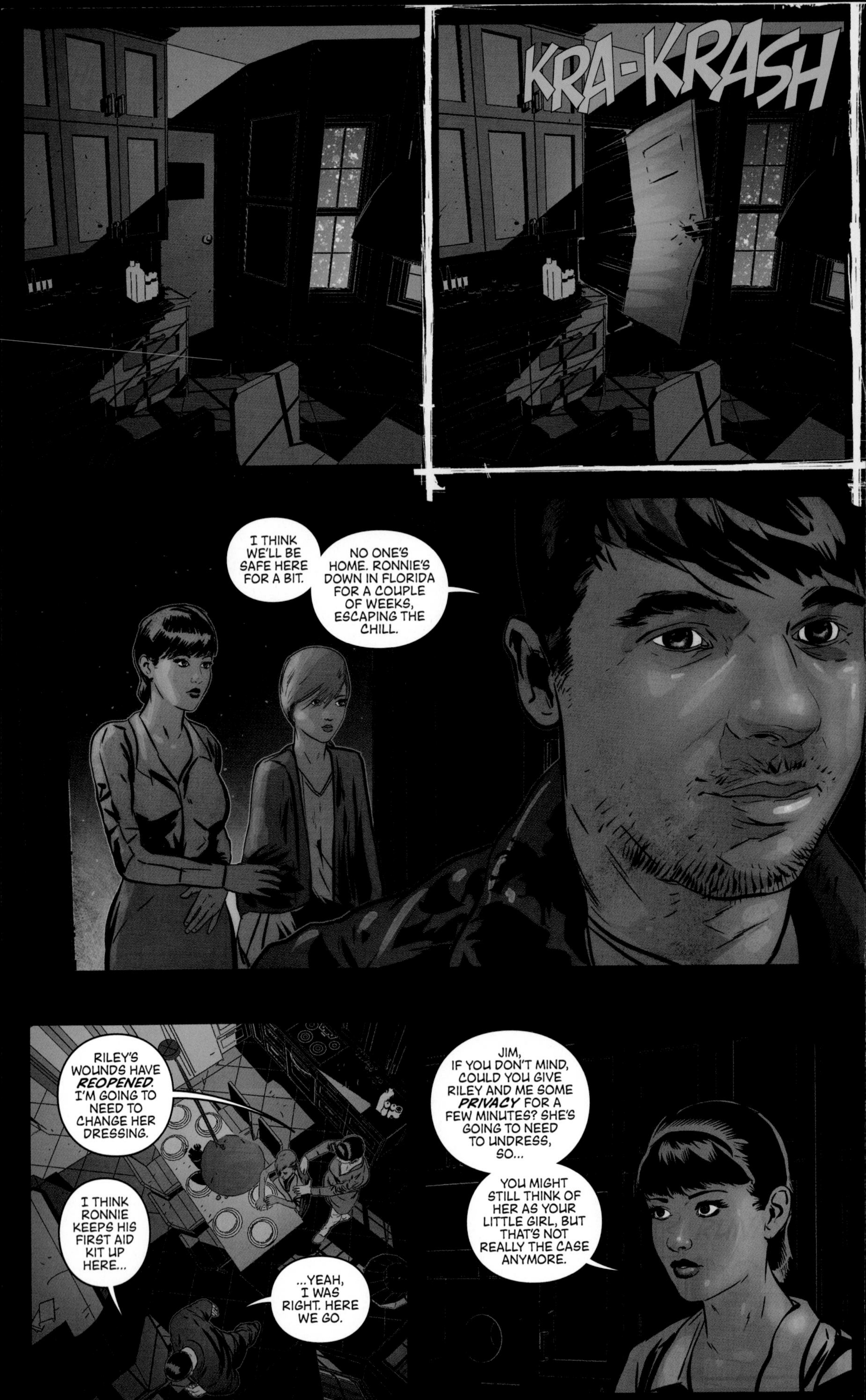
KRA-KRASH
I THINK WE'LL BE SAFE HERE FOR A BIT.
NO ONE'S HOME. RONNIE'S DOWN IN FLORIDA FOR A COUPLE OF WEEKS, ESCAPING THE CHILL.
RILEY'S WOUNDS HAVE *REOPENED*. I'M GOING TO NEED TO CHANGE HER DRESSING.
I THINK RONNIE KEEPS HIS FIRST AID KIT UP HERE...
...YEAH, I WAS RIGHT. HERE WE GO.
JIM, IF YOU DON'T MIND, COULD YOU GIVE RILEY AND ME SOME *PRIVACY* FOR A FEW MINUTES? SHE'S GOING TO NEED TO UNDRESS, SO...
YOU MIGHT STILL THINK OF HER AS YOUR LITTLE GIRL, BUT THAT'S NOT REALLY THE CASE ANYMORE.

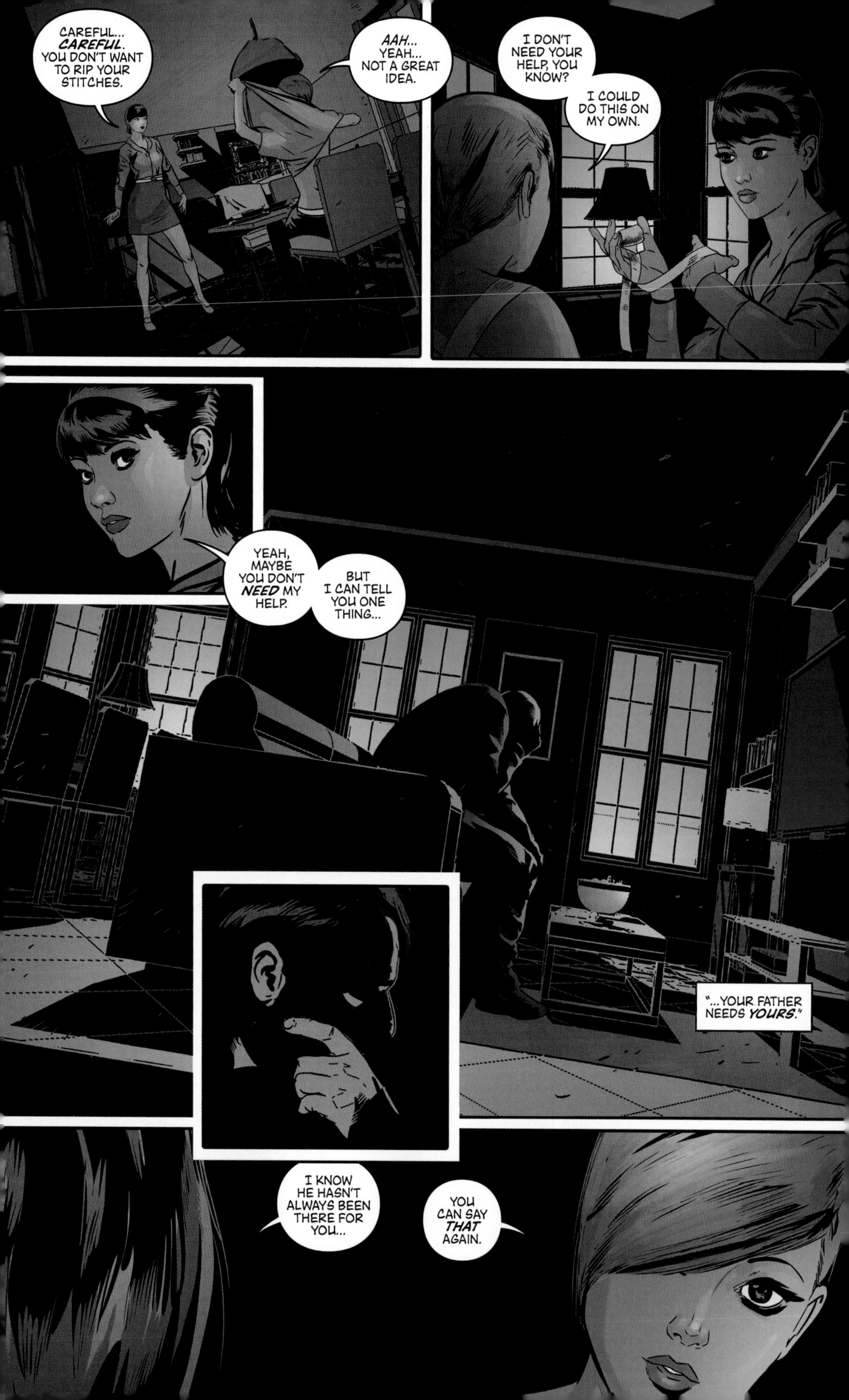
CAREFUL... CAREFUL. YOU DON'T WANT TO RIP YOUR STITCHES.
AAH... YEAH... NOT A GREAT IDEA.
I DON'T NEED YOUR HELP, YOU KNOW?
I COULD DO THIS ON MY OWN.
YEAH, MAYBE YOU DON'T NEED MY HELP.
BUT I CAN TELL YOU ONE THING...
"...YOUR FATHER NEEDS YOURS."
I KNOW HE HASN'T ALWAYS BEEN THERE FOR YOU...
YOU CAN SAY THAT AGAIN.

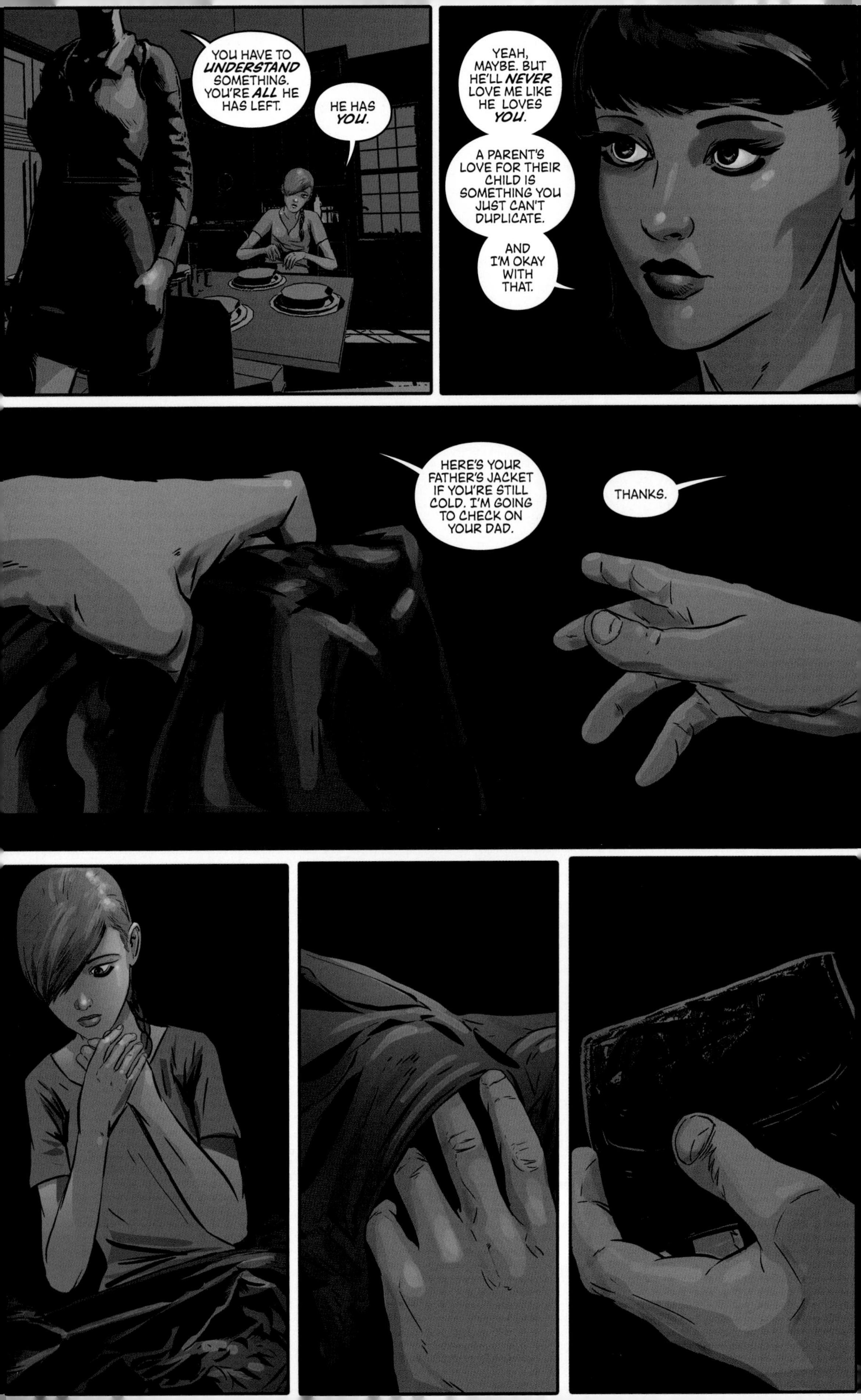
YOU HAVE TO UNDERSTAND SOMETHING. YOU'RE ALL HE HAS LEFT.
HE HAS YOU.
YEAH, MAYBE. BUT HE'LL NEVER LOVE ME LIKE HE LOVES YOU.
A PARENT'S LOVE FOR THEIR CHILD IS SOMETHING YOU JUST CAN'T DUPLICATE.
AND I'M OKAY WITH THAT.
HERE'S YOUR FATHER'S JACKET IF YOU'RE STILL COLD. I'M GOING TO CHECK ON YOUR DAD.
THANKS.

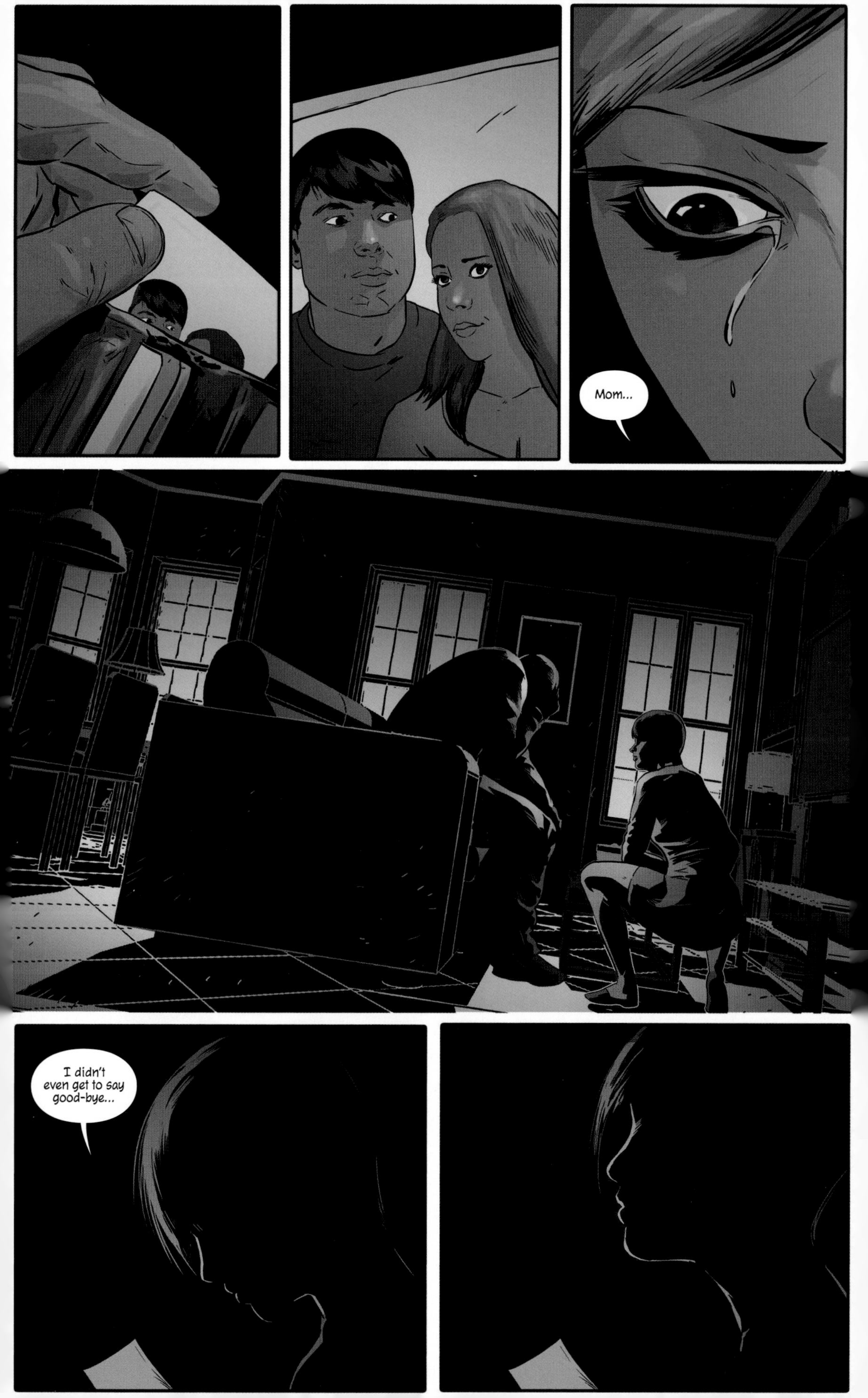
Mom...
I didn't even get to say good-bye...

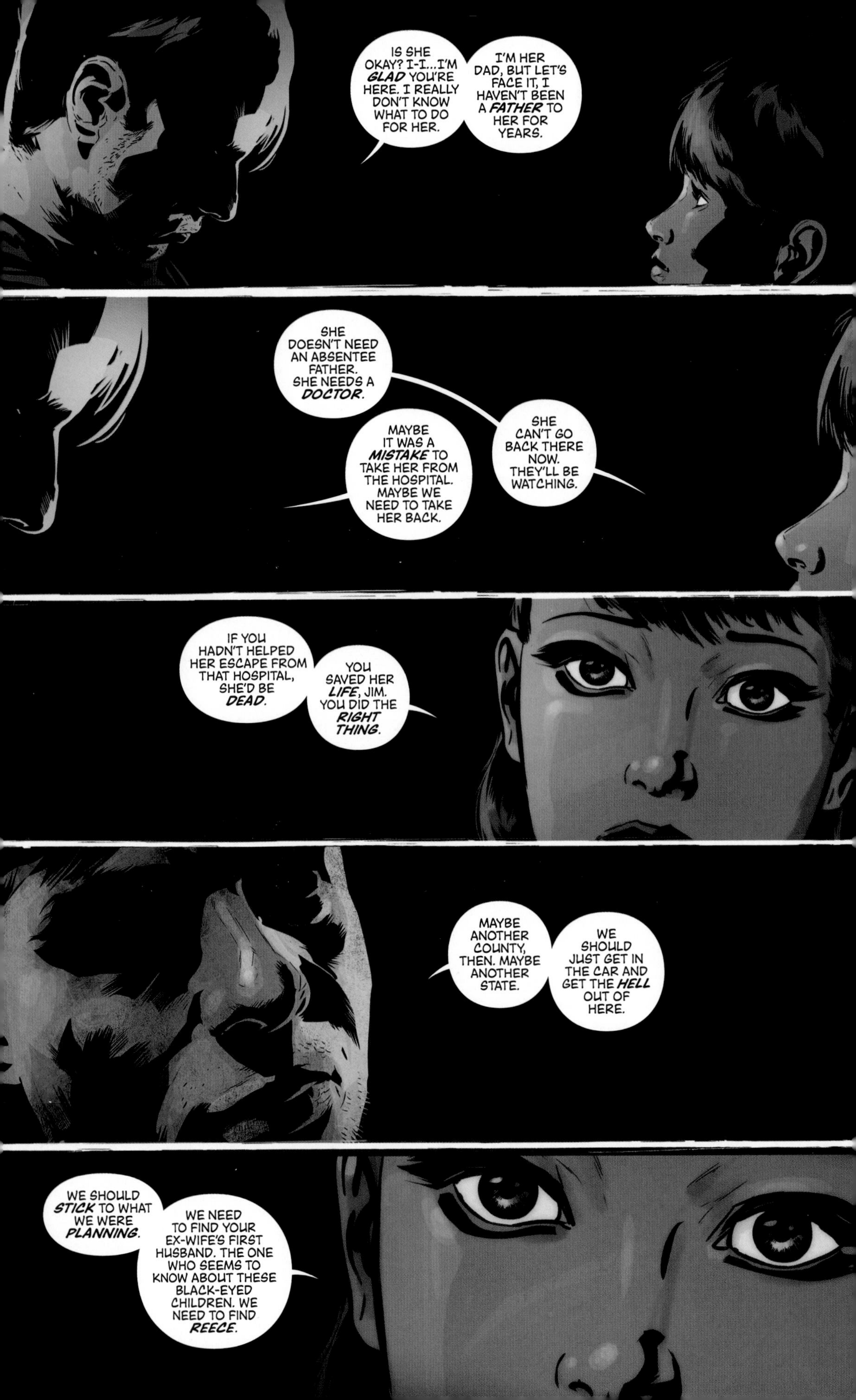
IS SHE OKAY? I-I...I'M GLAD YOU'RE HERE. I REALLY DON'T KNOW WHAT TO DO FOR HER.
I'M HER DAD, BUT LET'S FACE IT, I HAVEN'T BEEN A FATHER TO HER FOR YEARS.
SHE DOESN'T NEED AN ABSENTEE FATHER. SHE NEEDS A DOCTOR.
MAYBE IT WAS A MISTAKE TO TAKE HER FROM THE HOSPITAL. MAYBE WE NEED TO TAKE HER BACK.
SHE CAN'T GO BACK THERE NOW. THEY'LL BE WATCHING.
IF YOU HADN'T HELPED HER ESCAPE FROM THAT HOSPITAL, SHE'D BE DEAD.
YOU SAVED HER LIFE, JIM. YOU DID THE RIGHT THING.
MAYBE ANOTHER COUNTY, THEN. MAYBE ANOTHER STATE.
WE SHOULD JUST GET IN THE CAR AND GET THE HELL OUT OF HERE.
WE SHOULD STICK TO WHAT WE WERE PLANNING.
WE NEED TO FIND YOUR EX-WIFE'S FIRST HUSBAND. THE ONE WHO SEEMS TO KNOW ABOUT THESE BLACK-EYED CHILDREN. WE NEED TO FIND REECE.

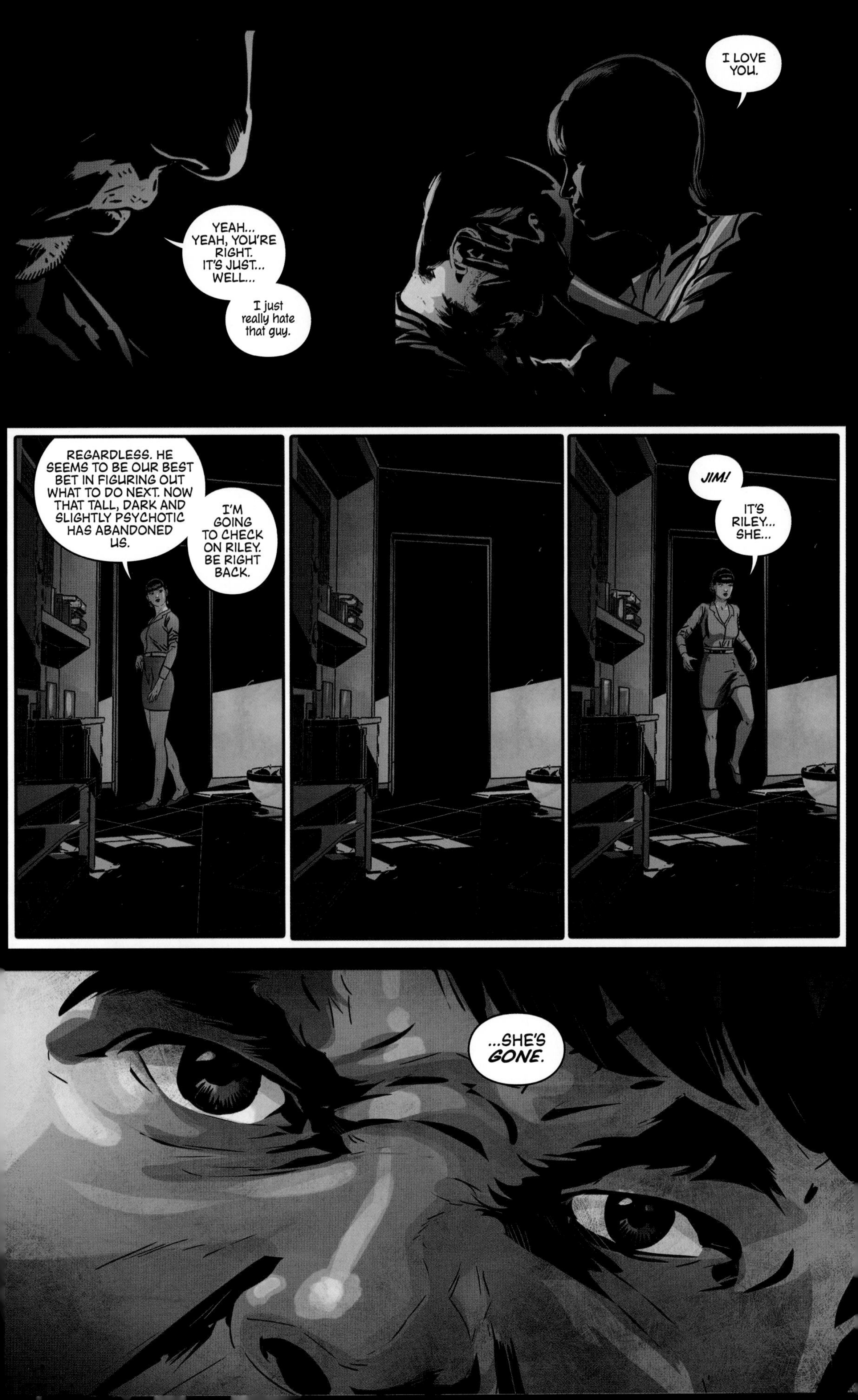
YEAH... YEAH, YOU'RE RIGHT. IT'S JUST... WELL...
I just really hate that guy.
I LOVE YOU.
REGARDLESS. HE SEEMS TO BE OUR BEST BET IN FIGURING OUT WHAT TO DO NEXT. NOW THAT TALL, DARK AND SLIGHTLY PSYCHOTIC HAS ABANDONED US.
I'M GOING TO CHECK ON RILEY. BE RIGHT BACK.
JIM!
IT'S RILEY... SHE...
...SHE'S GONE.

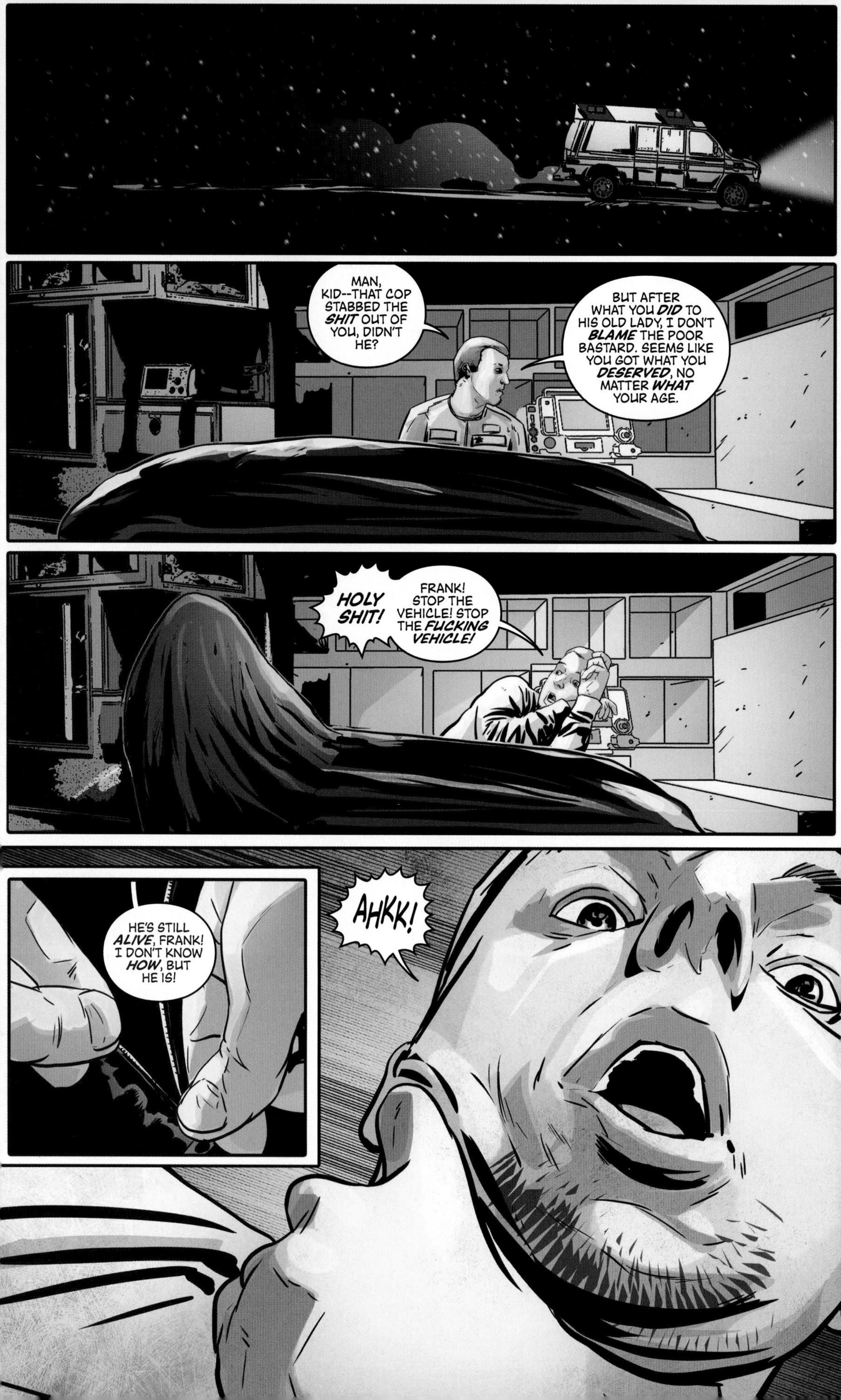

MAN, KID--THAT COP STABBED THE SHIT OUT OF YOU, DIDN'T HE?
BUT AFTER WHAT YOU DID TO HIS OLD LADY, I DON'T BLAME THE POOR BASTARD. SEEMS LIKE YOU GOT WHAT YOU DESERVED, NO MATTER WHAT YOUR AGE.
HOLY SHIT!
FRANK! STOP THE VEHICLE! STOP THE FUCKING VEHICLE!
HE'S STILL ALIVE, FRANK! I DON'T KNOW HOW, BUT HE IS!
AHKK!

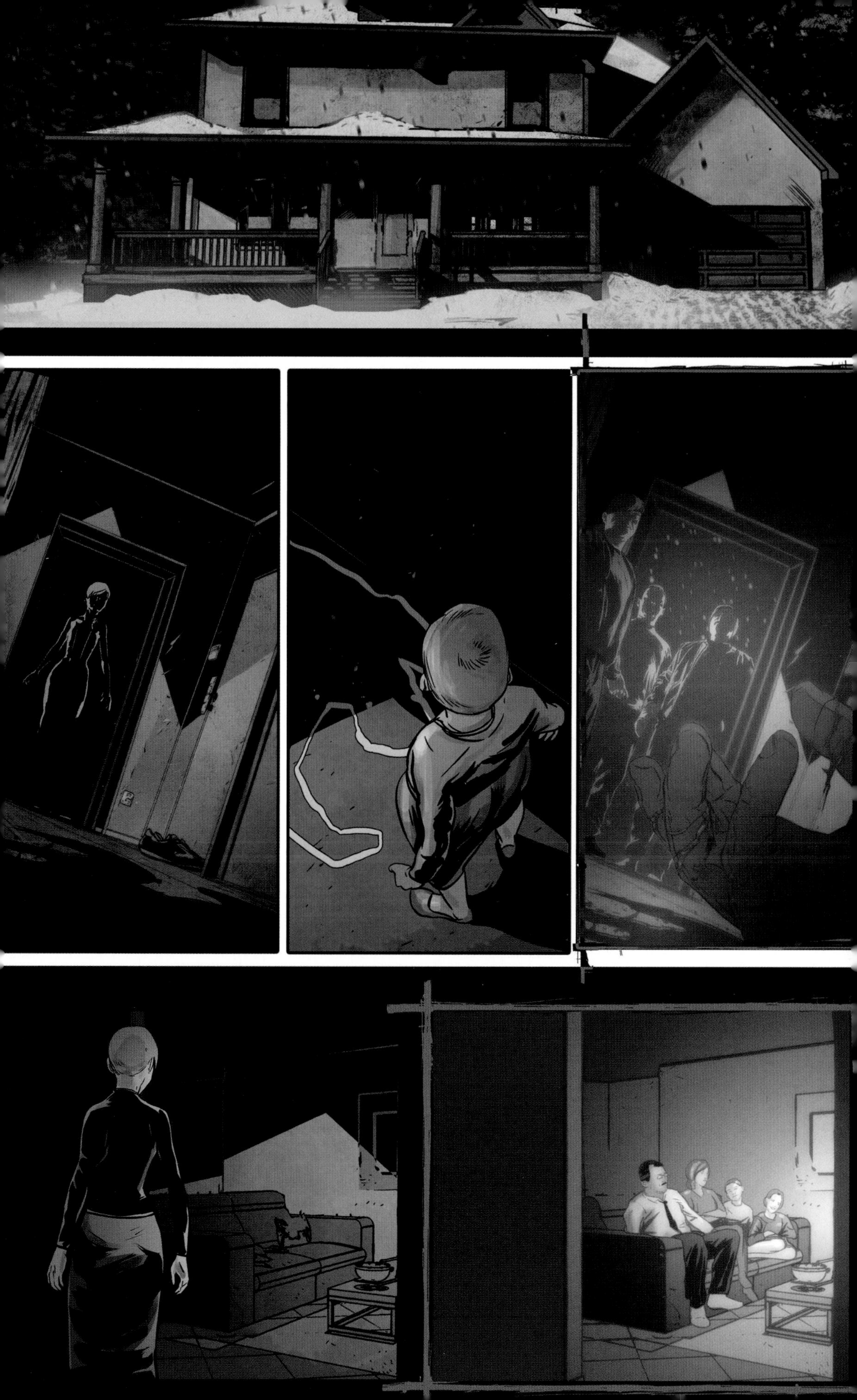

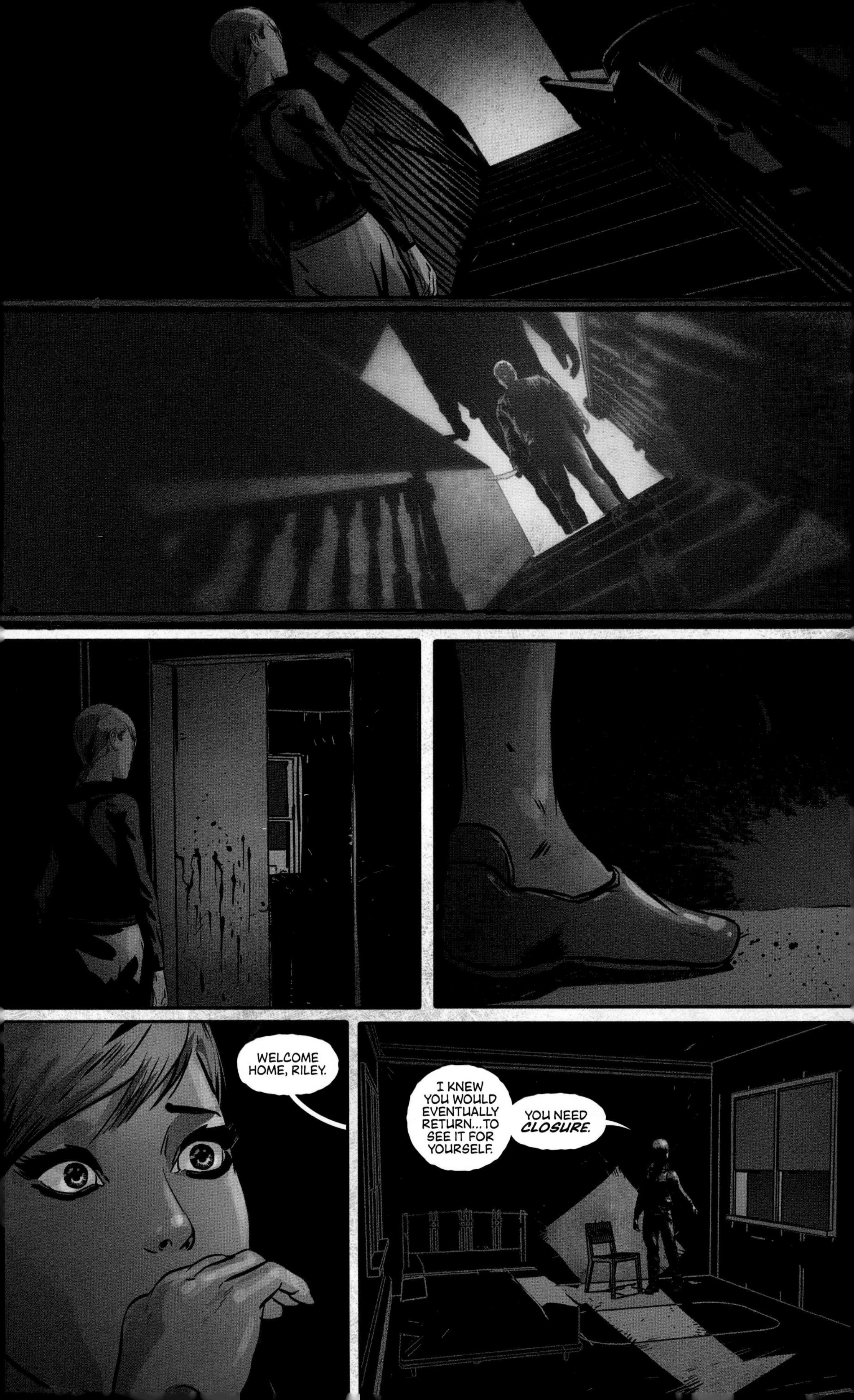
WELCOME HOME, RILEY.
I KNEW YOU WOULD EVENTUALLY RETURN...TO SEE IT FOR YOURSELF.
YOU NEED *CLOSURE*.

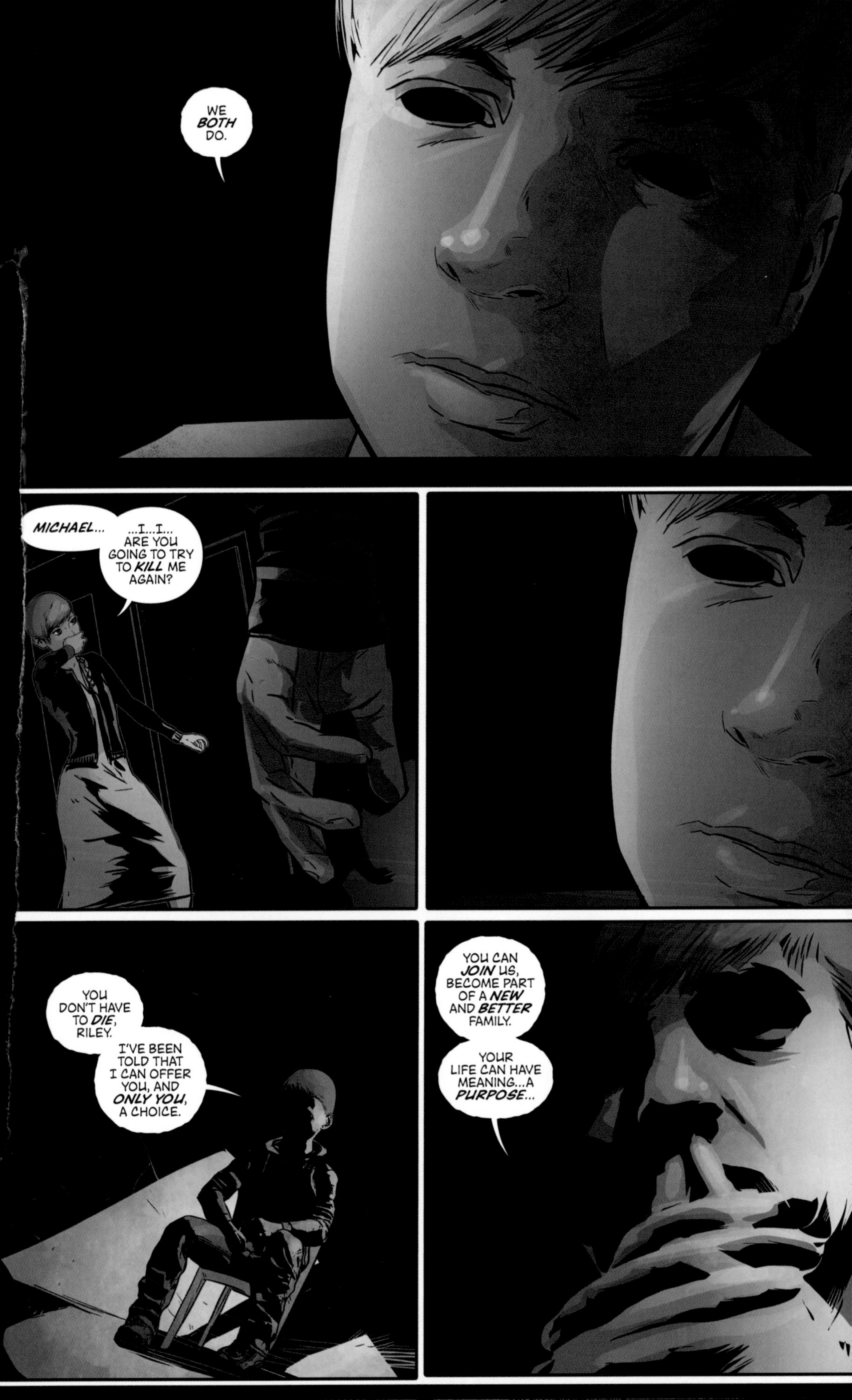
WE BOTH DO.
MICHAEL...
...I...I... ARE YOU GOING TO TRY TO KILL ME AGAIN?
YOU DON'T HAVE TO DIE, RILEY.
I'VE BEEN TOLD THAT I CAN OFFER YOU, AND ONLY YOU, A CHOICE.
YOU CAN JOIN US, BECOME PART OF A NEW AND BETTER FAMILY.
YOUR LIFE CAN HAVE MEANING...A PURPOSE...

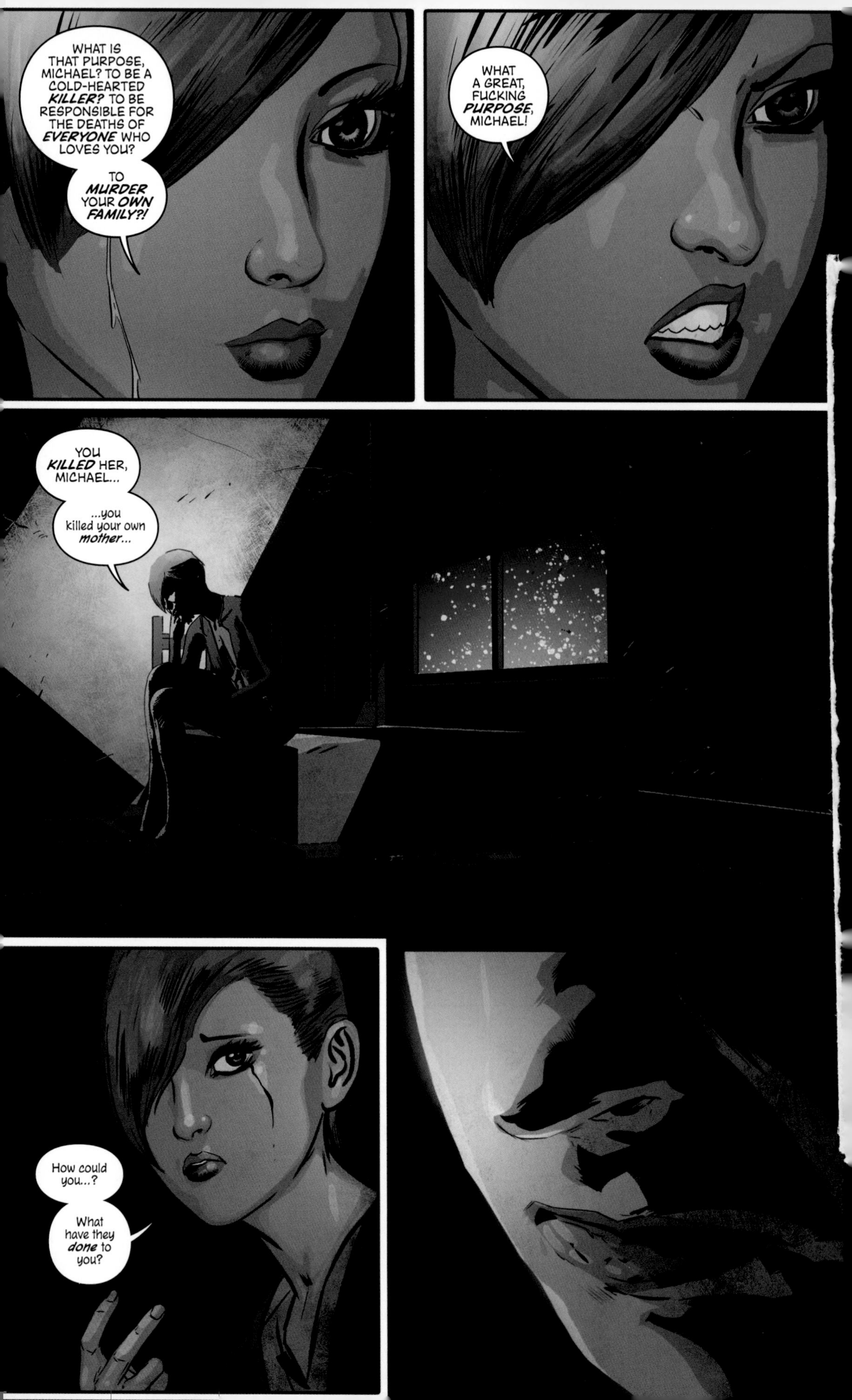
WHAT IS THAT PURPOSE, MICHAEL? TO BE A COLD-HEARTED KILLER? TO BE RESPONSIBLE FOR THE DEATHS OF EVERYONE WHO LOVES YOU?
TO MURDER YOUR OWN FAMILY?!
WHAT A GREAT, FUCKING PURPOSE, MICHAEL!
YOU KILLED HER, MICHAEL...
...you killed your own mother...
How could you...?
What have they done to you?

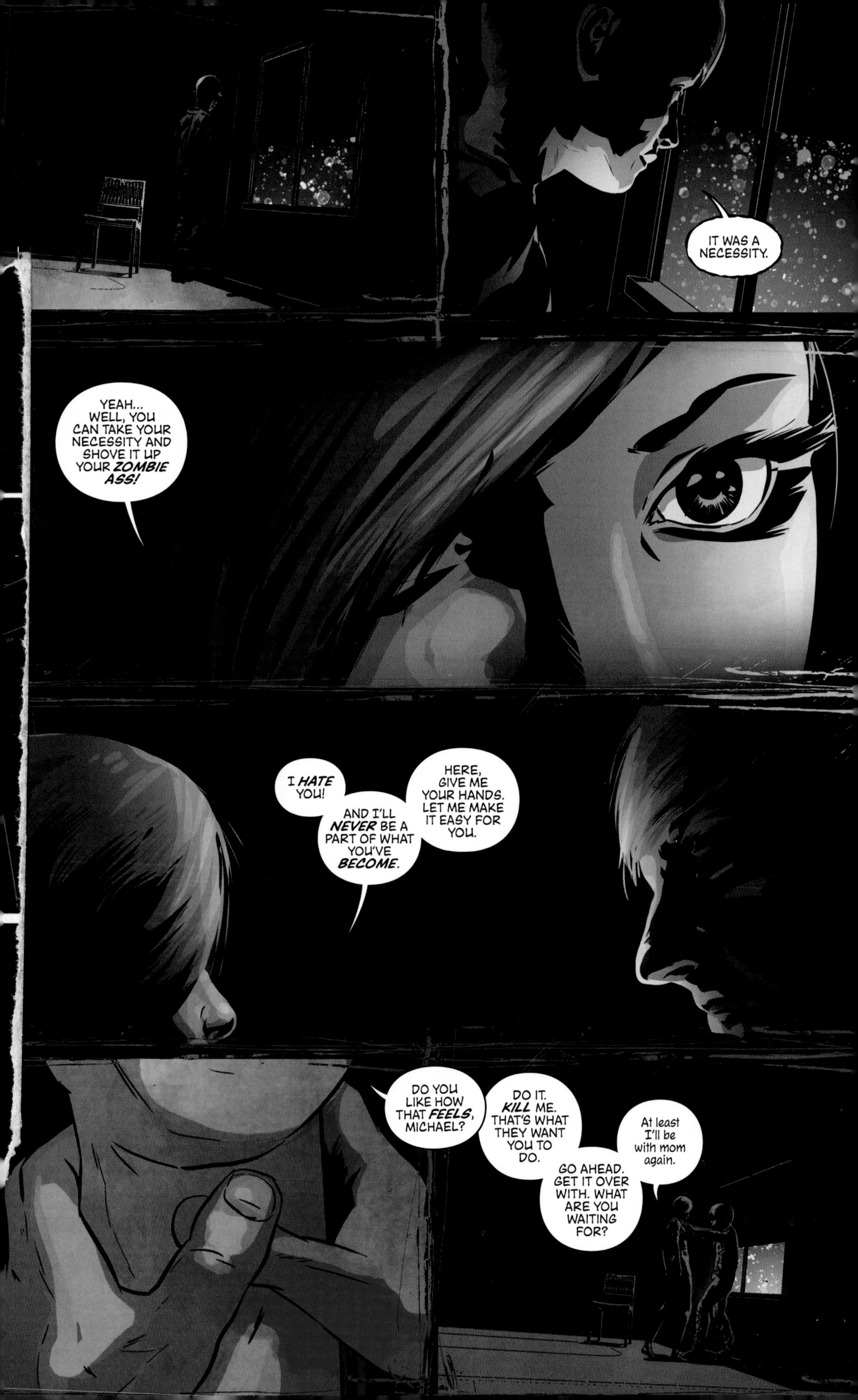
IT WAS A NECESSITY.
YEAH... WELL, YOU CAN TAKE YOUR NECESSITY AND SHOVE IT UP YOUR ZOMBIE ASS!
I HATE YOU!
AND I'LL NEVER BE A PART OF WHAT YOU'VE BECOME.
HERE, GIVE ME YOUR HANDS. LET ME MAKE IT EASY FOR YOU.
DO YOU LIKE HOW THAT FEELS, MICHAEL?
DO IT. KILL ME. THAT'S WHAT THEY WANT YOU TO DO.
GO AHEAD. GET IT OVER WITH. WHAT ARE YOU WAITING FOR?
At least I'll be with mom again.

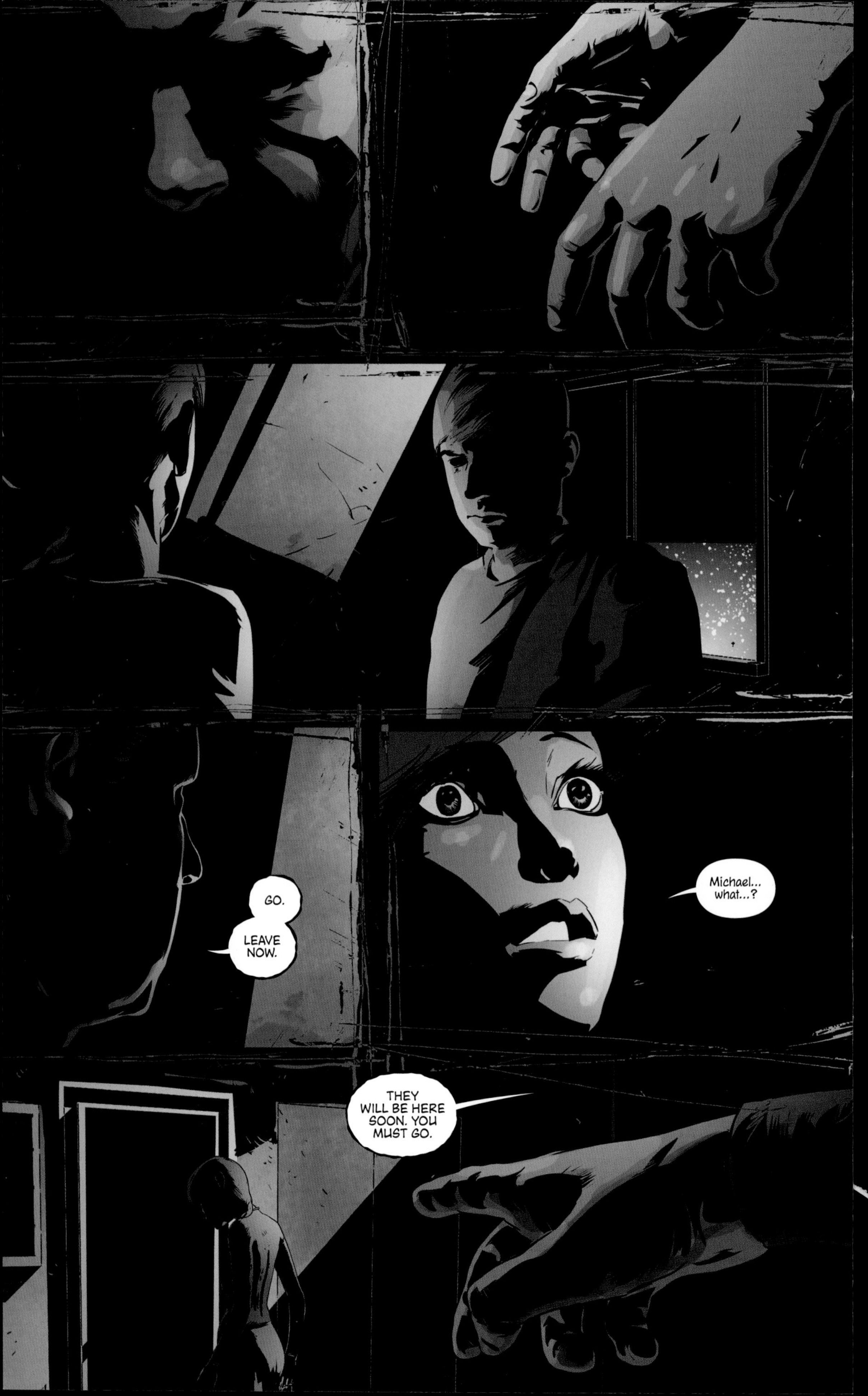
GO.
LEAVE NOW.
Michael... what...?
THEY WILL BE HERE SOON. YOU MUST GO.

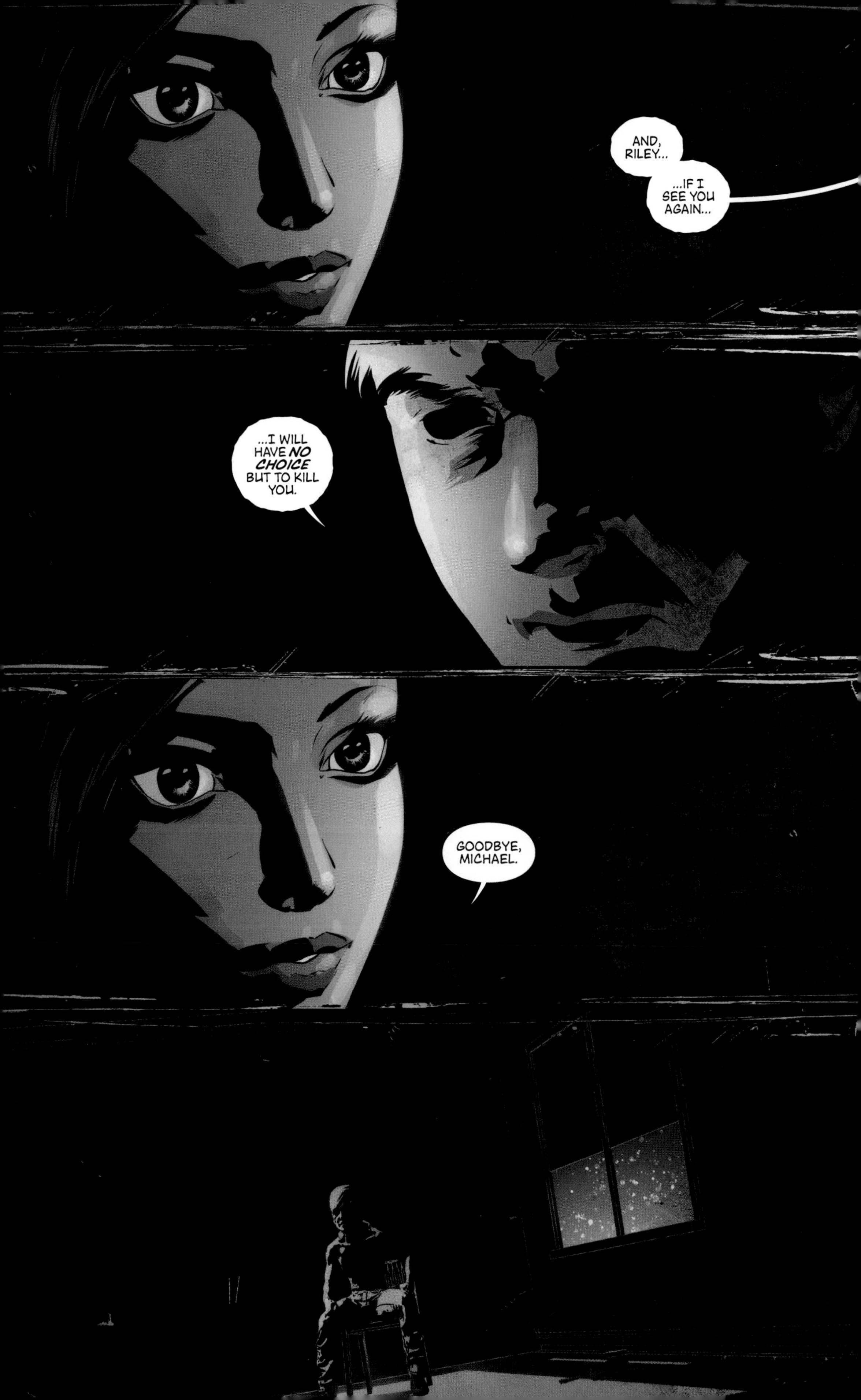
AND, RILEY...
...IF I SEE YOU AGAIN...
...I WILL HAVE NO CHOICE BUT TO KILL YOU.
GOODBYE, MICHAEL.

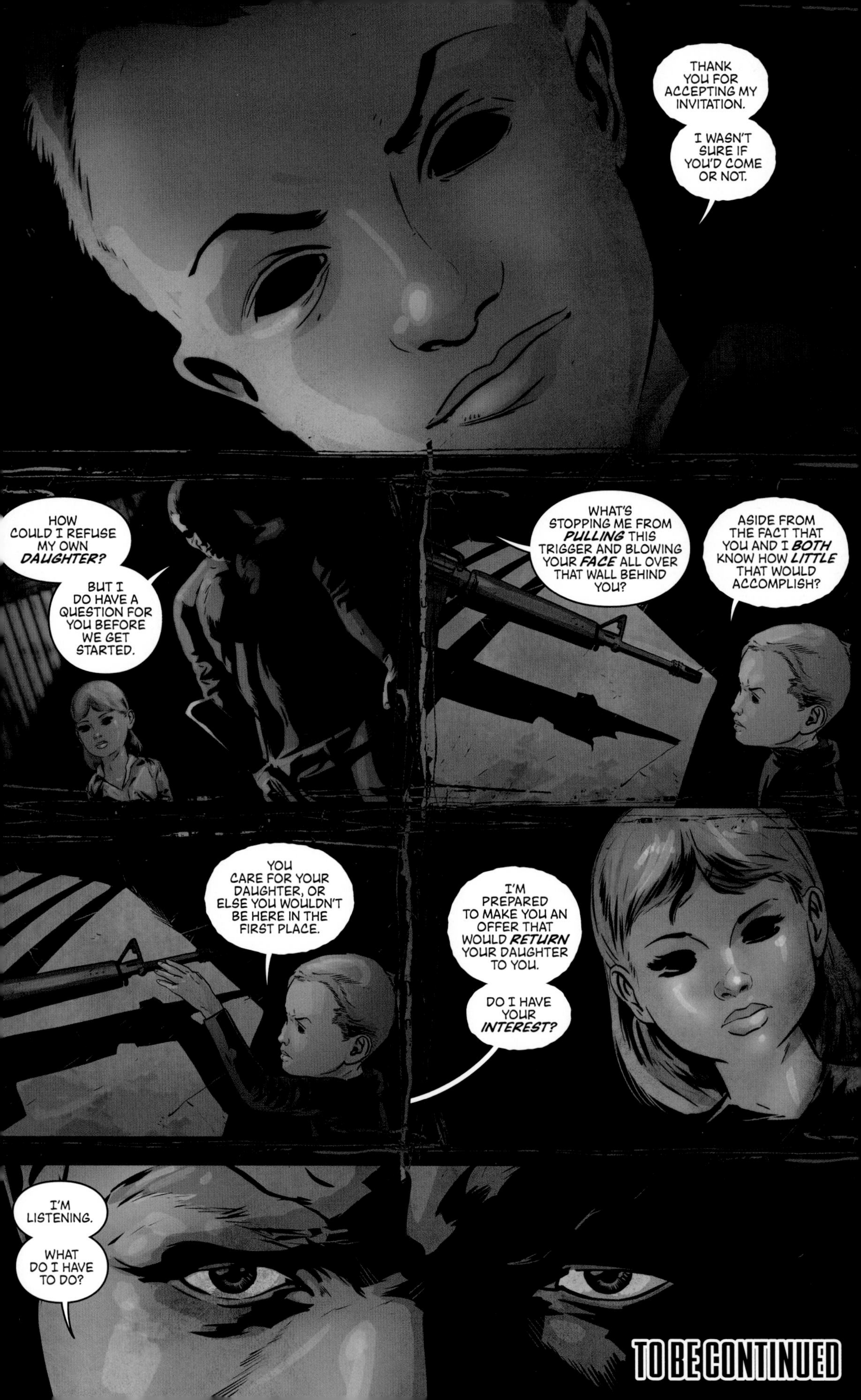
THANK YOU FOR ACCEPTING MY INVITATION.
I WASN'T SURE IF YOU'D COME OR NOT.
HOW COULD I REFUSE MY OWN *DAUGHTER?*
BUT I DO HAVE A QUESTION FOR YOU BEFORE WE GET STARTED.
WHAT'S STOPPING ME FROM *PULLING* THIS TRIGGER AND BLOWING YOUR *FACE* ALL OVER THAT WALL BEHIND YOU?
ASIDE FROM THE FACT THAT YOU AND I *BOTH* KNOW HOW *LITTLE* THAT WOULD ACCOMPLISH?
YOU CARE FOR YOUR DAUGHTER, OR ELSE YOU WOULDN'T BE HERE IN THE FIRST PLACE.
I'M PREPARED TO MAKE YOU AN OFFER THAT WOULD *RETURN* YOUR DAUGHTER TO YOU.
DO I HAVE YOUR *INTEREST?*
I'M LISTENING.
WHAT DO I HAVE TO DO?
TO BE CONTINUED

9

"DEALS WITH THE DEVIL"

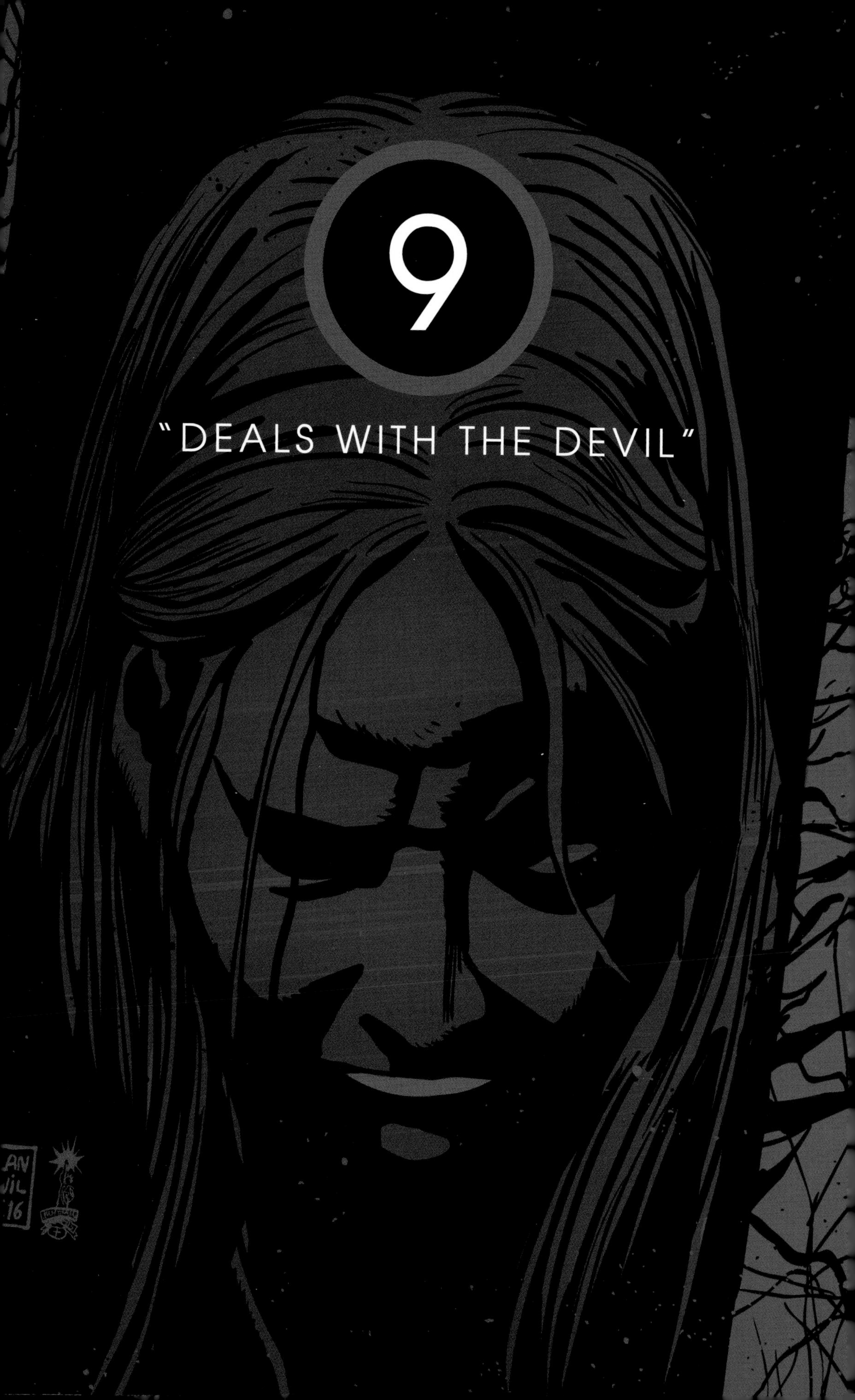

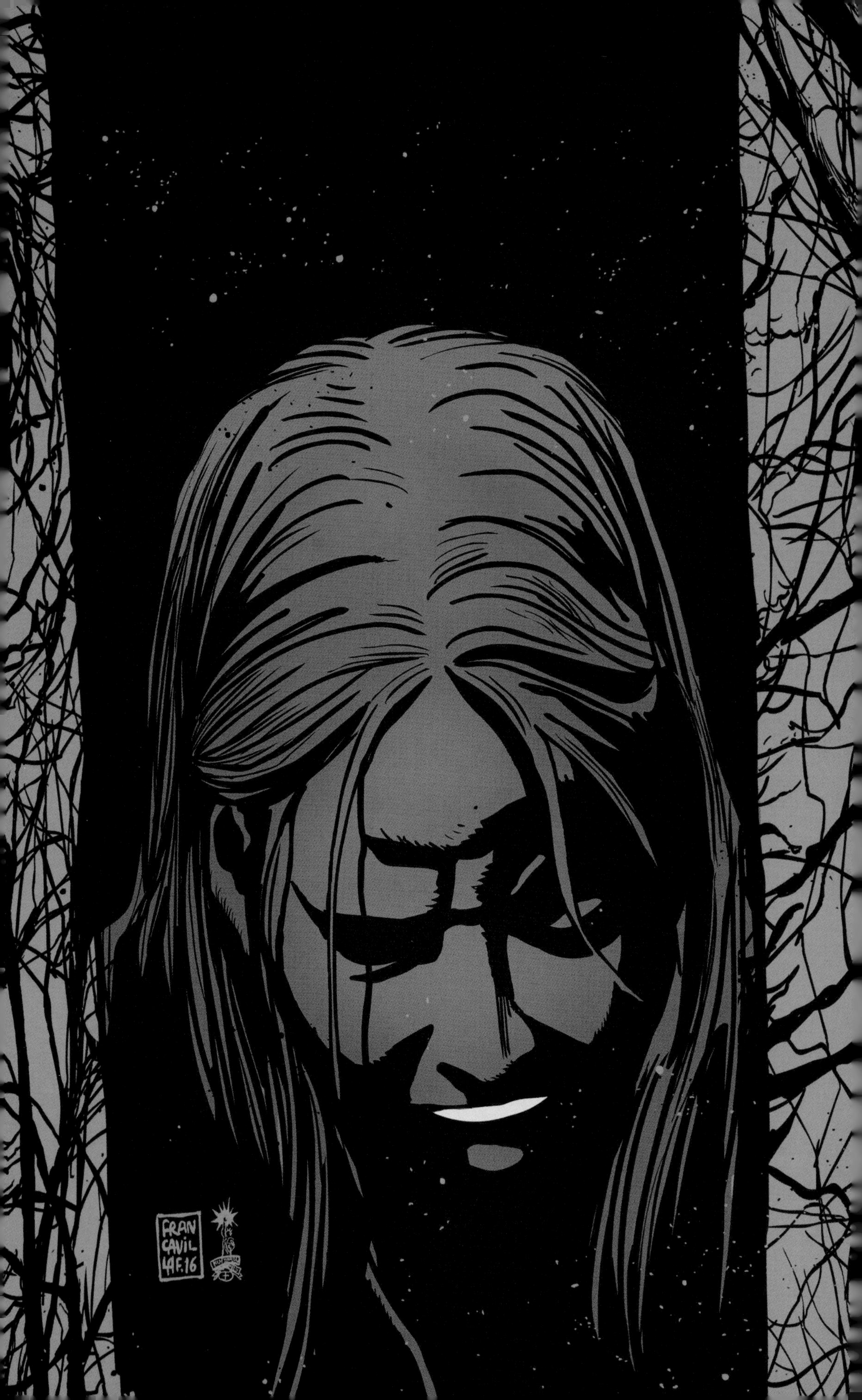
FRAN
CAVIL

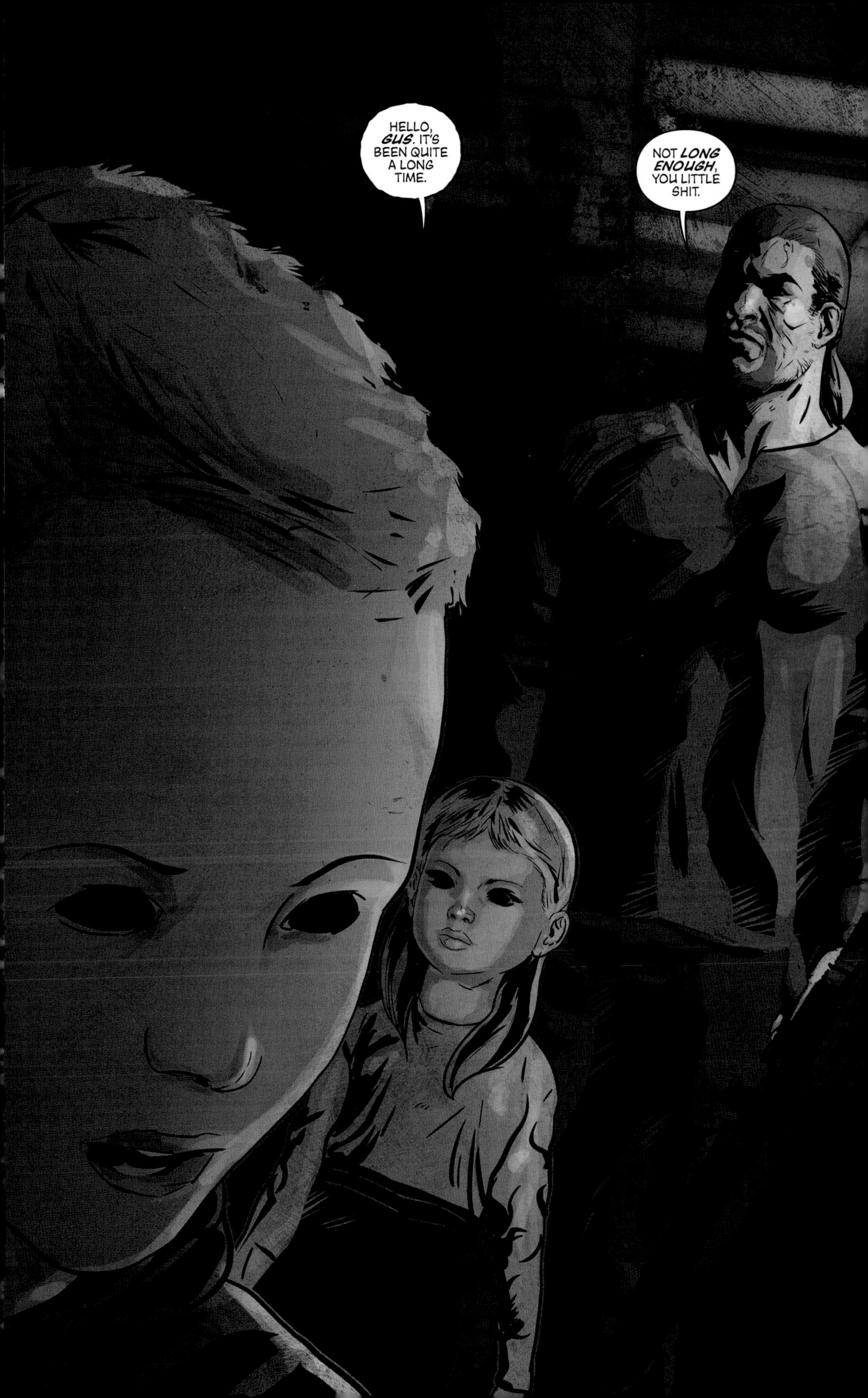
HELLO, GUS. IT'S BEEN QUITE A LONG TIME.
NOT LONG ENOUGH, YOU LITTLE SHIT.

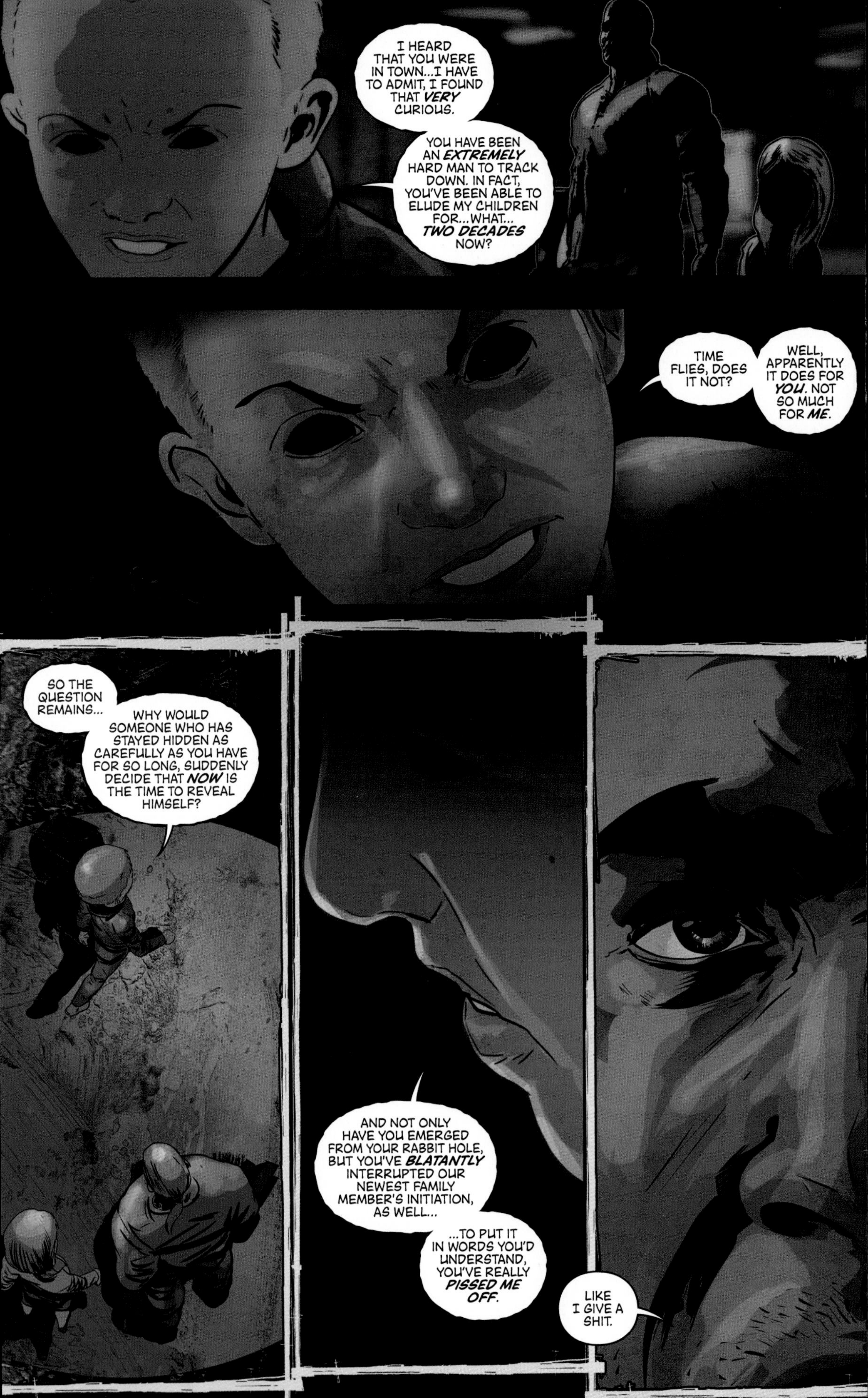
I HEARD THAT YOU WERE IN TOWN...I HAVE TO ADMIT, I FOUND THAT VERY CURIOUS.
YOU HAVE BEEN AN EXTREMELY HARD MAN TO TRACK DOWN. IN FACT, YOU'VE BEEN ABLE TO ELUDE MY CHILDREN FOR...WHAT... TWO DECADES NOW?
TIME FLIES, DOES IT NOT?
WELL, APPARENTLY IT DOES FOR YOU. NOT SO MUCH FOR ME.
SO THE QUESTION REMAINS...
WHY WOULD SOMEONE WHO HAS STAYED HIDDEN AS CAREFULLY AS YOU HAVE FOR SO LONG, SUDDENLY DECIDE THAT NOW IS THE TIME TO REVEAL HIMSELF?
AND NOT ONLY HAVE YOU EMERGED FROM YOUR RABBIT HOLE, BUT YOU'VE BLATANTLY INTERRUPTED OUR NEWEST FAMILY MEMBER'S INITIATION, AS WELL...
...TO PUT IT IN WORDS YOU'D UNDERSTAND, YOU'VE REALLY PISSED ME OFF.
LIKE I GIVE A SHIT.

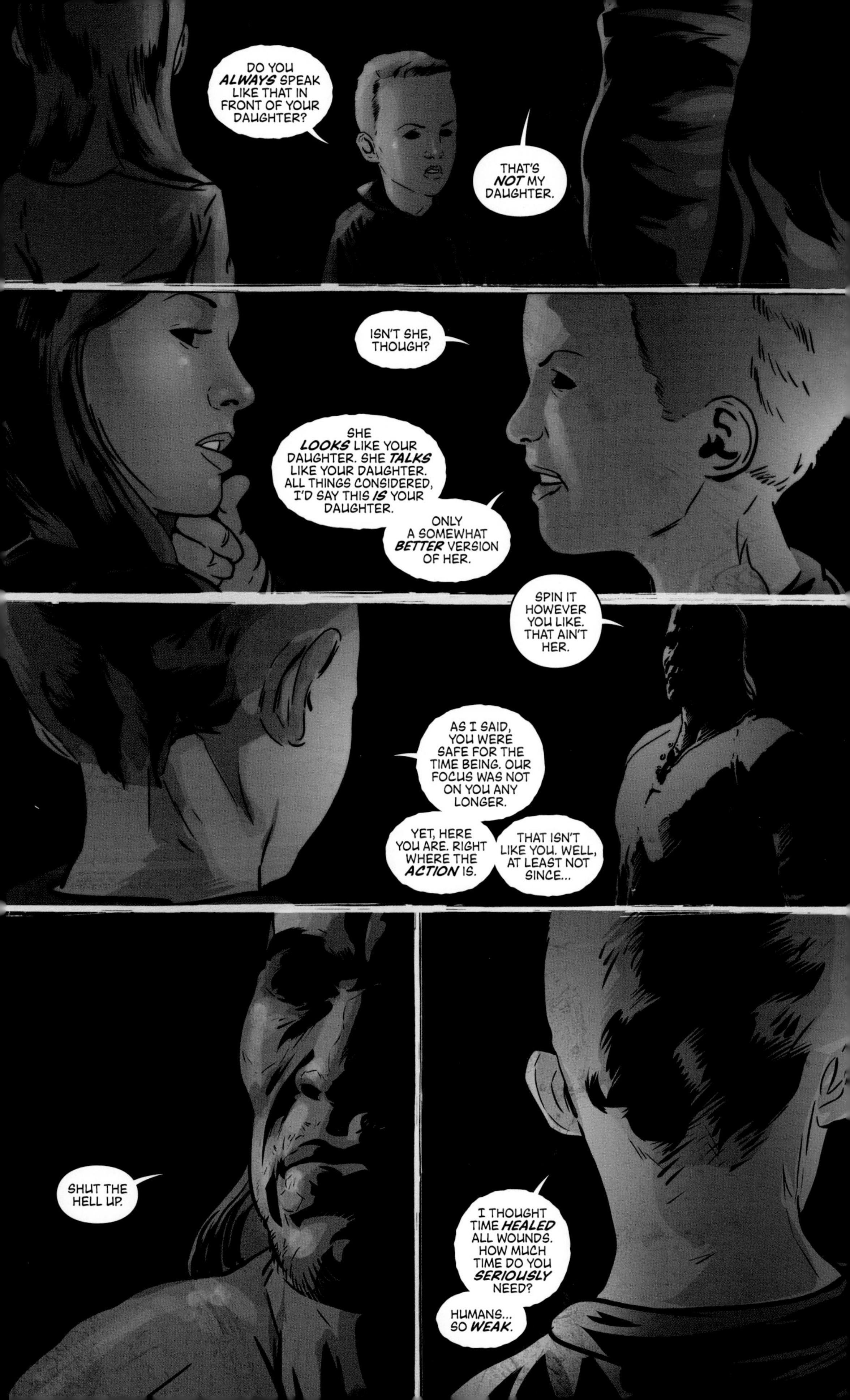
DO YOU ALWAYS SPEAK LIKE THAT IN FRONT OF YOUR DAUGHTER?
THAT'S NOT MY DAUGHTER.
ISN'T SHE, THOUGH?
SHE LOOKS LIKE YOUR DAUGHTER. SHE TALKS LIKE YOUR DAUGHTER. ALL THINGS CONSIDERED, I'D SAY THIS IS YOUR DAUGHTER.
ONLY A SOMEWHAT BETTER VERSION OF HER.
SPIN IT HOWEVER YOU LIKE. THAT AIN'T HER.
AS I SAID, YOU WERE SAFE FOR THE TIME BEING. OUR FOCUS WAS NOT ON YOU ANY LONGER.
YET, HERE YOU ARE. RIGHT WHERE THE ACTION IS.
THAT ISN'T LIKE YOU. WELL, AT LEAST NOT SINCE...
SHUT THE HELL UP.
I THOUGHT TIME HEALED ALL WOUNDS. HOW MUCH TIME DO YOU SERIOUSLY NEED?
HUMANS... SO WEAK.

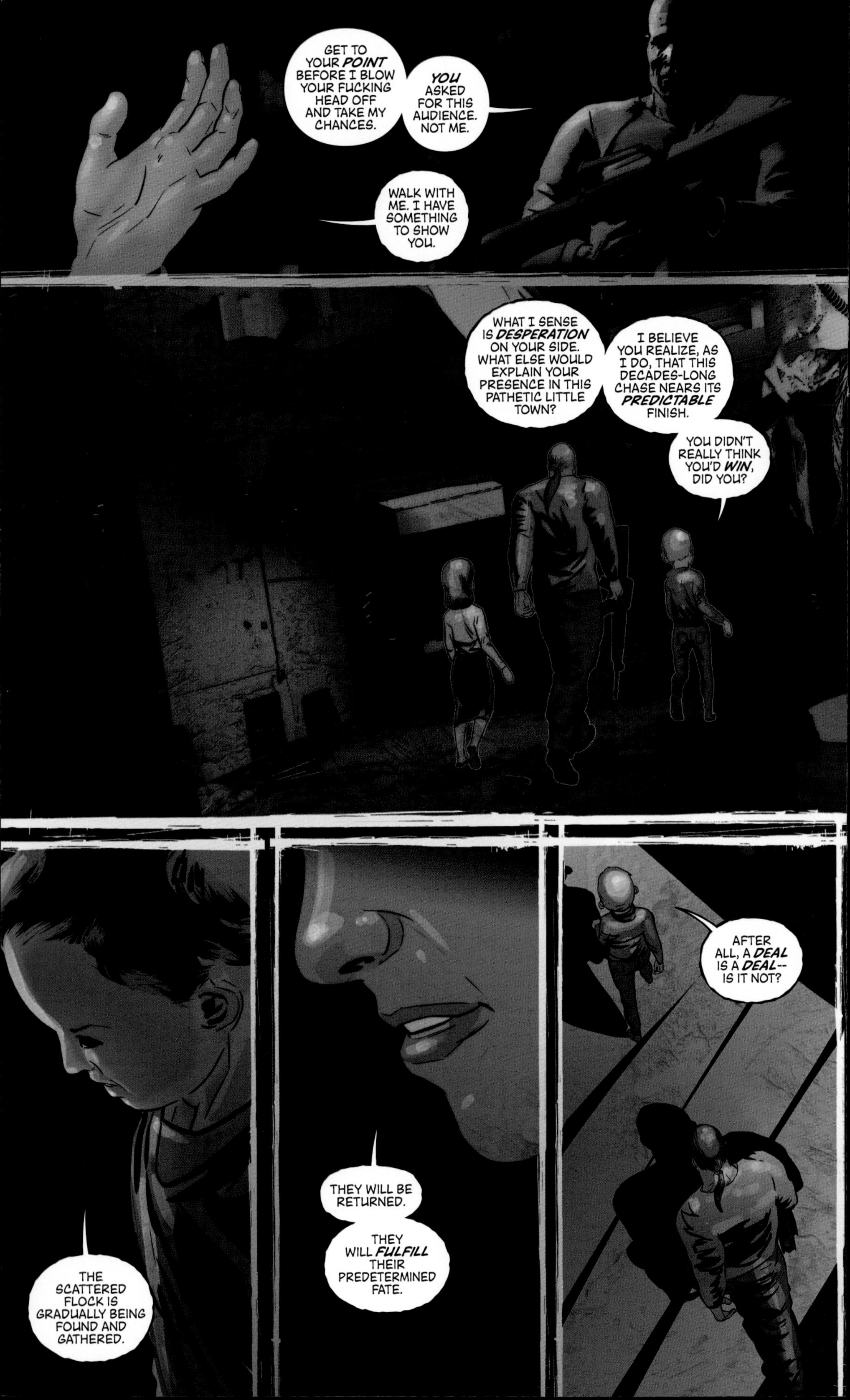
GET TO YOUR *POINT* BEFORE I BLOW YOUR FUCKING HEAD OFF AND TAKE MY CHANCES.
YOU ASKED FOR THIS AUDIENCE. NOT ME.
WALK WITH ME. I HAVE SOMETHING TO SHOW YOU.
WHAT I SENSE IS *DESPERATION* ON YOUR SIDE. WHAT ELSE WOULD EXPLAIN YOUR PRESENCE IN THIS PATHETIC LITTLE TOWN?
I BELIEVE YOU REALIZE, AS I DO, THAT THIS DECADES-LONG CHASE NEARS ITS *PREDICTABLE* FINISH.
YOU DIDN'T REALLY THINK YOU'D *WIN*, DID YOU?
THE SCATTERED FLOCK IS GRADUALLY BEING FOUND AND GATHERED.
THEY WILL BE RETURNED.
THEY WILL *FULFILL* THEIR PREDETERMINED FATE.
AFTER ALL, A *DEAL* IS A *DEAL*-- IS IT NOT?

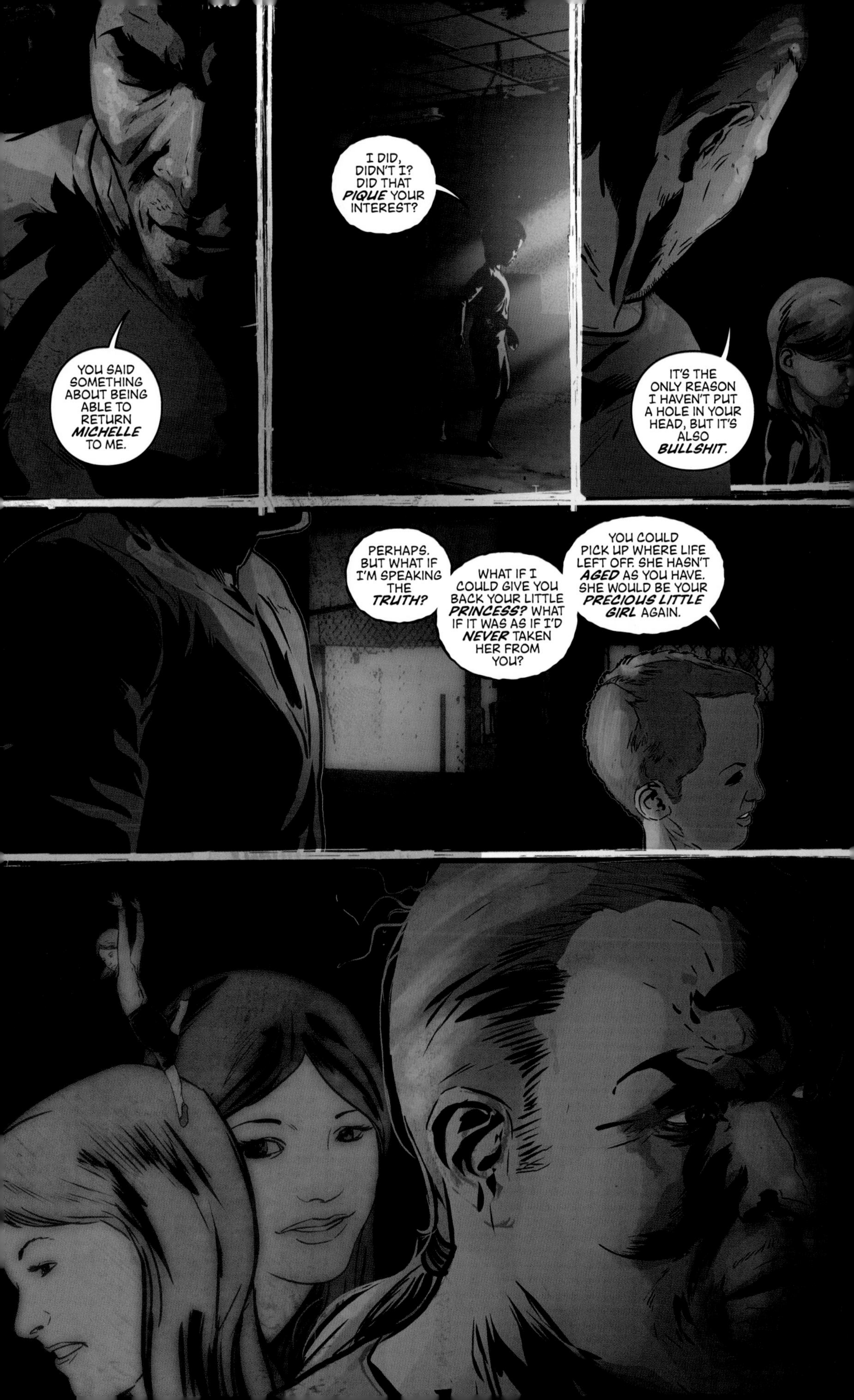
YOU SAID SOMETHING ABOUT BEING ABLE TO RETURN MICHELLE TO ME.
I DID, DIDN'T I? DID THAT PIQUE YOUR INTEREST?
IT'S THE ONLY REASON I HAVEN'T PUT A HOLE IN YOUR HEAD, BUT IT'S ALSO BULLSHIT.
PERHAPS. BUT WHAT IF I'M SPEAKING THE TRUTH?
WHAT IF I COULD GIVE YOU BACK YOUR LITTLE PRINCESS? WHAT IF IT WAS AS IF I'D NEVER TAKEN HER FROM YOU?
YOU COULD PICK UP WHERE LIFE LEFT OFF. SHE HASN'T AGED AS YOU HAVE. SHE WOULD BE YOUR PRECIOUS LITTLE GIRL AGAIN.

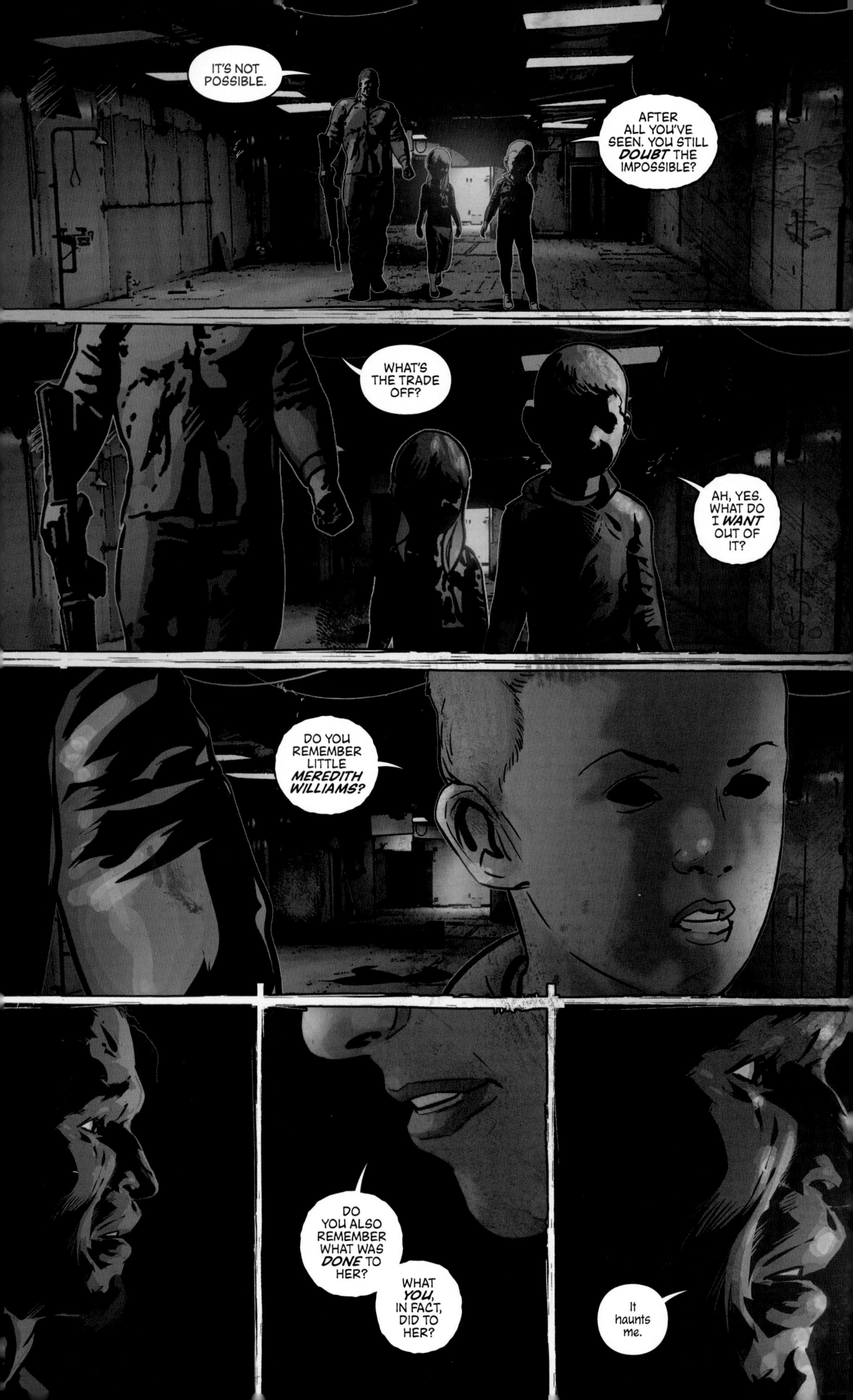
IT'S NOT POSSIBLE.
AFTER ALL YOU'VE SEEN. YOU STILL DOUBT THE IMPOSSIBLE?
WHAT'S THE TRADE OFF?
AH, YES. WHAT DO I WANT OUT OF IT?
DO YOU REMEMBER LITTLE MEREDITH WILLIAMS?
DO YOU ALSO REMEMBER WHAT WAS DONE TO HER?
WHAT YOU, IN FACT, DID TO HER?
It haunts me.

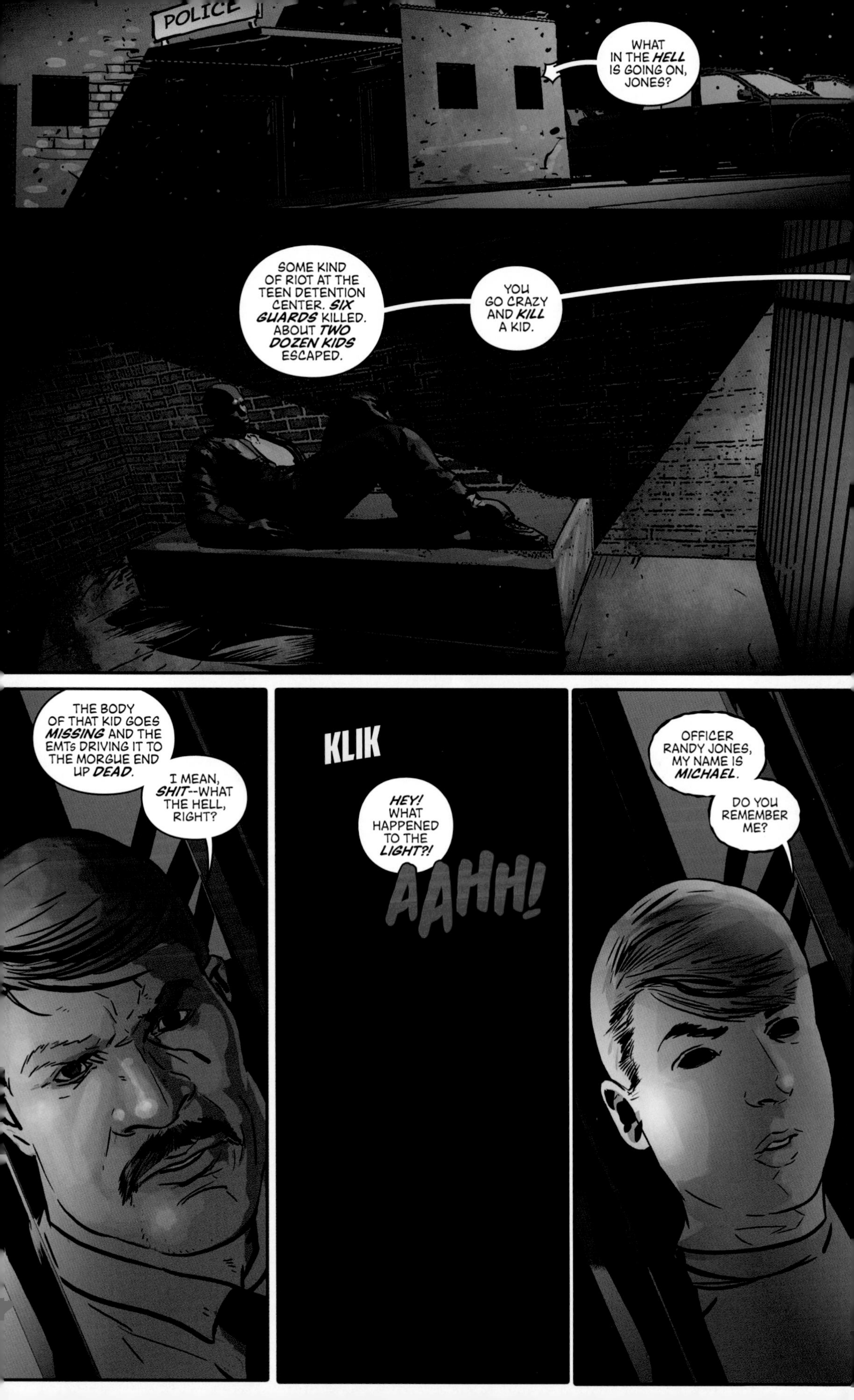
POLICE
WHAT IN THE HELL IS GOING ON, JONES?
SOME KIND OF RIOT AT THE TEEN DETENTION CENTER. SIX GUARDS KILLED. ABOUT TWO DOZEN KIDS ESCAPED.
YOU GO CRAZY AND KILL A KID.
THE BODY OF THAT KID GOES MISSING AND THE EMTs DRIVING IT TO THE MORGUE END UP DEAD.
I MEAN, SHIT--WHAT THE HELL, RIGHT?
KLIK
HEY! WHAT HAPPENED TO THE LIGHT?!
AAHH!
OFFICER RANDY JONES, MY NAME IS MICHAEL.
DO YOU REMEMBER ME?

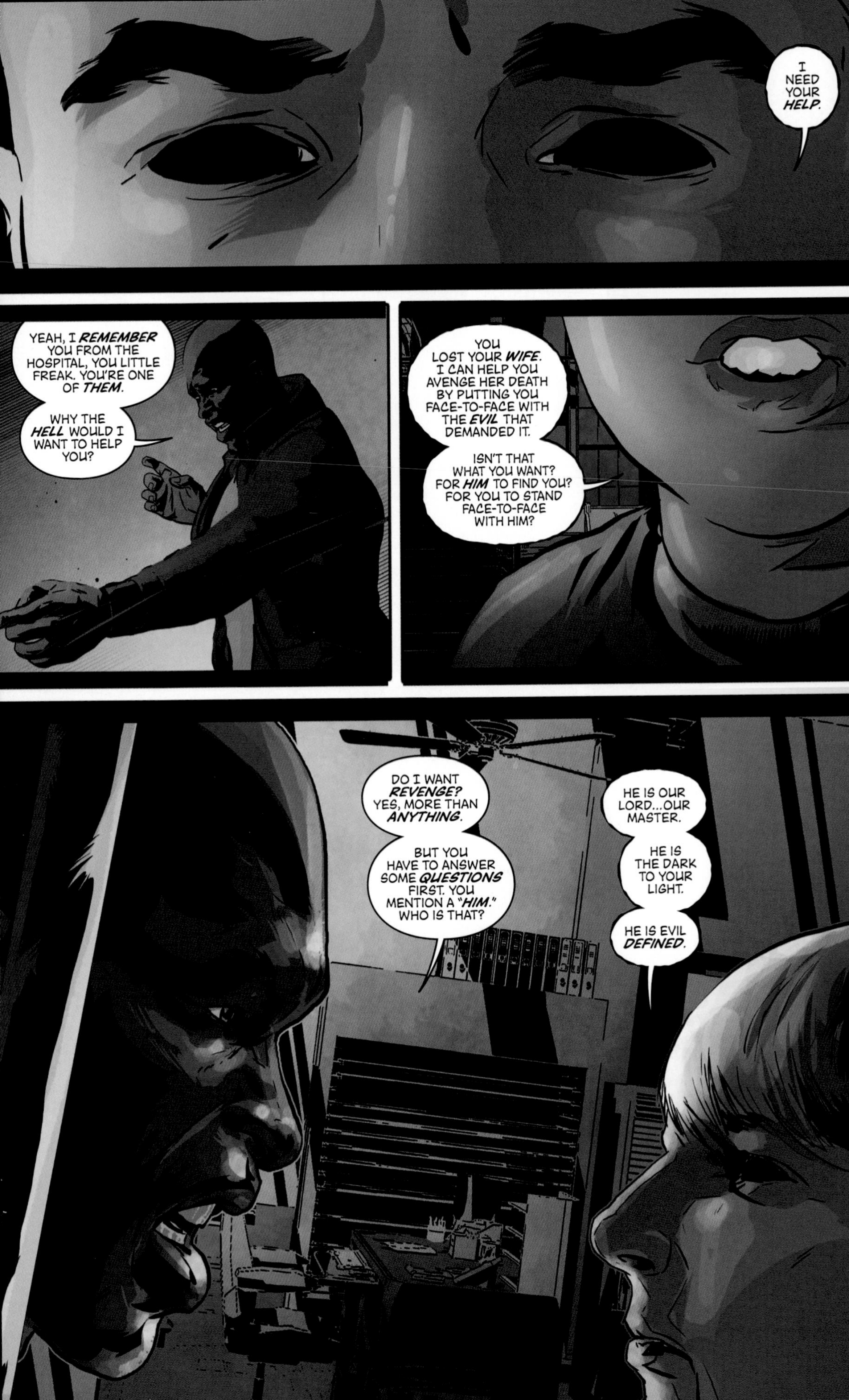

I NEED YOUR HELP.
YEAH, I REMEMBER YOU FROM THE HOSPITAL, YOU LITTLE FREAK. YOU'RE ONE OF THEM.
WHY THE HELL WOULD I WANT TO HELP YOU?
YOU LOST YOUR WIFE. I CAN HELP YOU AVENGE HER DEATH BY PUTTING YOU FACE-TO-FACE WITH THE EVIL THAT DEMANDED IT.
ISN'T THAT WHAT YOU WANT? FOR HIM TO FIND YOU? FOR YOU TO STAND FACE-TO-FACE WITH HIM?
DO I WANT REVENGE? YES, MORE THAN ANYTHING.
BUT YOU HAVE TO ANSWER SOME QUESTIONS FIRST. YOU MENTION A "HIM." WHO IS THAT?
HE IS OUR LORD...OUR MASTER.
HE IS THE DARK TO YOUR LIGHT.
HE IS EVIL DEFINED.

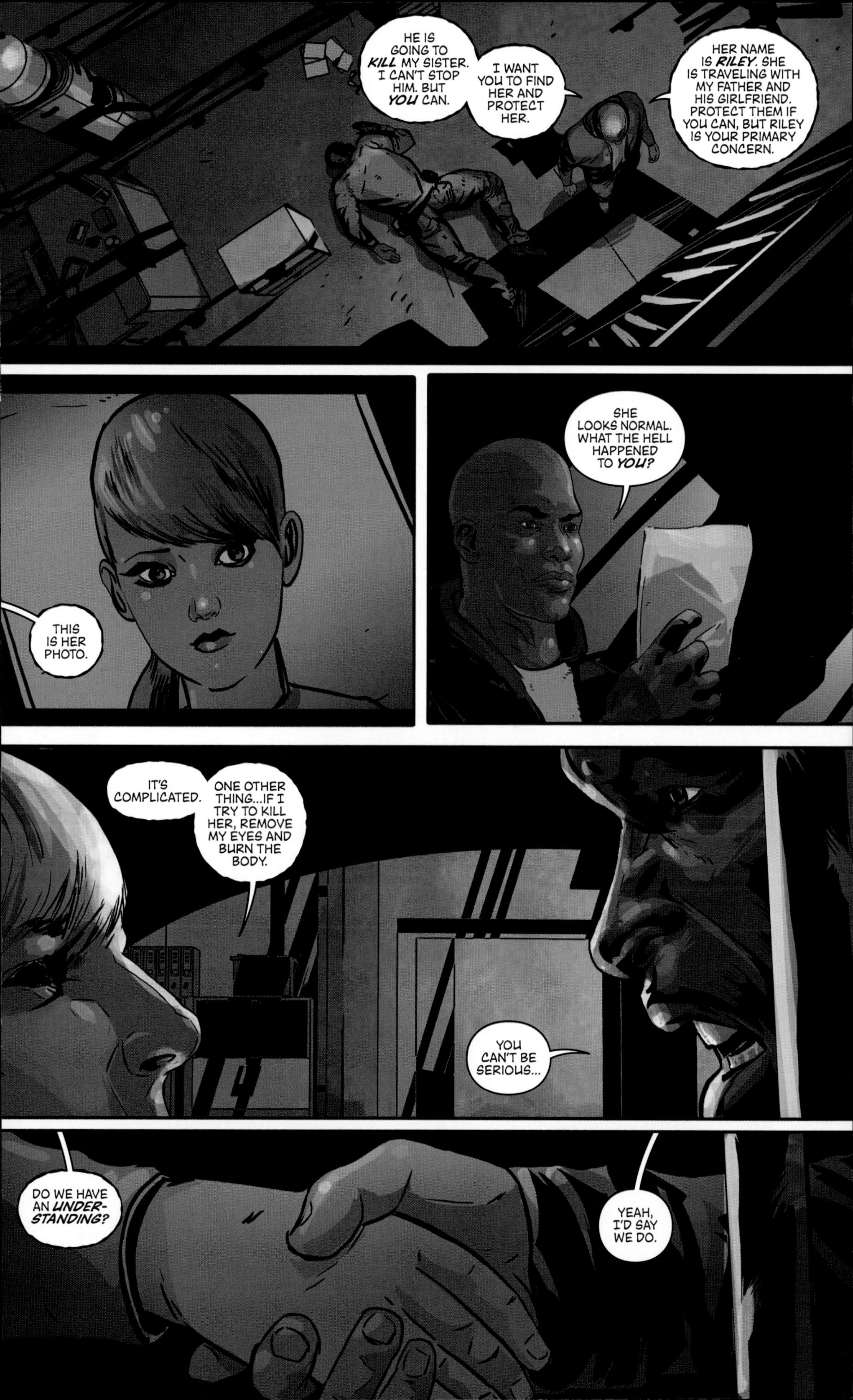
HE IS GOING TO KILL MY SISTER. I CAN'T STOP HIM. BUT YOU CAN.
I WANT YOU TO FIND HER AND PROTECT HER.
HER NAME IS RILEY. SHE IS TRAVELING WITH MY FATHER AND HIS GIRLFRIEND. PROTECT THEM IF YOU CAN, BUT RILEY IS YOUR PRIMARY CONCERN.
THIS IS HER PHOTO.
SHE LOOKS NORMAL. WHAT THE HELL HAPPENED TO YOU?
IT'S COMPLICATED.
ONE OTHER THING...IF I TRY TO KILL HER, REMOVE MY EYES AND BURN THE BODY.
YOU CAN'T BE SERIOUS...
DO WE HAVE AN UNDER-STANDING?
YEAH, I'D SAY WE DO.

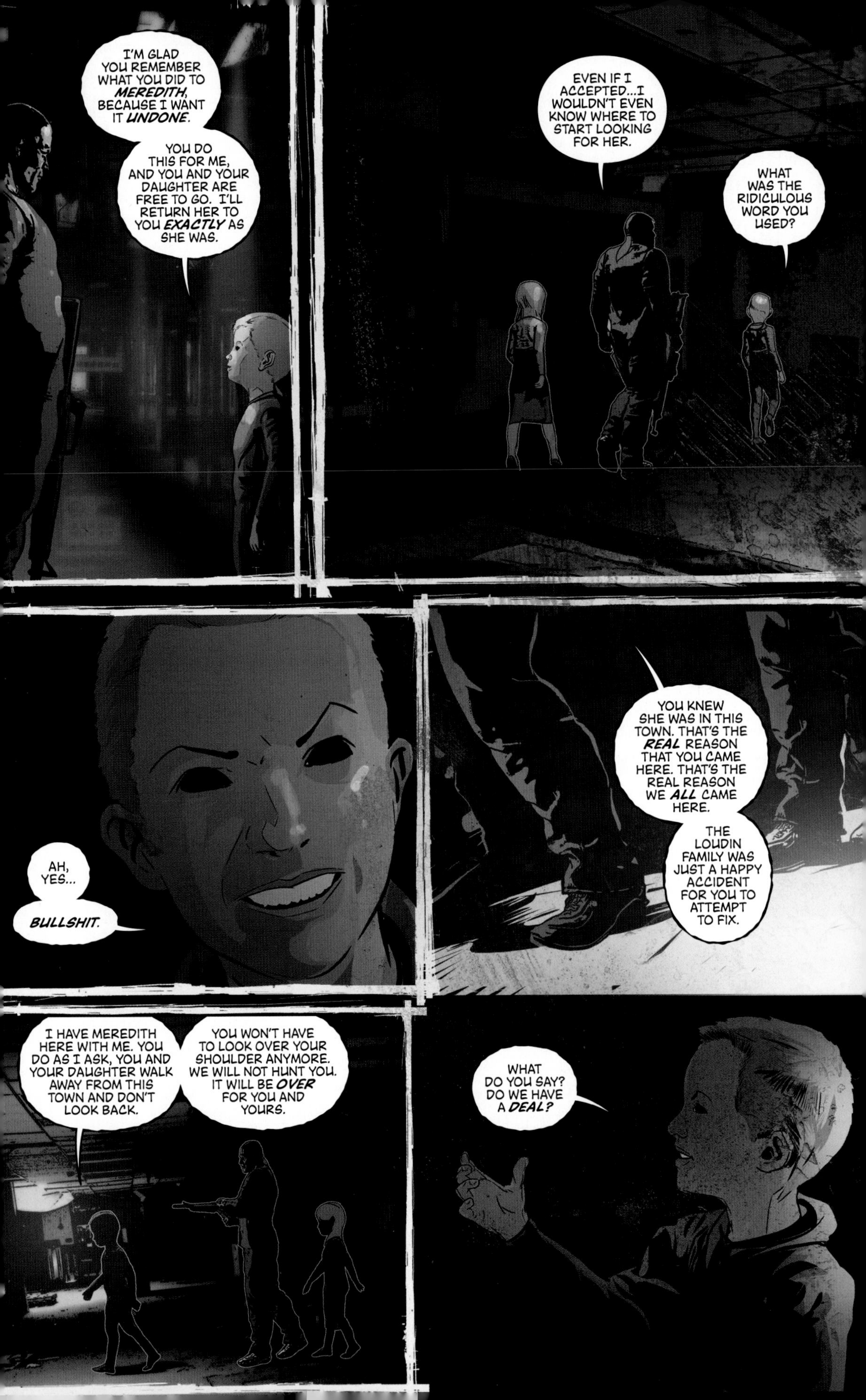
I'M GLAD YOU REMEMBER WHAT YOU DID TO MEREDITH, BECAUSE I WANT IT UNDONE.
YOU DO THIS FOR ME, AND YOU AND YOUR DAUGHTER ARE FREE TO GO. I'LL RETURN HER TO YOU EXACTLY AS SHE WAS.
EVEN IF I ACCEPTED...I WOULDN'T EVEN KNOW WHERE TO START LOOKING FOR HER.
WHAT WAS THE RIDICULOUS WORD YOU USED?
AH, YES...
BULLSHIT.
YOU KNEW SHE WAS IN THIS TOWN. THAT'S THE REAL REASON THAT YOU CAME HERE. THAT'S THE REAL REASON WE ALL CAME HERE.
THE LOUDIN FAMILY WAS JUST A HAPPY ACCIDENT FOR YOU TO ATTEMPT TO FIX.
I HAVE MEREDITH HERE WITH ME. YOU DO AS I ASK, YOU AND YOUR DAUGHTER WALK AWAY FROM THIS TOWN AND DON'T LOOK BACK.
YOU WON'T HAVE TO LOOK OVER YOUR SHOULDER ANYMORE. WE WILL NOT HUNT YOU. IT WILL BE OVER FOR YOU AND YOURS.
WHAT DO YOU SAY? DO WE HAVE A DEAL?

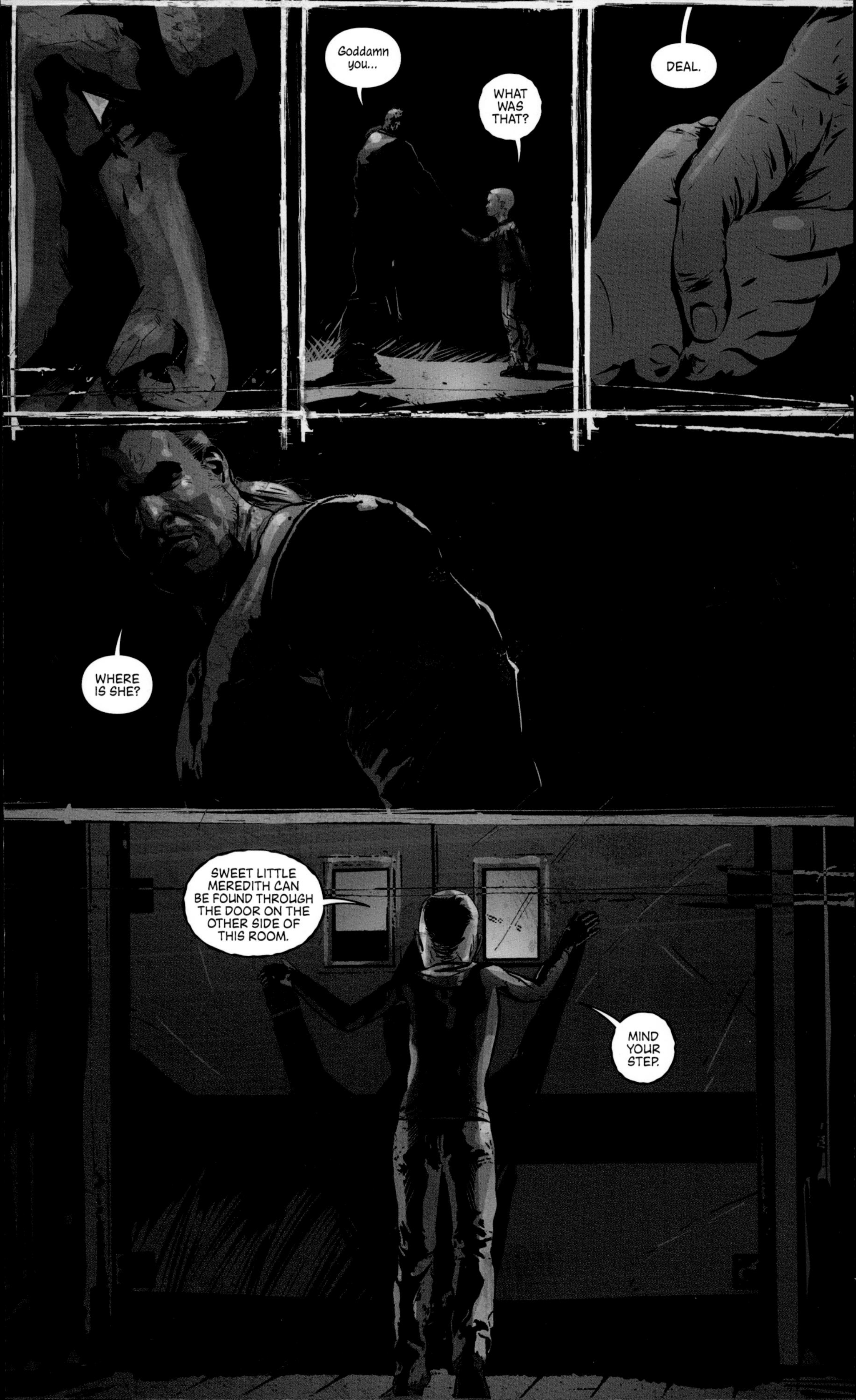

Goddamn you...
WHAT WAS THAT?
DEAL.
WHERE IS SHE?
SWEET LITTLE MEREDITH CAN BE FOUND THROUGH THE DOOR ON THE OTHER SIDE OF THIS ROOM.
MIND YOUR STEP.

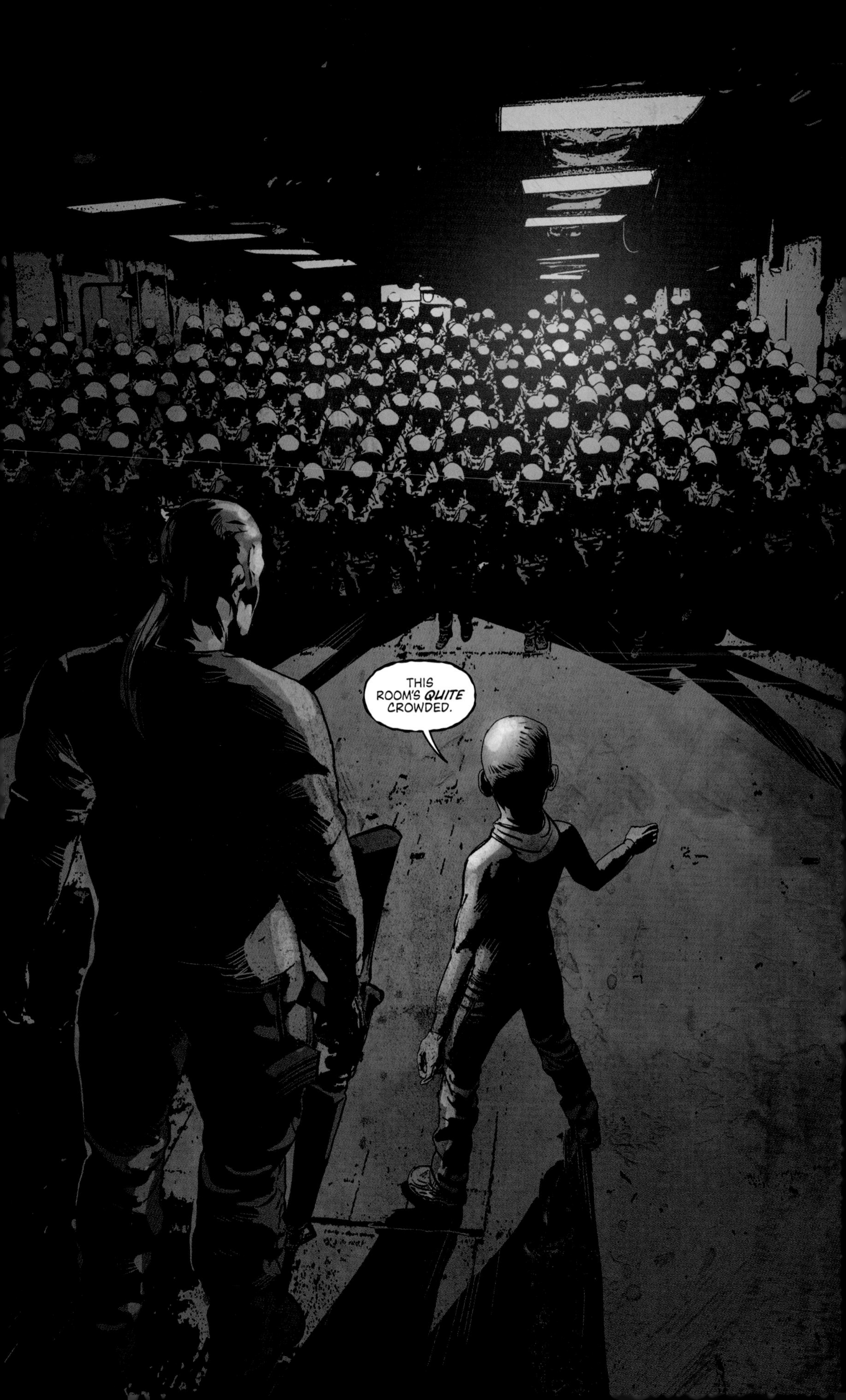
THIS ROOM'S QUITE CROWDED.

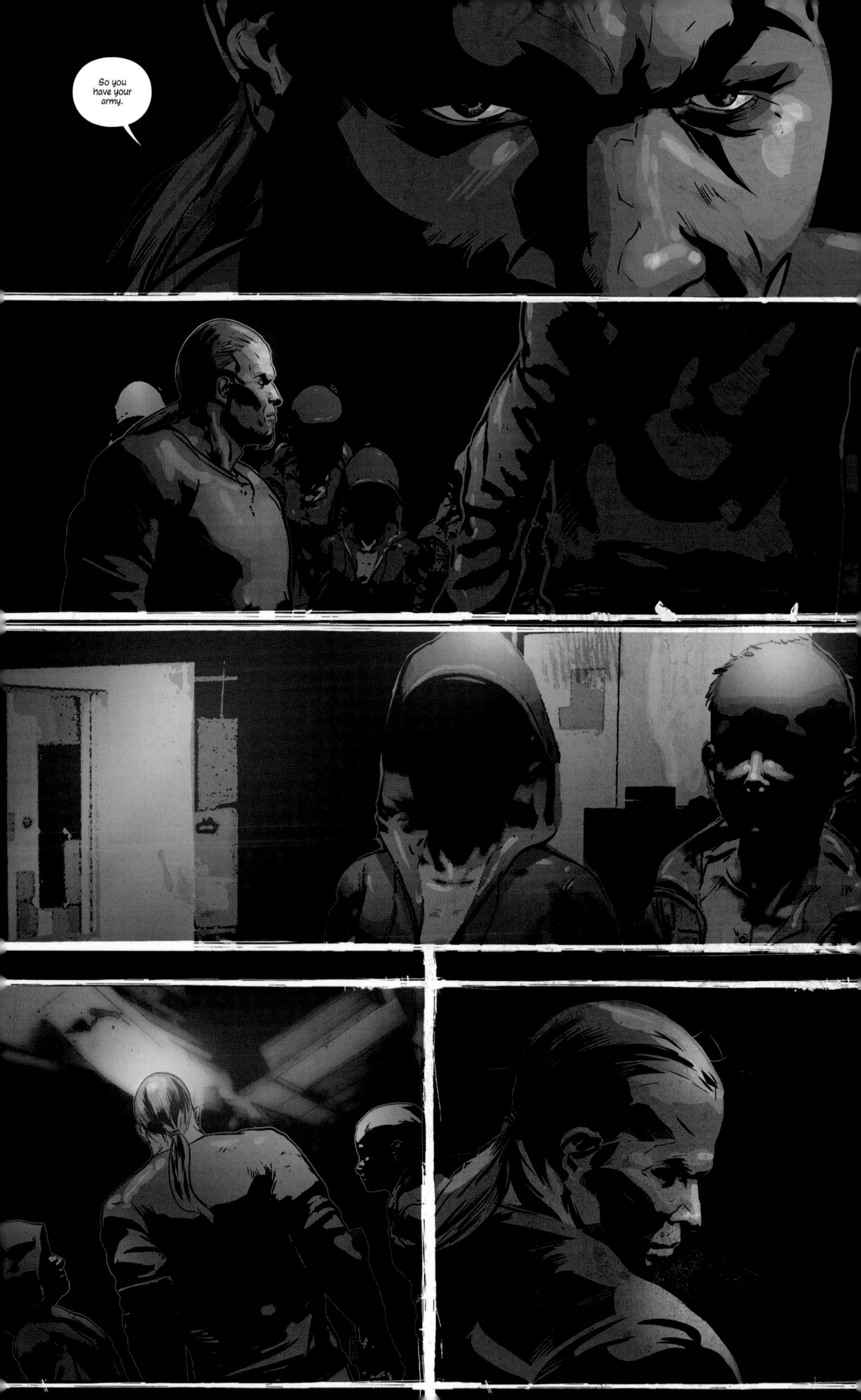
So you have your army.

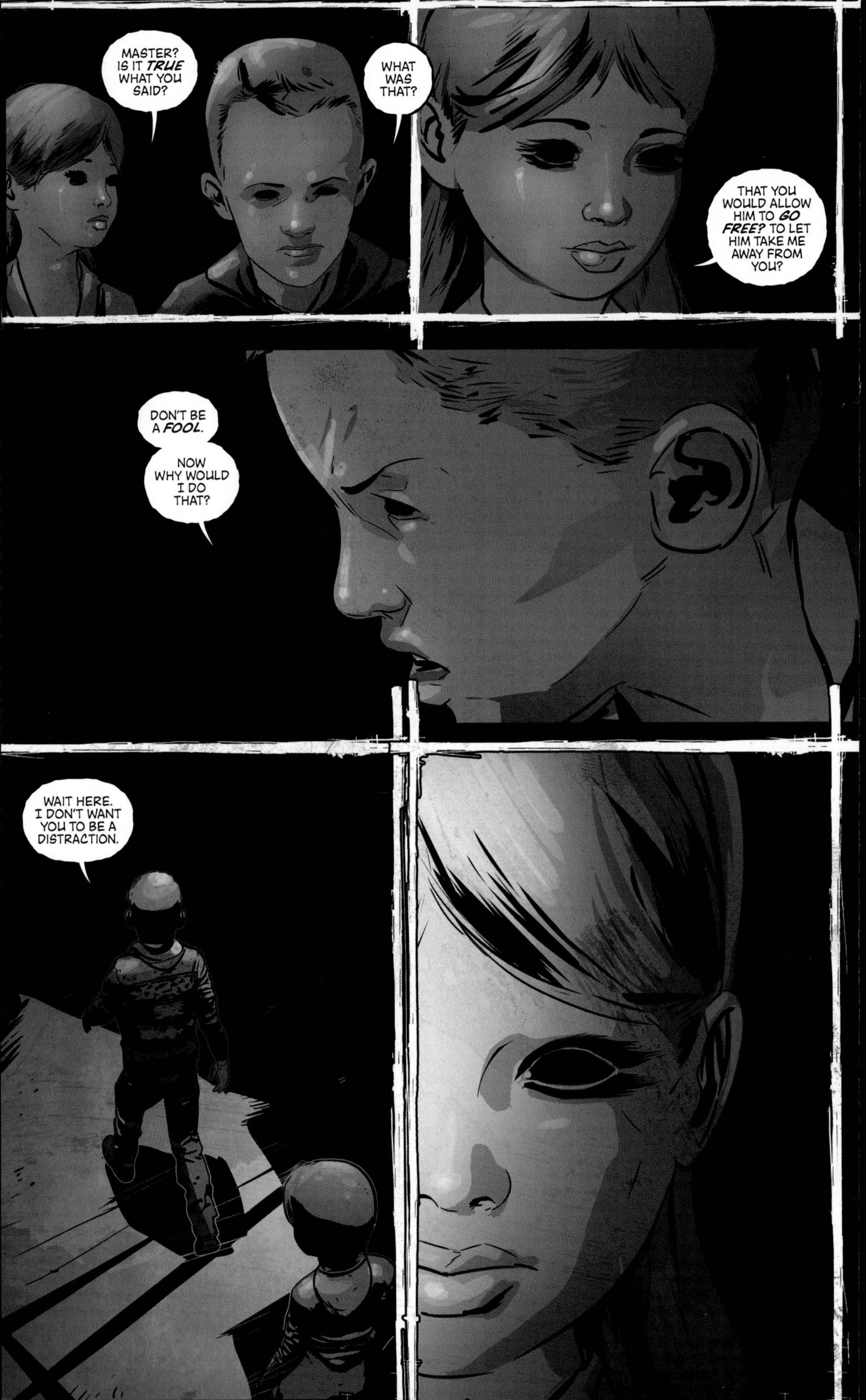

MASTER? IS IT TRUE WHAT YOU SAID?
WHAT WAS THAT?
THAT YOU WOULD ALLOW HIM TO GO FREE? TO LET HIM TAKE ME AWAY FROM YOU?
DON'T BE A FOOL.
NOW WHY WOULD I DO THAT?
WAIT HERE. I DON'T WANT YOU TO BE A DISTRACTION.

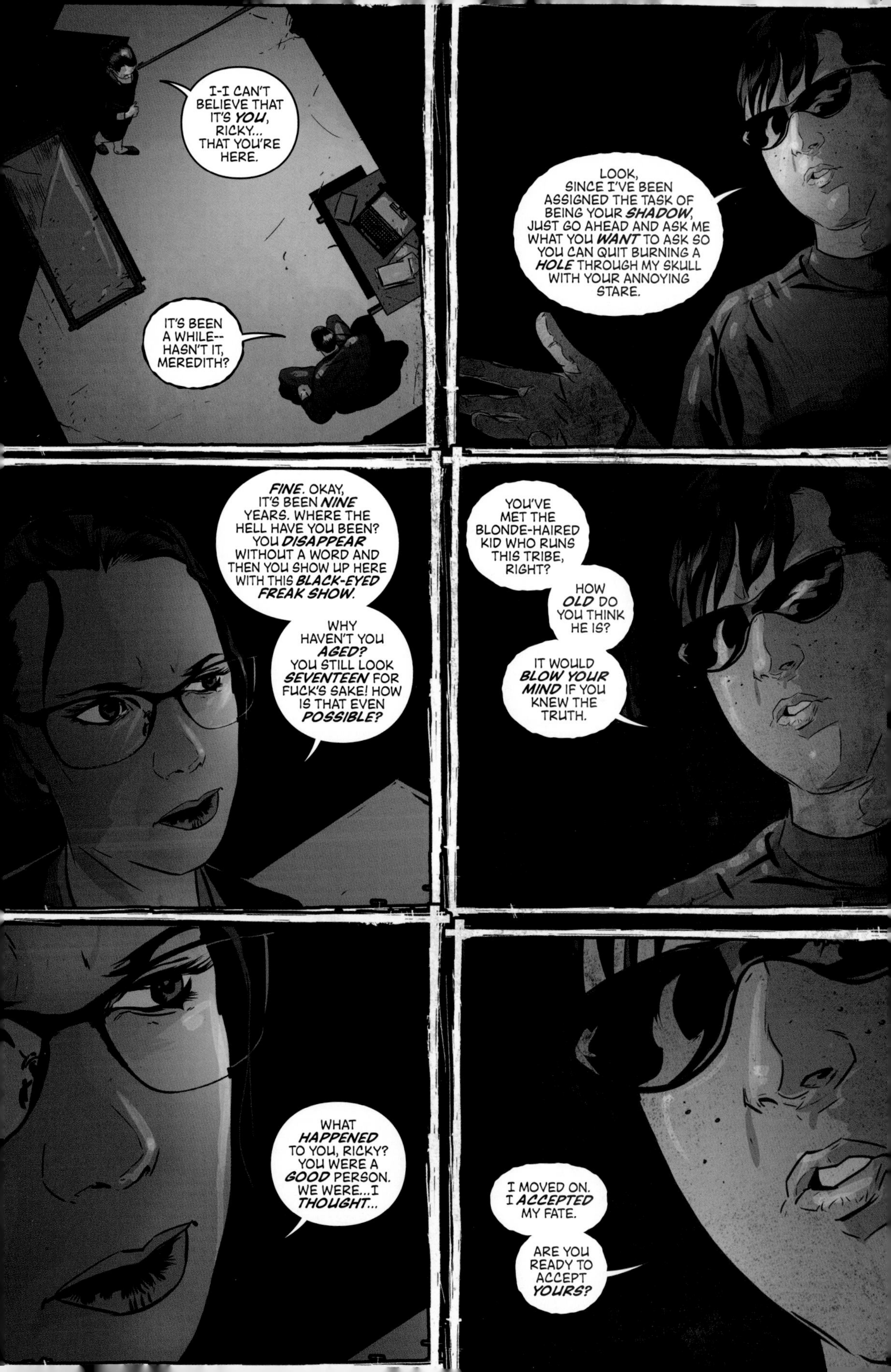
I-I CAN'T BELIEVE THAT IT'S YOU, RICKY... THAT YOU'RE HERE.
IT'S BEEN A WHILE-- HASN'T IT, MEREDITH?
LOOK, SINCE I'VE BEEN ASSIGNED THE TASK OF BEING YOUR SHADOW, JUST GO AHEAD AND ASK ME WHAT YOU WANT TO ASK SO YOU CAN QUIT BURNING A HOLE THROUGH MY SKULL WITH YOUR ANNOYING STARE.
FINE. OKAY, IT'S BEEN NINE YEARS. WHERE THE HELL HAVE YOU BEEN? YOU DISAPPEAR WITHOUT A WORD AND THEN YOU SHOW UP HERE WITH THIS BLACK-EYED FREAK SHOW.
WHY HAVEN'T YOU AGED? YOU STILL LOOK SEVENTEEN FOR FUCK'S SAKE! HOW IS THAT EVEN POSSIBLE?
YOU'VE MET THE BLONDE-HAIRED KID WHO RUNS THIS TRIBE, RIGHT?
HOW OLD DO YOU THINK HE IS?
IT WOULD BLOW YOUR MIND IF YOU KNEW THE TRUTH.
WHAT HAPPENED TO YOU, RICKY? YOU WERE A GOOD PERSON. WE WERE...I THOUGHT...
I MOVED ON. I ACCEPTED MY FATE.
ARE YOU READY TO ACCEPT YOURS?

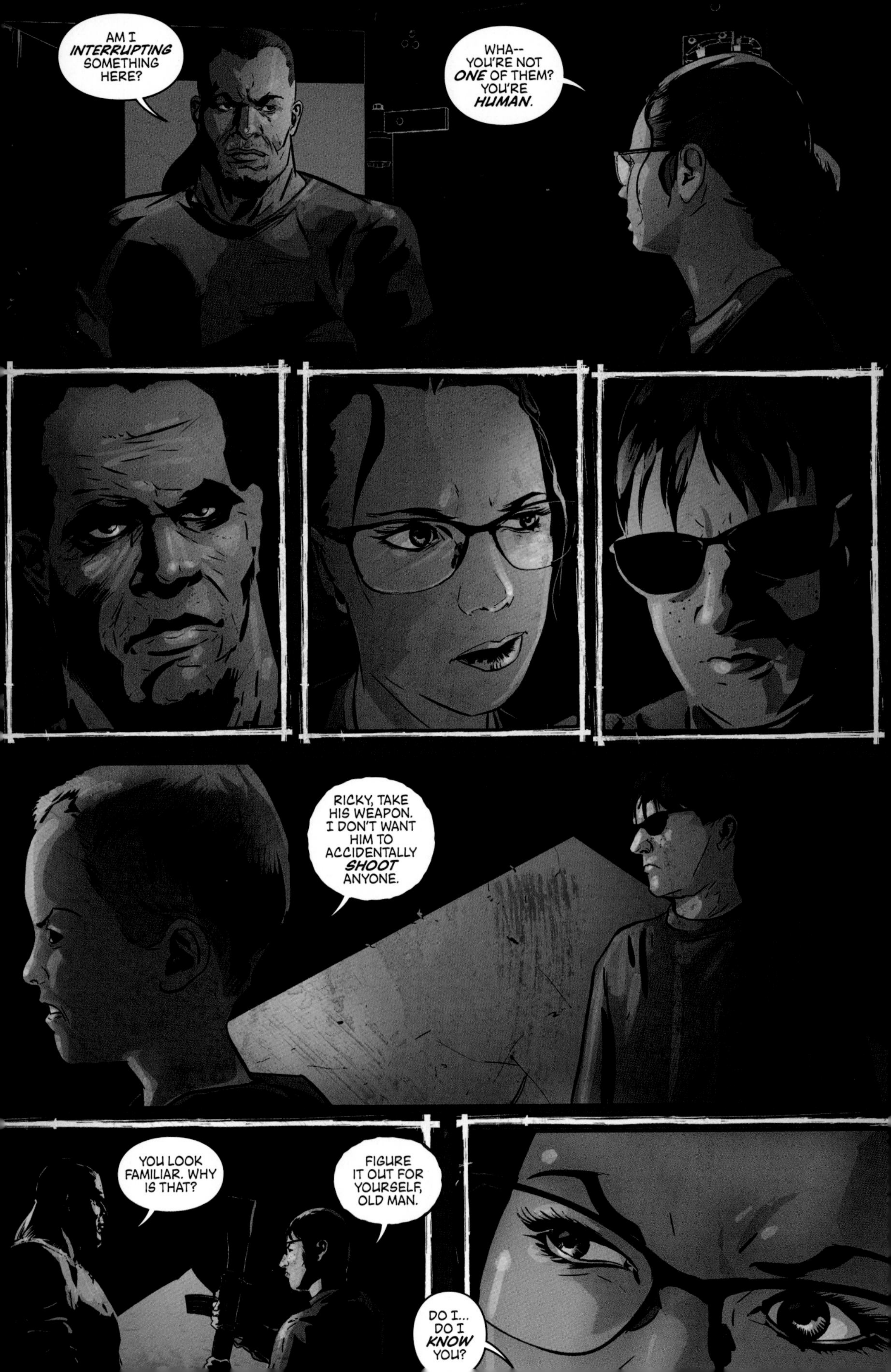
AM I *INTERRUPTING* SOMETHING HERE?
WHA-- YOU'RE NOT *ONE* OF THEM? YOU'RE *HUMAN*.
RICKY, TAKE HIS WEAPON. I DON'T WANT HIM TO ACCIDENTALLY *SHOOT* ANYONE.
YOU LOOK FAMILIAR. WHY IS THAT?
FIGURE IT OUT FOR YOURSELF, OLD MAN.
DO I... DO I *KNOW* YOU?

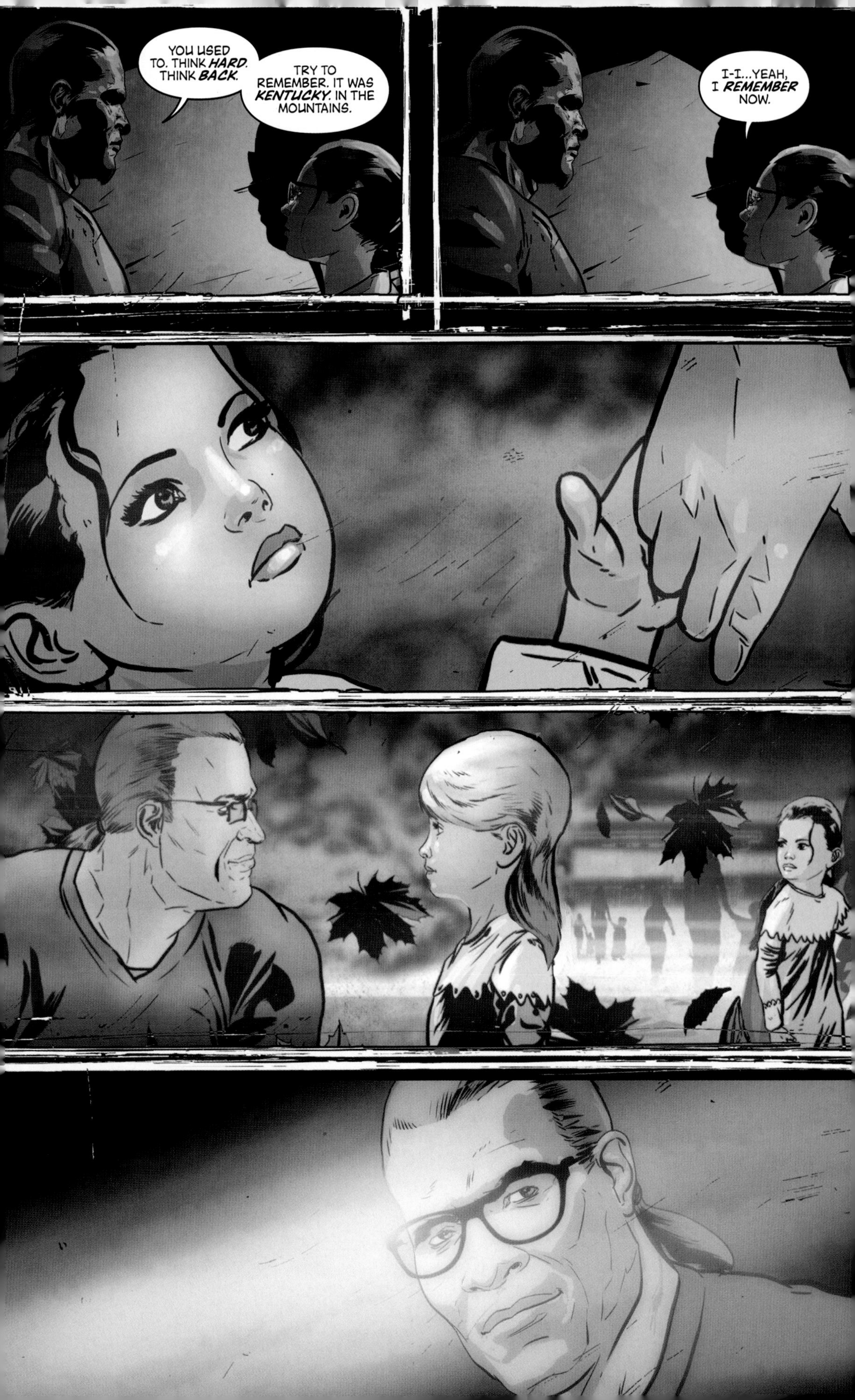
YOU USED TO. THINK HARD. THINK BACK.
TRY TO REMEMBER. IT WAS KENTUCKY. IN THE MOUNTAINS.
I-I...YEAH, I REMEMBER NOW.

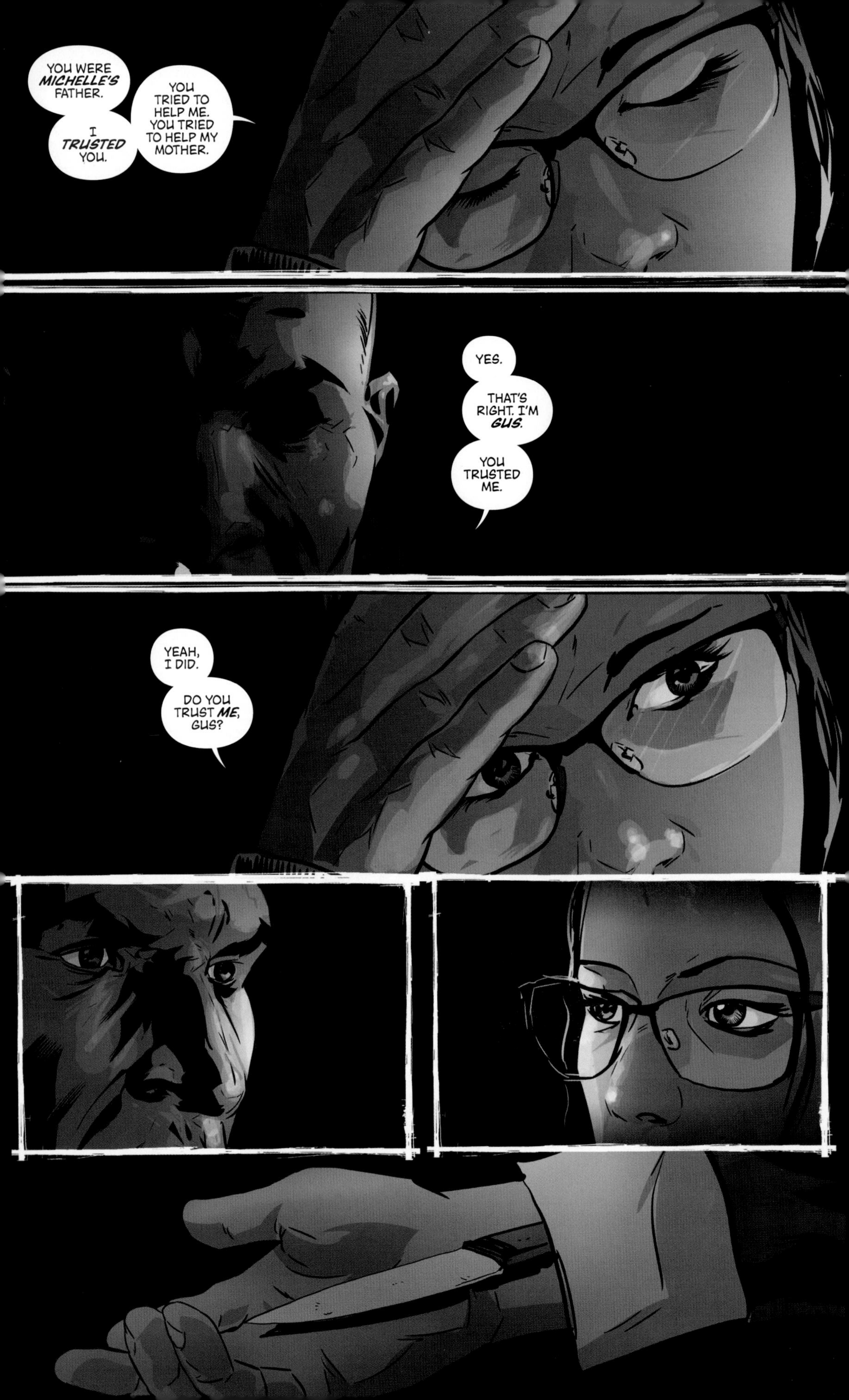
YOU WERE MICHELLE'S FATHER.
I TRUSTED YOU.
YOU TRIED TO HELP ME. YOU TRIED TO HELP MY MOTHER.
YES.
THAT'S RIGHT. I'M GUS.
YOU TRUSTED ME.
YEAH, I DID.
DO YOU TRUST ME, GUS?

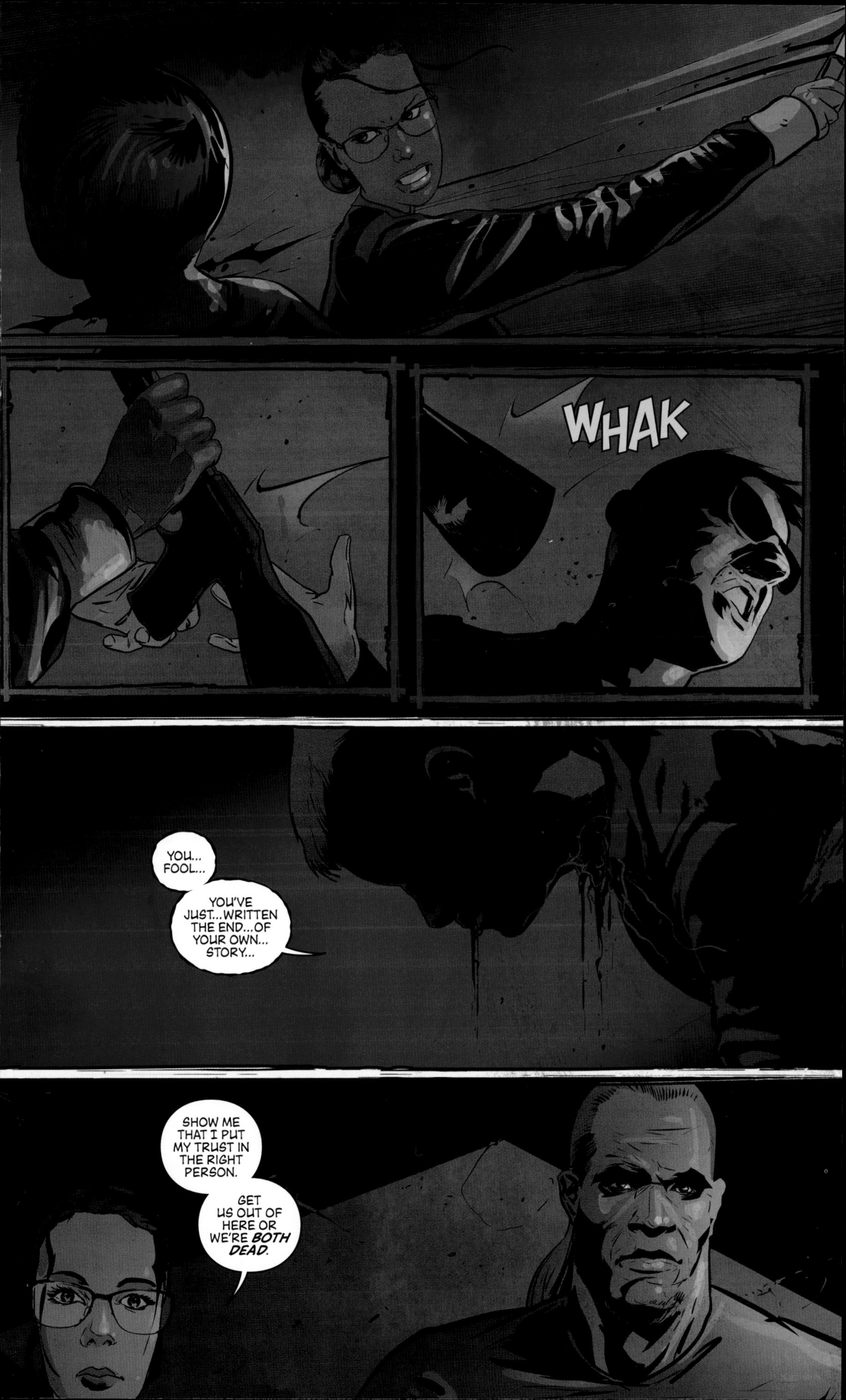
WHAK
YOU... FOOL...
YOU'VE JUST...WRITTEN THE END...OF YOUR OWN... STORY...
SHOW ME THAT I PUT MY TRUST IN THE RIGHT PERSON.
GET US OUT OF HERE OR WE'RE *BOTH DEAD*.

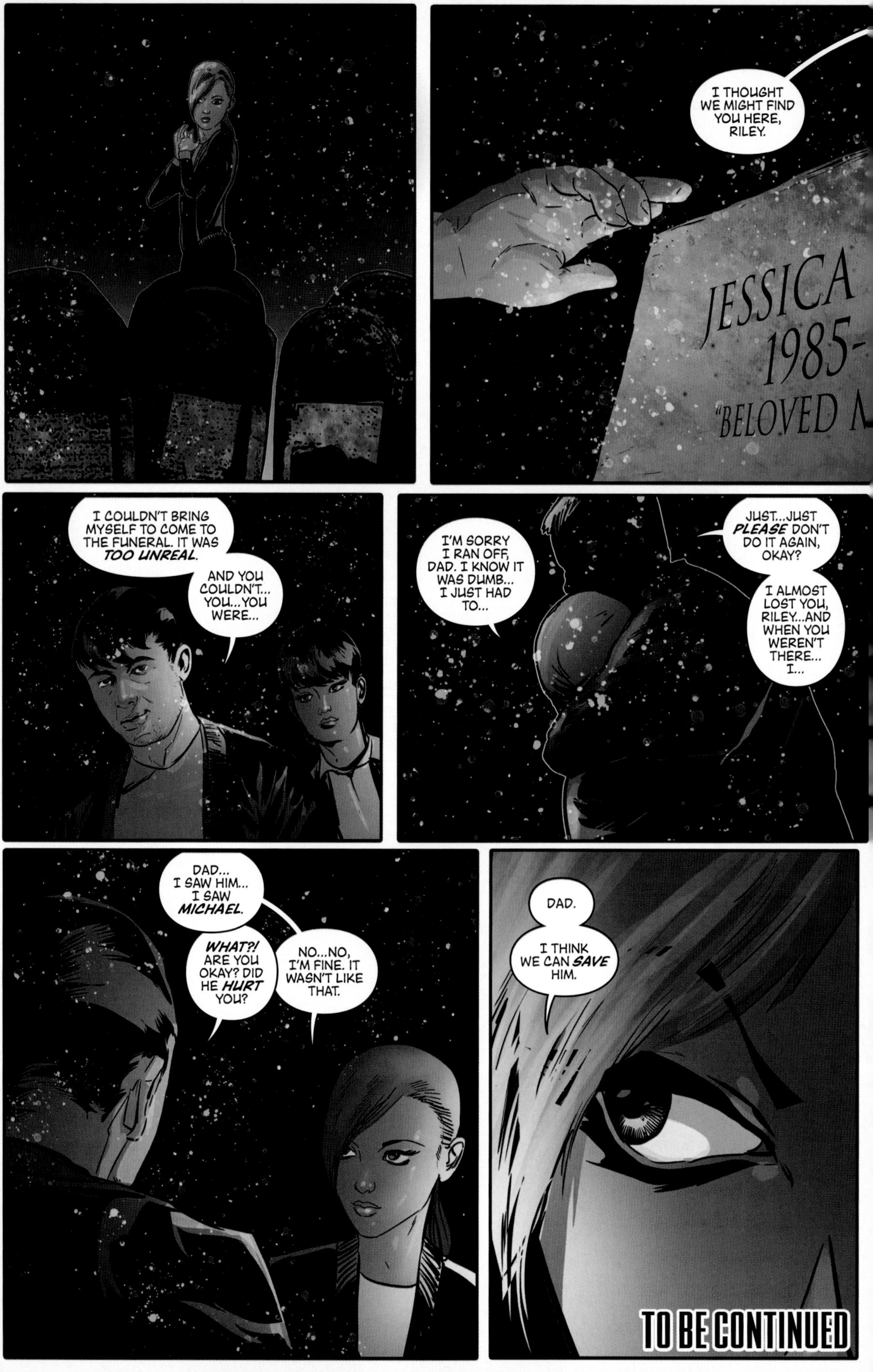

I THOUGHT WE MIGHT FIND YOU HERE, RILEY.
JESSICA
1985-
"BELOVED
I COULDN'T BRING MYSELF TO COME TO THE FUNERAL. IT WAS *TOO UNREAL*.
AND YOU COULDN'T... YOU...YOU WERE...
I'M SORRY I RAN OFF, DAD. I KNOW IT WAS DUMB... I JUST HAD TO...
JUST...JUST *PLEASE* DON'T DO IT AGAIN, OKAY?
I ALMOST LOST YOU, RILEY...AND WHEN YOU WEREN'T THERE... I...
DAD... I SAW HIM... I SAW *MICHAEL*.
WHAT?! ARE YOU OKAY? DID HE *HURT* YOU?
NO...NO, I'M FINE. IT WASN'T LIKE THAT.
DAD.
I THINK WE CAN *SAVE* HIM.
TO BE CONTINUED

10

"HIDE AND SEEK"

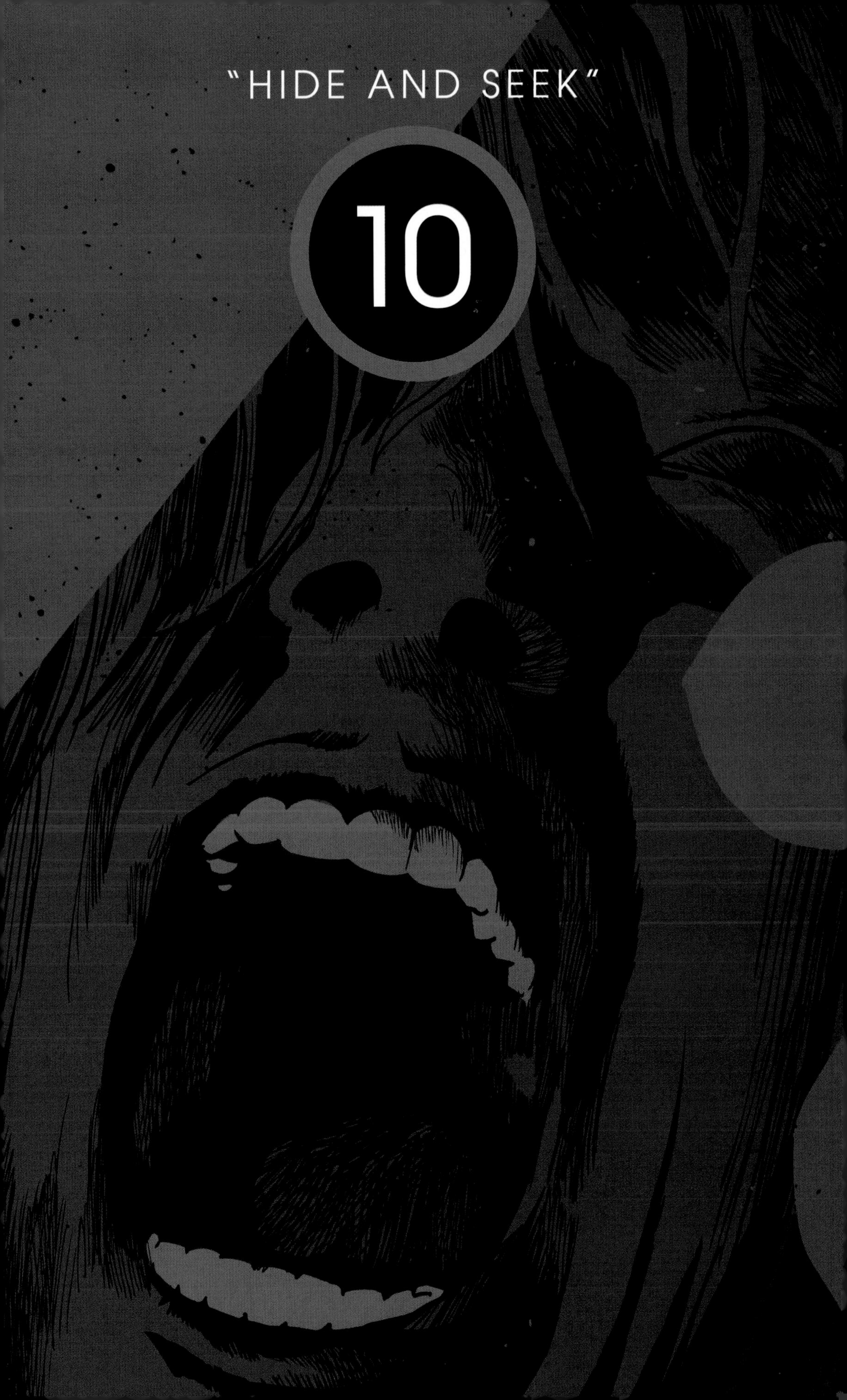

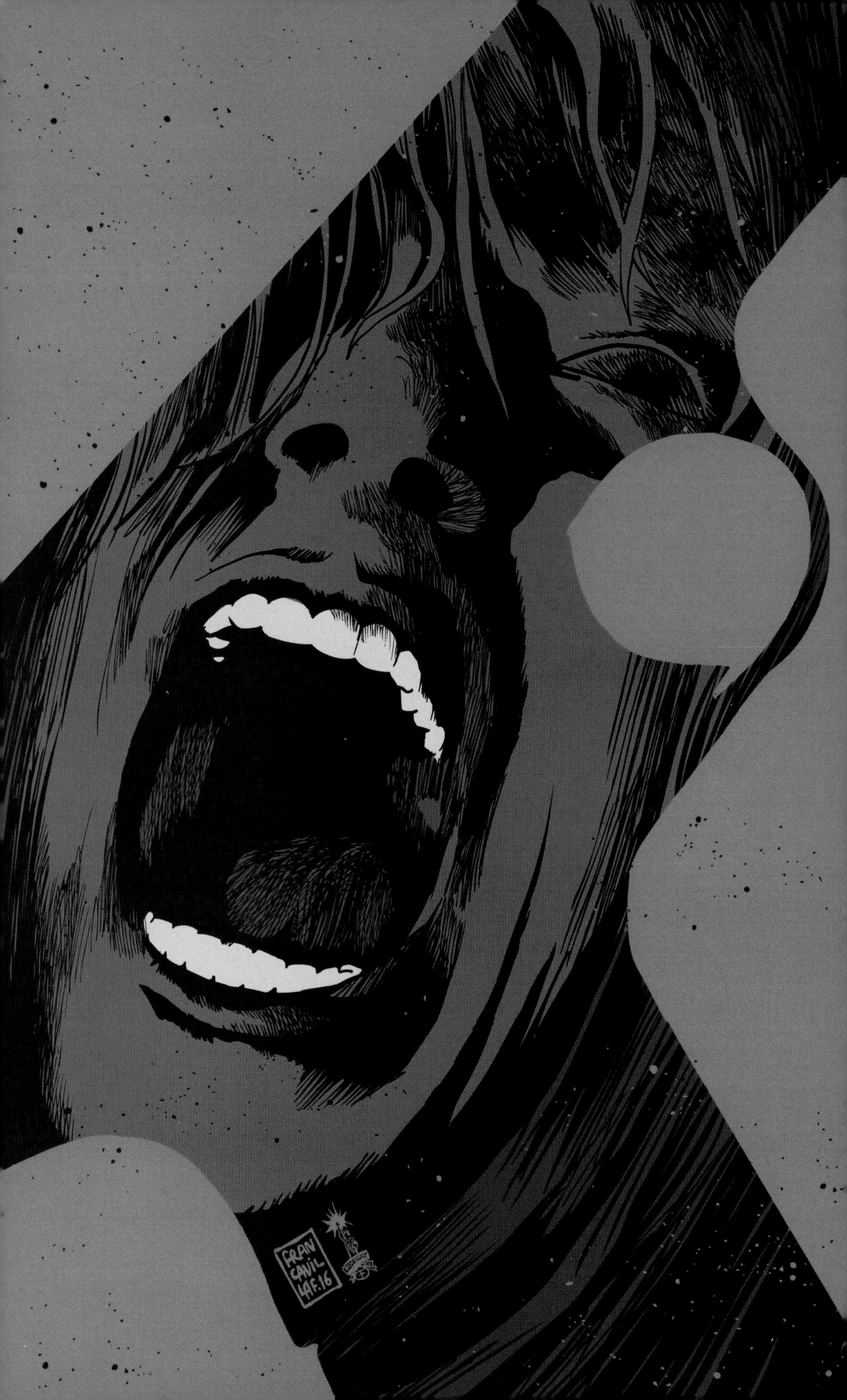

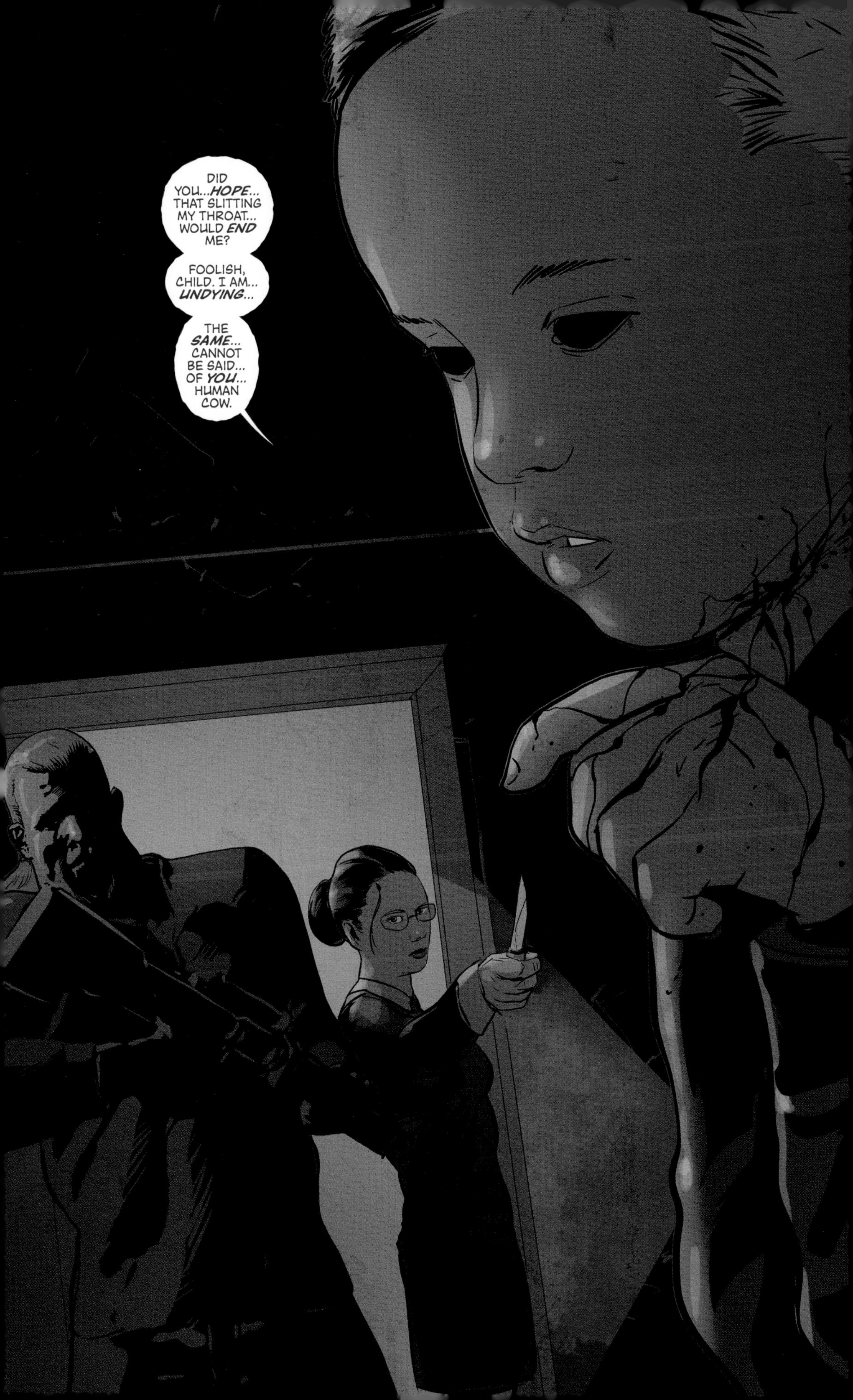
DID YOU...*HOPE*... THAT SLITTING MY THROAT... WOULD *END* ME?
FOOLISH, CHILD. I AM... *UNDYING*...
THE *SAME*... CANNOT BE SAID... OF *YOU*... HUMAN COW.

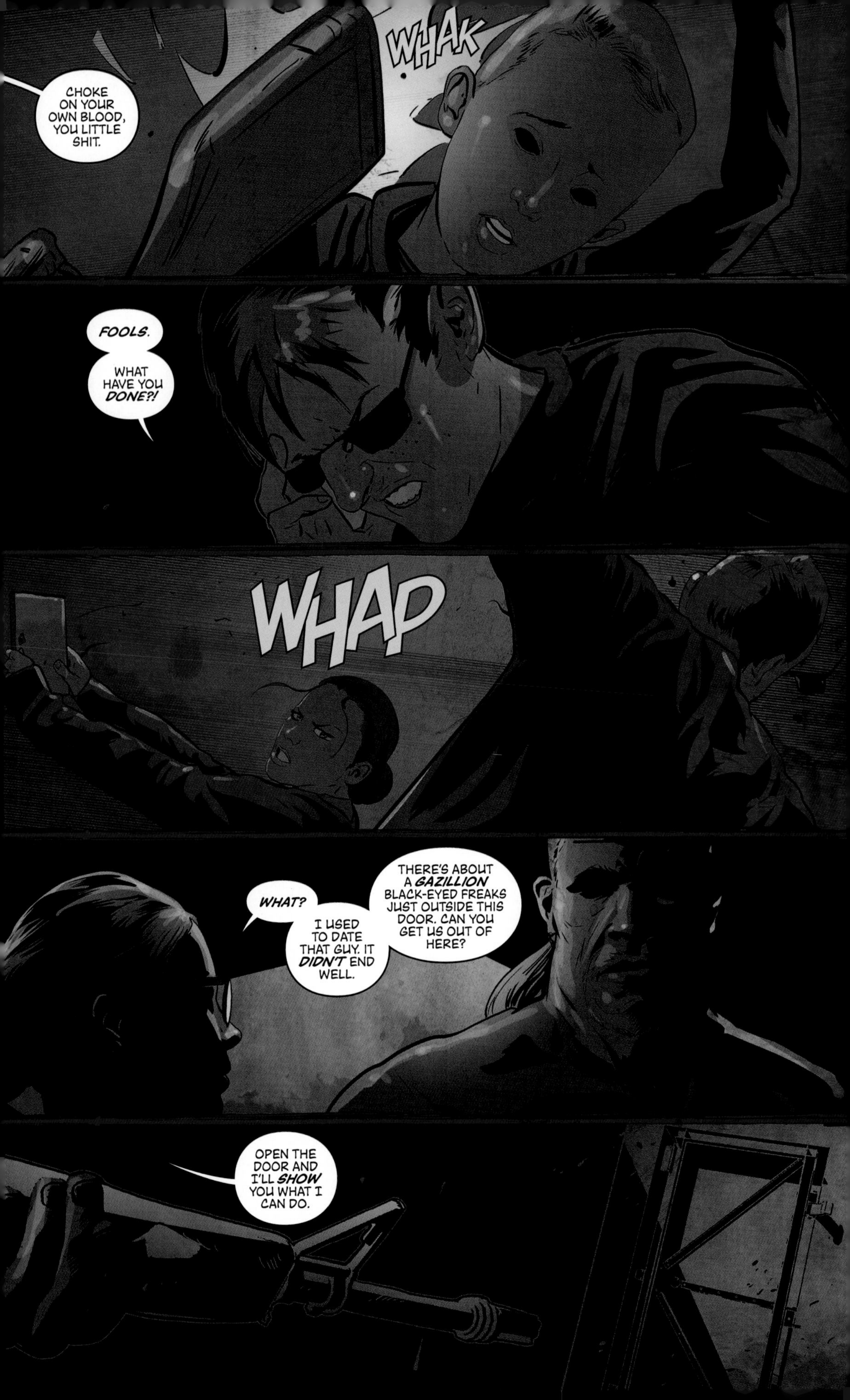
WHAK
CHOKE ON YOUR OWN BLOOD, YOU LITTLE SHIT.
FOOLS.
WHAT HAVE YOU DONE?!
WHAP
WHAT?
I USED TO DATE THAT GUY. IT DIDN'T END WELL.
THERE'S ABOUT A GAZILLION BLACK-EYED FREAKS JUST OUTSIDE THIS DOOR. CAN YOU GET US OUT OF HERE?
OPEN THE DOOR AND I'LL SHOW YOU WHAT I CAN DO.

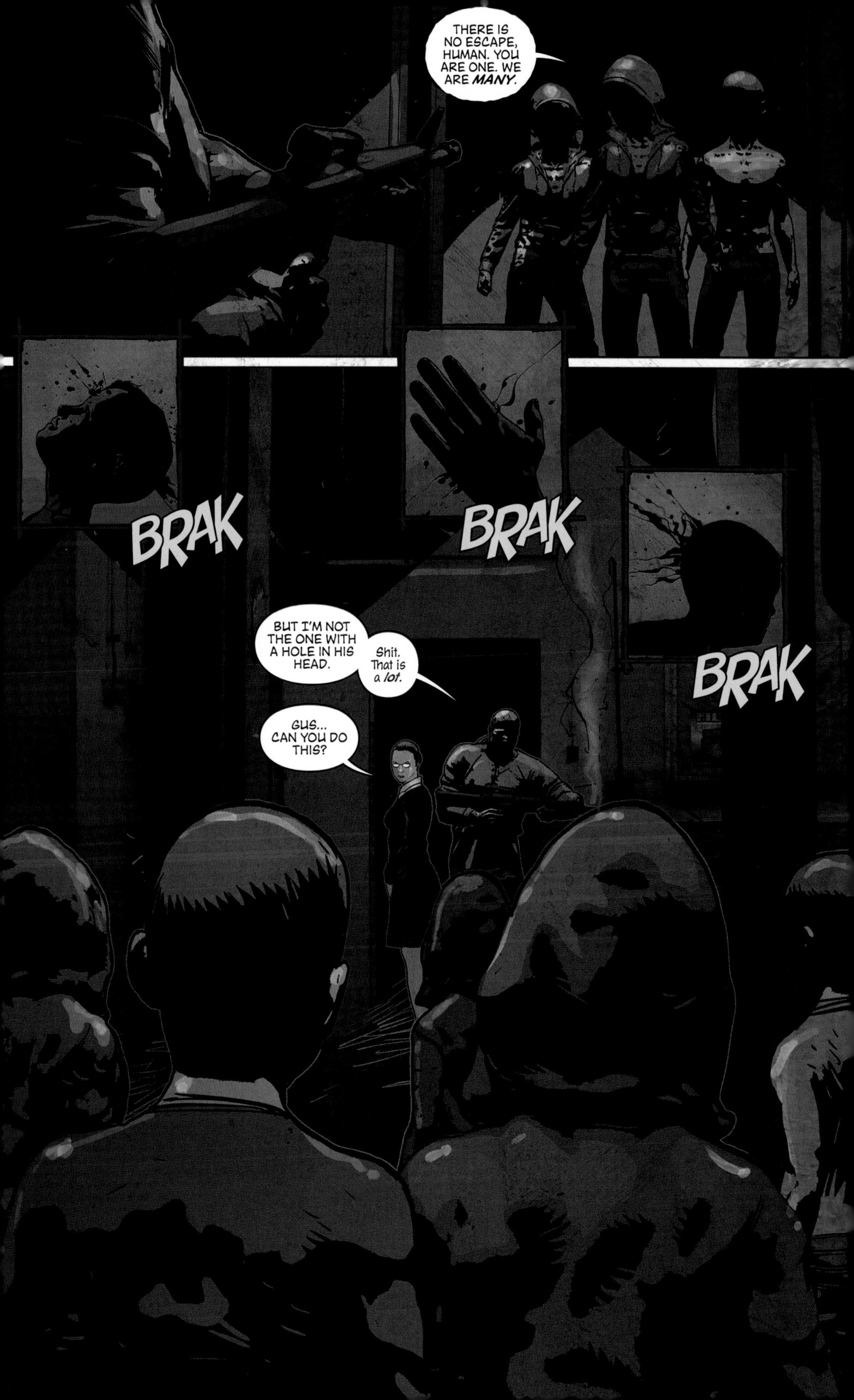
THERE IS NO ESCAPE, HUMAN. YOU ARE ONE. WE ARE *MANY*.
BRAK
BRAK
BRAK
BUT I'M NOT THE ONE WITH A HOLE IN HIS HEAD.
Shit. That is a *lot*.
GUS... CAN YOU DO THIS?

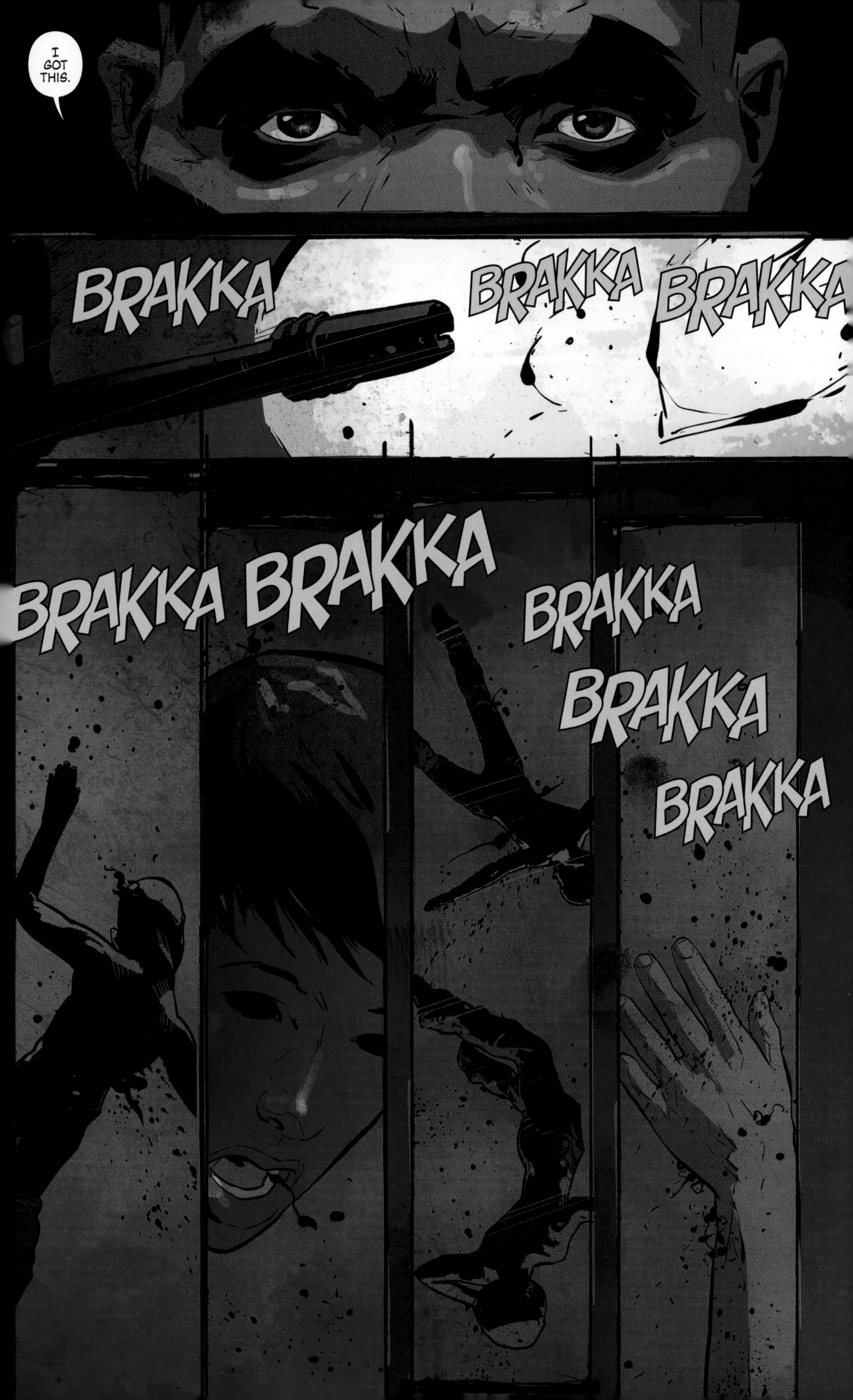
I GOT THIS.
BRAKKA
BRAKKA
BRAKKA
BRAKKA
BRAKKA
BRAKKA
BRAKKA
BRAKKA

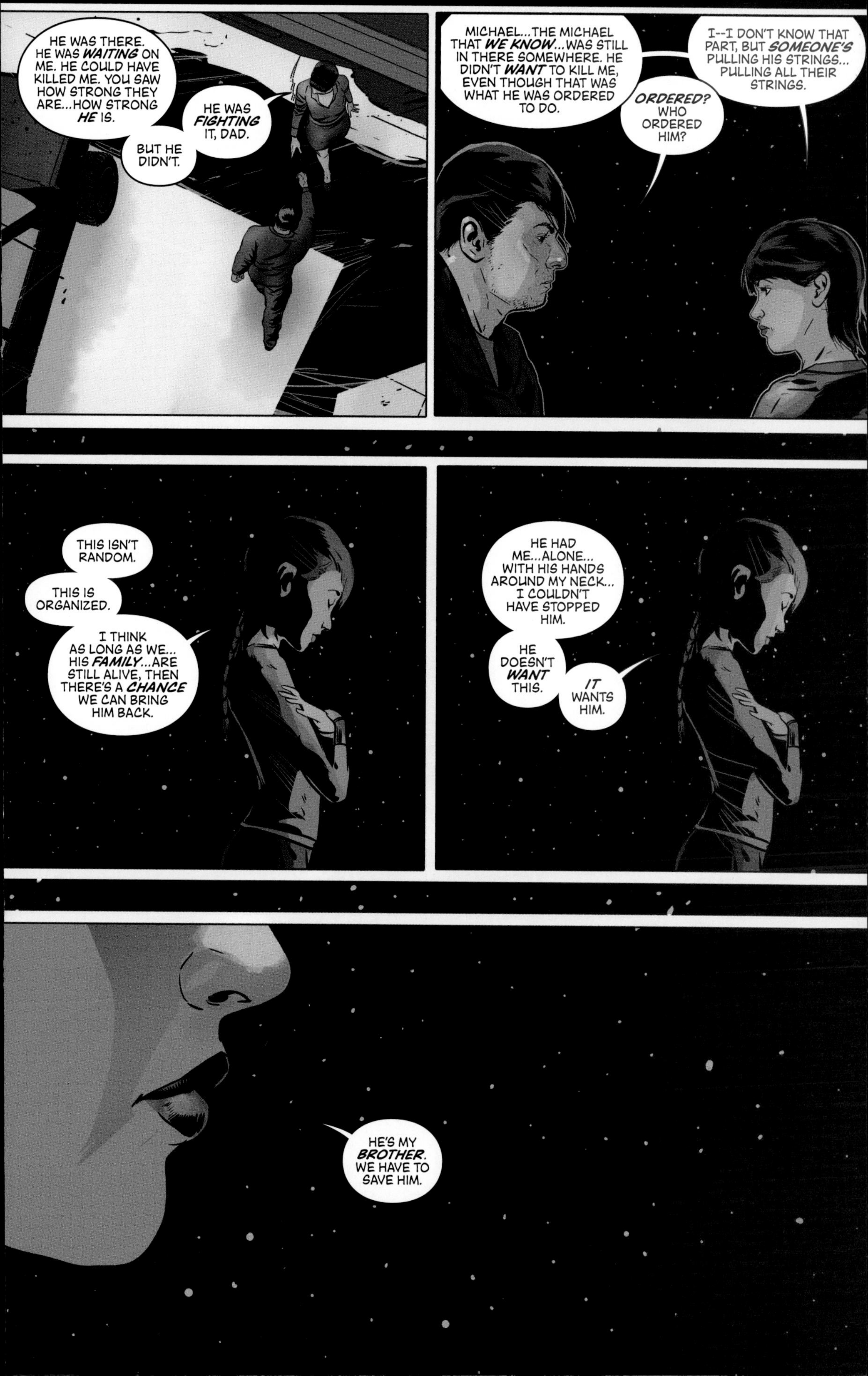
HE WAS THERE. HE WAS WAITING ON ME. HE COULD HAVE KILLED ME. YOU SAW HOW STRONG THEY ARE...HOW STRONG HE IS.
BUT HE DIDN'T.
HE WAS FIGHTING IT, DAD.
MICHAEL...THE MICHAEL THAT WE KNOW...WAS STILL IN THERE SOMEWHERE. HE DIDN'T WANT TO KILL ME, EVEN THOUGH THAT WAS WHAT HE WAS ORDERED TO DO.
ORDERED? WHO ORDERED HIM?
I--I DON'T KNOW THAT PART, BUT SOMEONE'S PULLING HIS STRINGS... PULLING ALL THEIR STRINGS.
THIS ISN'T RANDOM.
THIS IS ORGANIZED.
I THINK AS LONG AS WE... HIS FAMILY...ARE STILL ALIVE, THEN THERE'S A CHANCE WE CAN BRING HIM BACK.
HE HAD ME...ALONE... WITH HIS HANDS AROUND MY NECK... I COULDN'T HAVE STOPPED HIM.
HE DOESN'T WANT THIS.
IT WANTS HIM.
HE'S MY BROTHER. WE HAVE TO SAVE HIM.

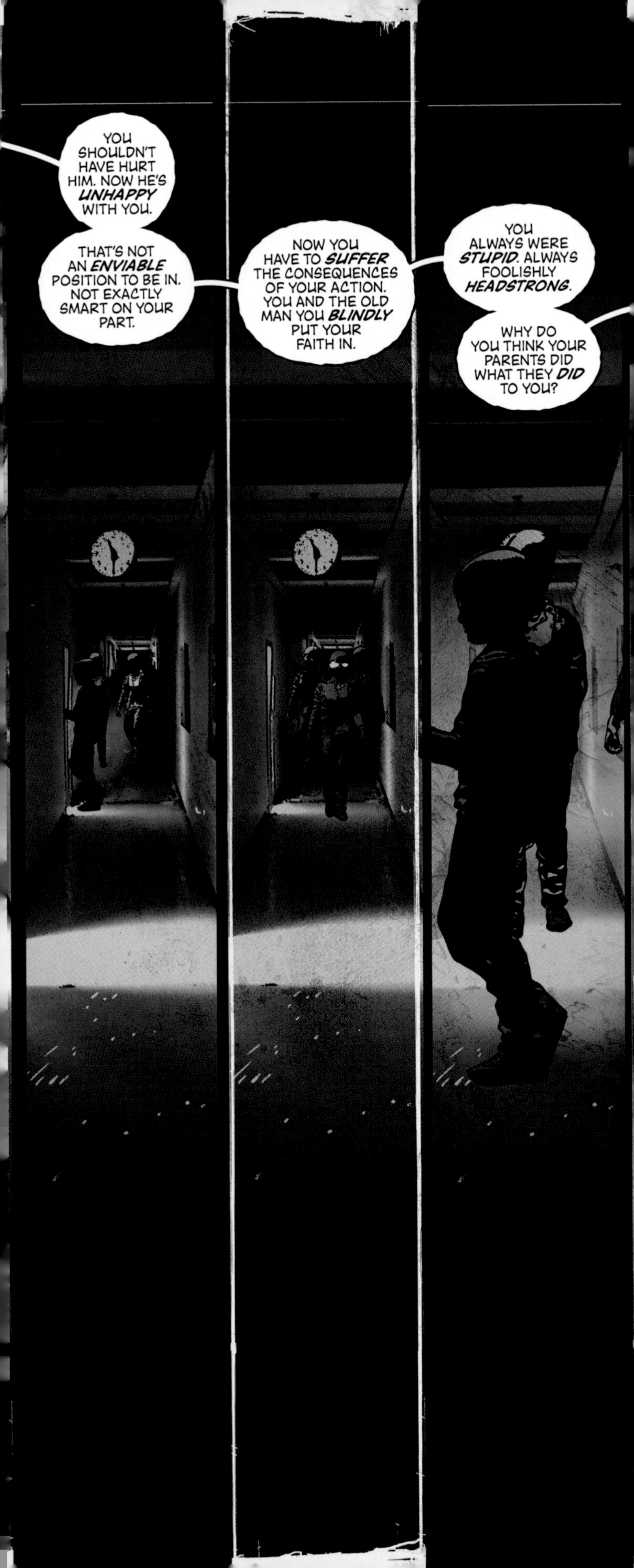
YOU SHOULDN'T HAVE HURT HIM. NOW HE'S UNHAPPY WITH YOU.
THAT'S NOT AN ENVIABLE POSITION TO BE IN. NOT EXACTLY SMART ON YOUR PART.
NOW YOU HAVE TO SUFFER THE CONSEQUENCES OF YOUR ACTION. YOU AND THE OLD MAN YOU BLINDLY PUT YOUR FAITH IN.
YOU ALWAYS WERE STUPID. ALWAYS FOOLISHLY HEADSTRONG.
WHY DO YOU THINK YOUR PARENTS DID WHAT THEY DID TO YOU?

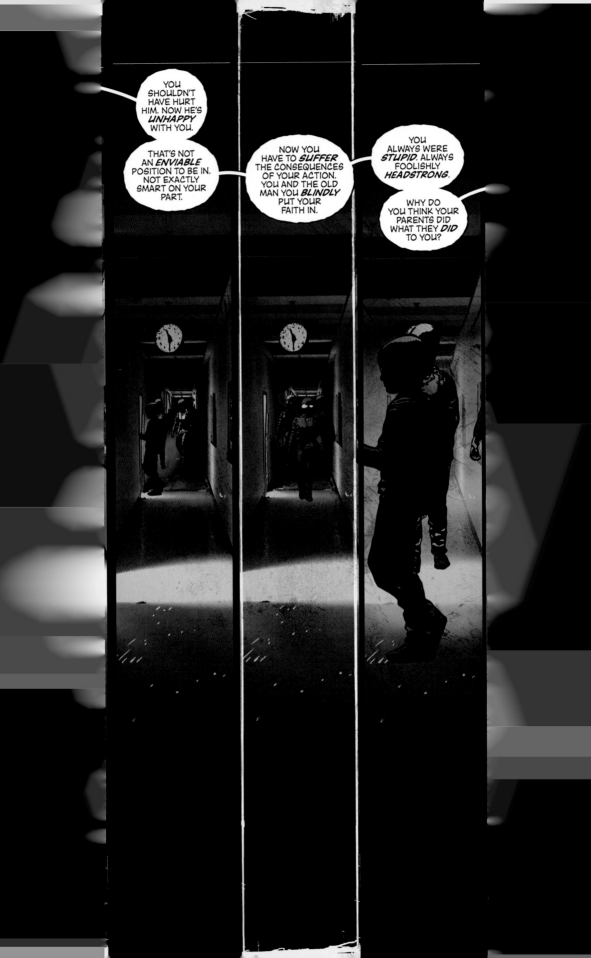

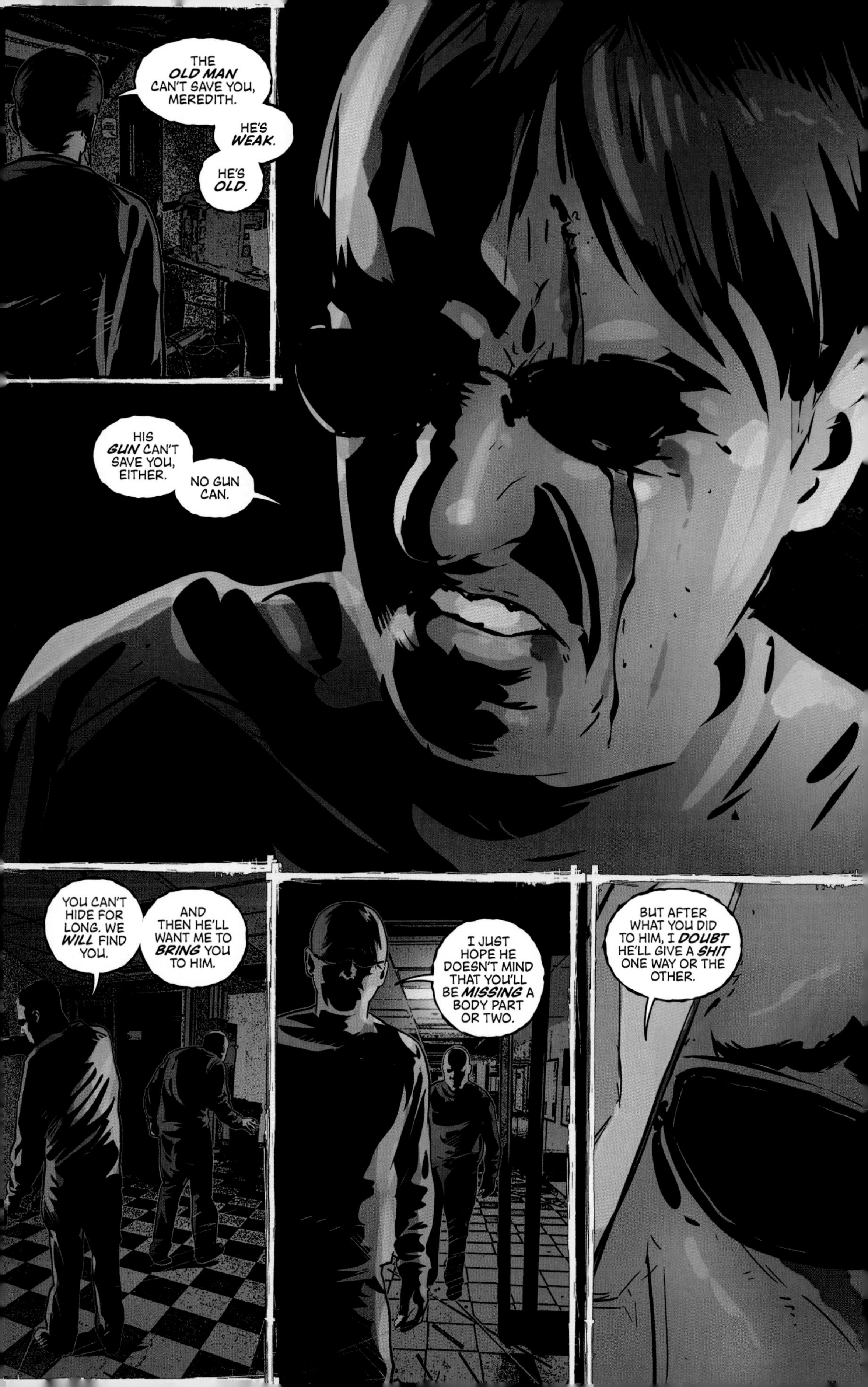
THE OLD MAN CAN'T SAVE YOU, MEREDITH.
HE'S WEAK.
HE'S OLD.
HIS GUN CAN'T SAVE YOU, EITHER.
NO GUN CAN.
YOU CAN'T HIDE FOR LONG. WE WILL FIND YOU.
AND THEN HE'LL WANT ME TO BRING YOU TO HIM.
I JUST HOPE HE DOESN'T MIND THAT YOU'LL BE MISSING A BODY PART OR TWO.
BUT AFTER WHAT YOU DID TO HIM, I DOUBT HE'LL GIVE A SHIT ONE WAY OR THE OTHER.

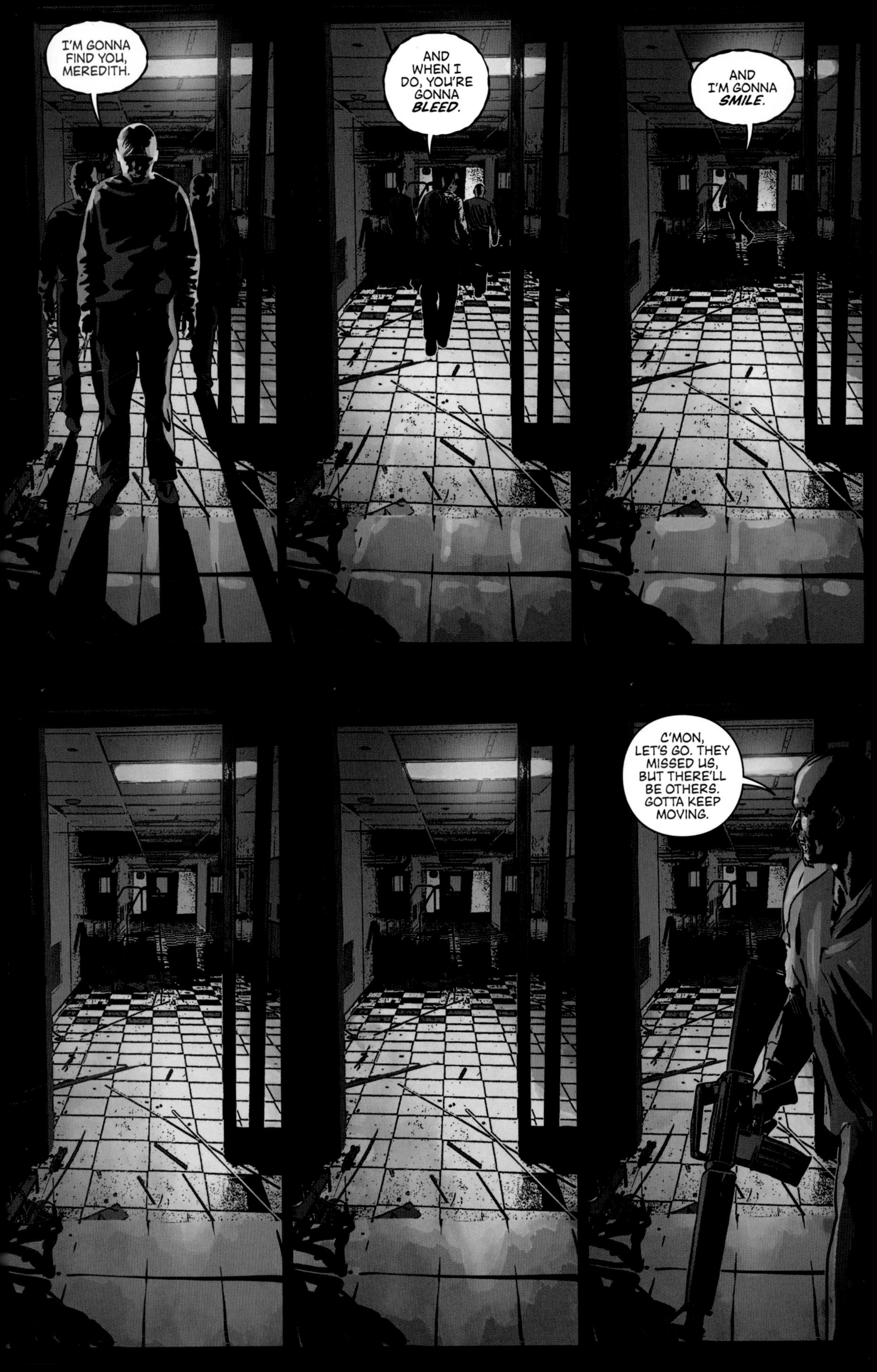
I'M GONNA FIND YOU, MEREDITH.
AND WHEN I DO, YOU'RE GONNA *BLEED*.
AND I'M GONNA *SMILE*.
C'MON, LET'S GO. THEY MISSED US, BUT THERE'LL BE OTHERS. GOTTA KEEP MOVING.

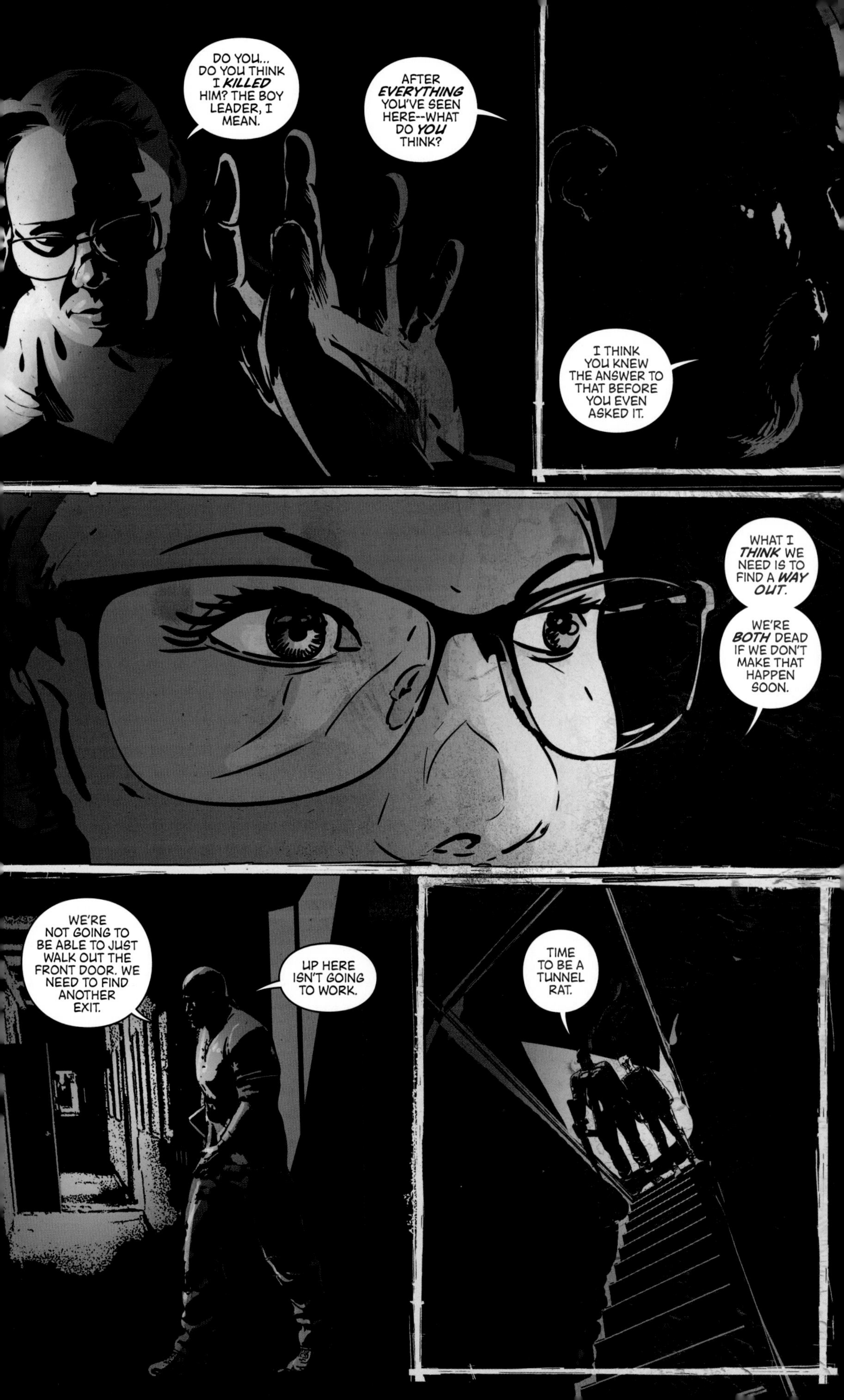
DO YOU... DO YOU THINK I KILLED HIM? THE BOY LEADER, I MEAN.
AFTER EVERYTHING YOU'VE SEEN HERE--WHAT DO YOU THINK?
I THINK YOU KNEW THE ANSWER TO THAT BEFORE YOU EVEN ASKED IT.
WHAT I THINK WE NEED IS TO FIND A WAY OUT.
WE'RE BOTH DEAD IF WE DON'T MAKE THAT HAPPEN SOON.
WE'RE NOT GOING TO BE ABLE TO JUST WALK OUT THE FRONT DOOR. WE NEED TO FIND ANOTHER EXIT.
UP HERE ISN'T GOING TO WORK.
TIME TO BE A TUNNEL RAT.

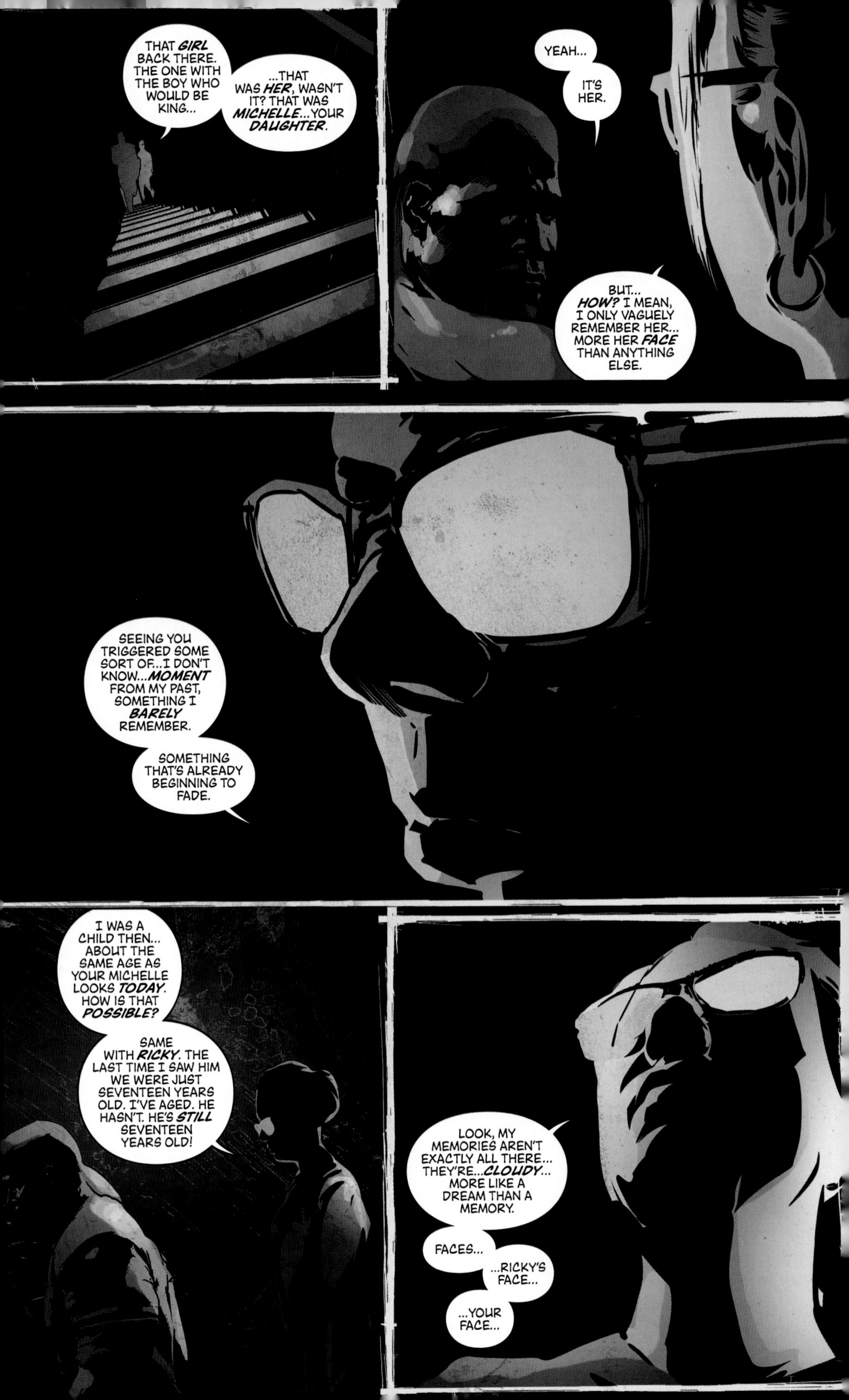
THAT GIRL BACK THERE. THE ONE WITH THE BOY WHO WOULD BE KING...
...THAT WAS HER, WASN'T IT? THAT WAS MICHELLE...YOUR DAUGHTER.
YEAH...
IT'S HER.
BUT... HOW? I MEAN, I ONLY VAGUELY REMEMBER HER... MORE HER FACE THAN ANYTHING ELSE.
SEEING YOU TRIGGERED SOME SORT OF...I DON'T KNOW...MOMENT FROM MY PAST, SOMETHING I BARELY REMEMBER.
SOMETHING THAT'S ALREADY BEGINNING TO FADE.
I WAS A CHILD THEN... ABOUT THE SAME AGE AS YOUR MICHELLE LOOKS TODAY. HOW IS THAT POSSIBLE?
SAME WITH RICKY. THE LAST TIME I SAW HIM WE WERE JUST SEVENTEEN YEARS OLD. I'VE AGED. HE HASN'T. HE'S STILL SEVENTEEN YEARS OLD!
LOOK, MY MEMORIES AREN'T EXACTLY ALL THERE... THEY'RE...CLOUDY... MORE LIKE A DREAM THAN A MEMORY.
FACES...
...RICKY'S FACE...
...YOUR FACE...

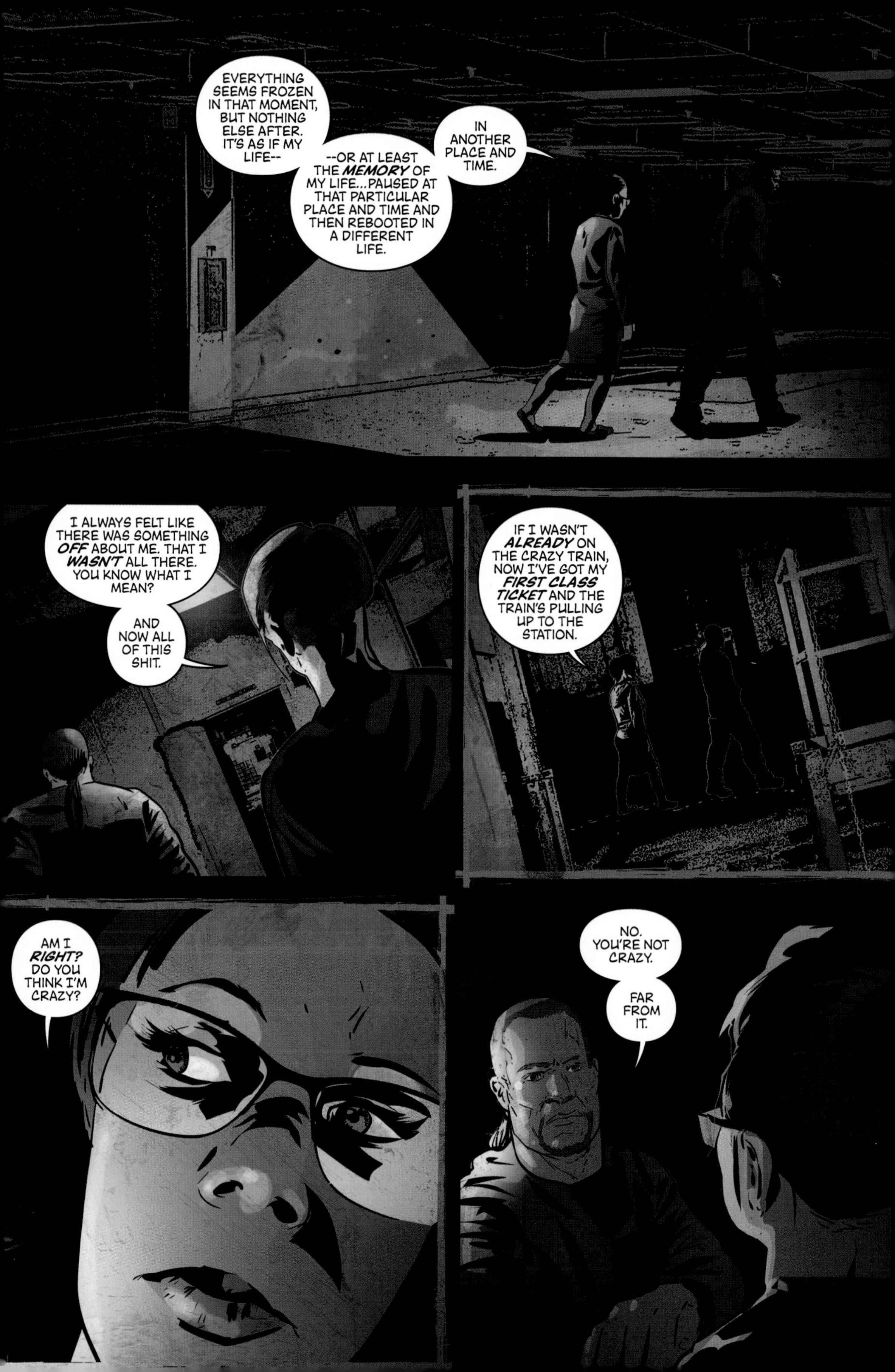
EVERYTHING SEEMS FROZEN IN THAT MOMENT, BUT NOTHING ELSE AFTER. IT'S AS IF MY LIFE--
--OR AT LEAST THE *MEMORY* OF MY LIFE...PAUSED AT THAT PARTICULAR PLACE AND TIME AND THEN REBOOTED IN A DIFFERENT LIFE.
IN ANOTHER PLACE AND TIME.
I ALWAYS FELT LIKE THERE WAS SOMETHING *OFF* ABOUT ME. THAT I *WASN'T* ALL THERE. YOU KNOW WHAT I MEAN?
AND NOW ALL OF THIS SHIT.
IF I WASN'T *ALREADY* ON THE CRAZY TRAIN, NOW I'VE GOT MY *FIRST CLASS TICKET* AND THE TRAIN'S PULLING UP TO THE STATION.
AM I *RIGHT?* DO YOU THINK I'M CRAZY?
NO. YOU'RE NOT CRAZY.
FAR FROM IT.

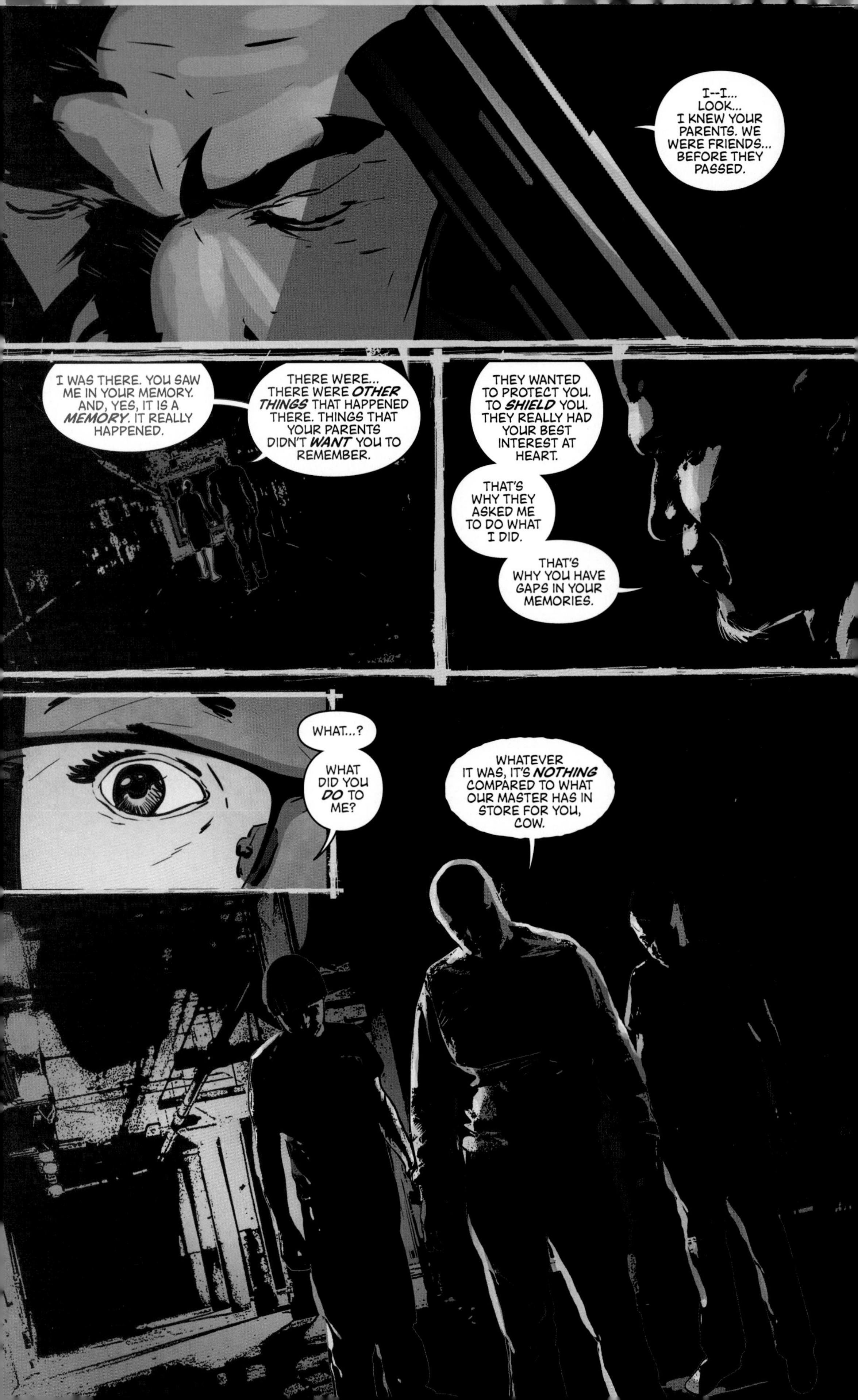
I--I... LOOK... I KNEW YOUR PARENTS. WE WERE FRIENDS... BEFORE THEY PASSED.
I WAS THERE. YOU SAW ME IN YOUR MEMORY. AND, YES, IT IS A MEMORY. IT REALLY HAPPENED.
THERE WERE... THERE WERE OTHER THINGS THAT HAPPENED THERE. THINGS THAT YOUR PARENTS DIDN'T WANT YOU TO REMEMBER.
THEY WANTED TO PROTECT YOU. TO SHIELD YOU. THEY REALLY HAD YOUR BEST INTEREST AT HEART.
THAT'S WHY THEY ASKED ME TO DO WHAT I DID.
THAT'S WHY YOU HAVE GAPS IN YOUR MEMORIES.
WHAT...?
WHAT DID YOU DO TO ME?
WHATEVER IT WAS, IT'S NOTHING COMPARED TO WHAT OUR MASTER HAS IN STORE FOR YOU, COW.

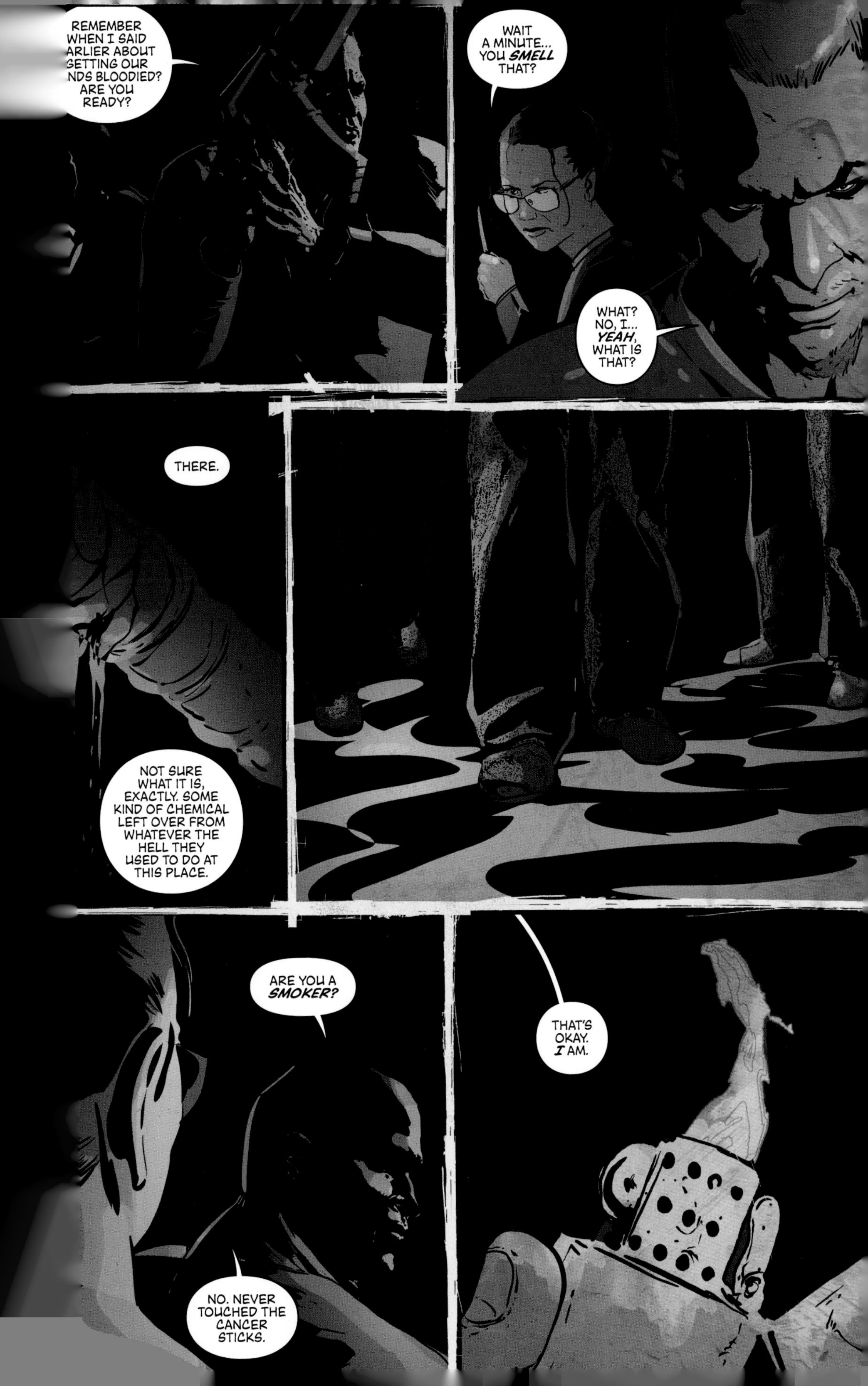
REMEMBER WHEN I SAID ARLIER ABOUT GETTING OUR NDS BLOODIED? ARE YOU READY?
WAIT A MINUTE... YOU SMELL THAT?
WHAT? NO, I... YEAH, WHAT IS THAT?
THERE.
NOT SURE WHAT IT IS, EXACTLY. SOME KIND OF CHEMICAL LEFT OVER FROM WHATEVER THE HELL THEY USED TO DO AT THIS PLACE.
ARE YOU A SMOKER?
NO. NEVER TOUCHED THE CANCER STICKS.
THAT'S OKAY. I AM.

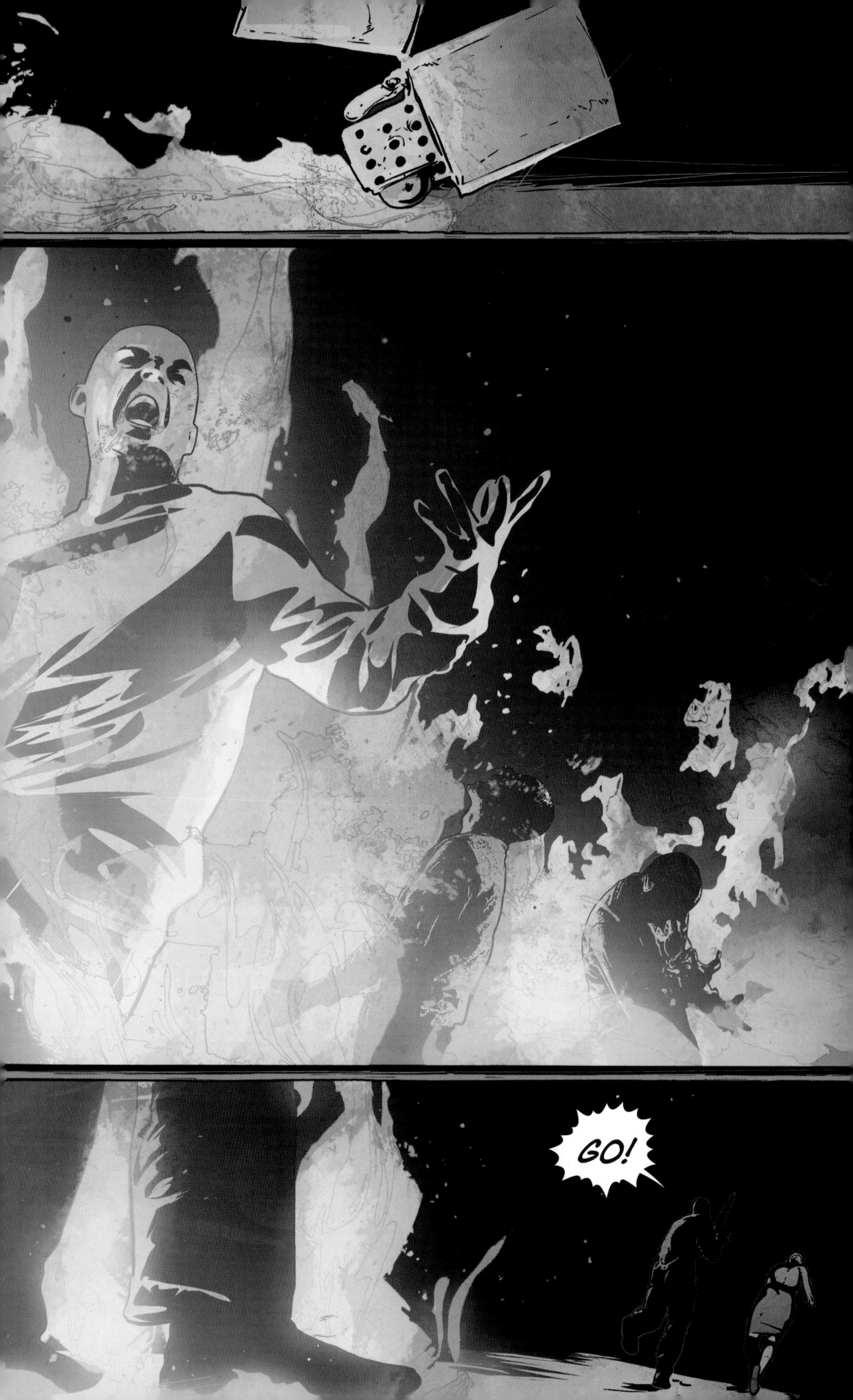
GO!

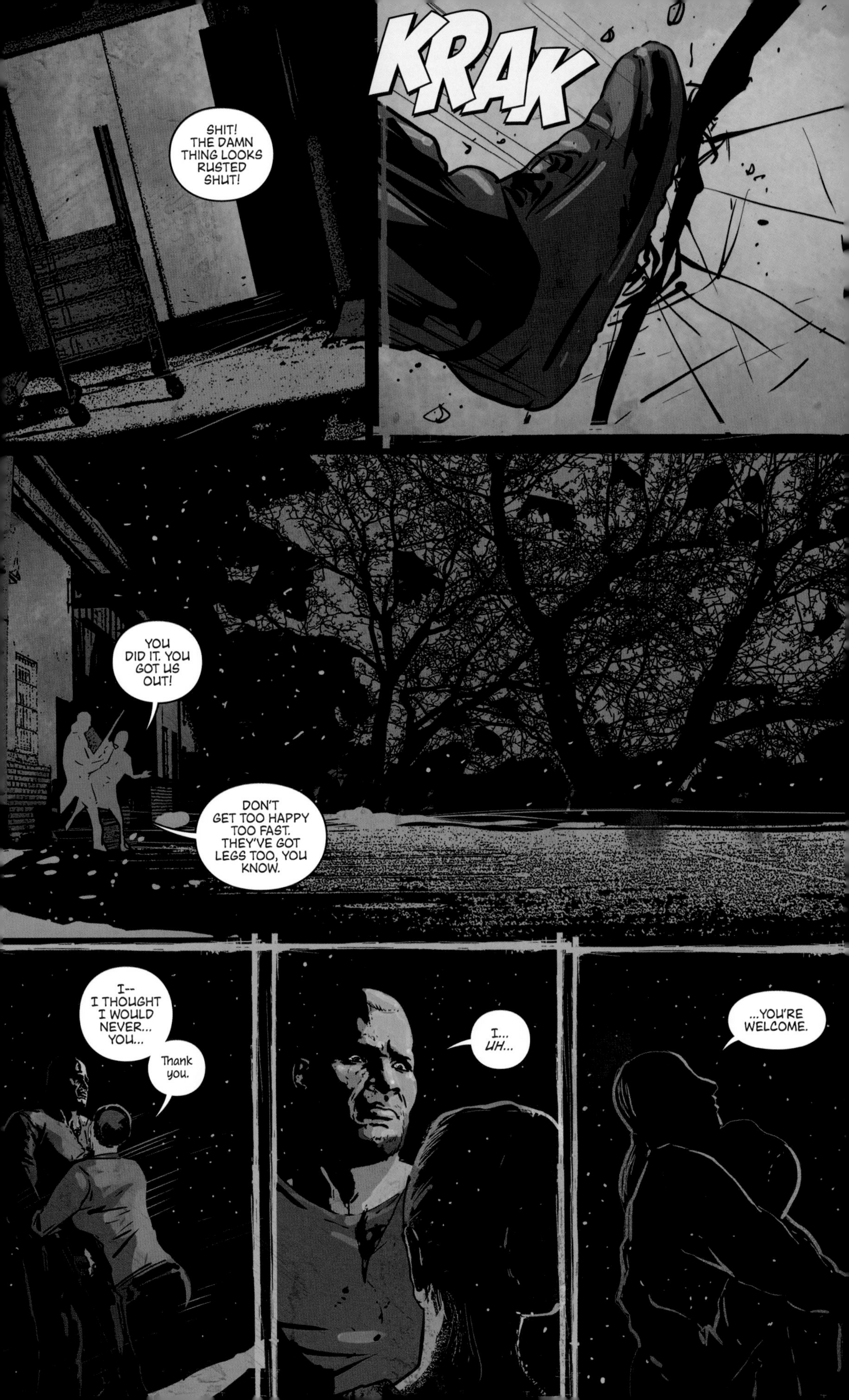
SHIT! THE DAMN THING LOOKS RUSTED SHUT!
KRAK
YOU DID IT. YOU GOT US OUT!
DON'T GET TOO HAPPY TOO FAST. THEY'VE GOT LEGS TOO, YOU KNOW.
I-- I THOUGHT I WOULD NEVER... YOU...
Thank you.
I... UH...
...YOU'RE WELCOME.

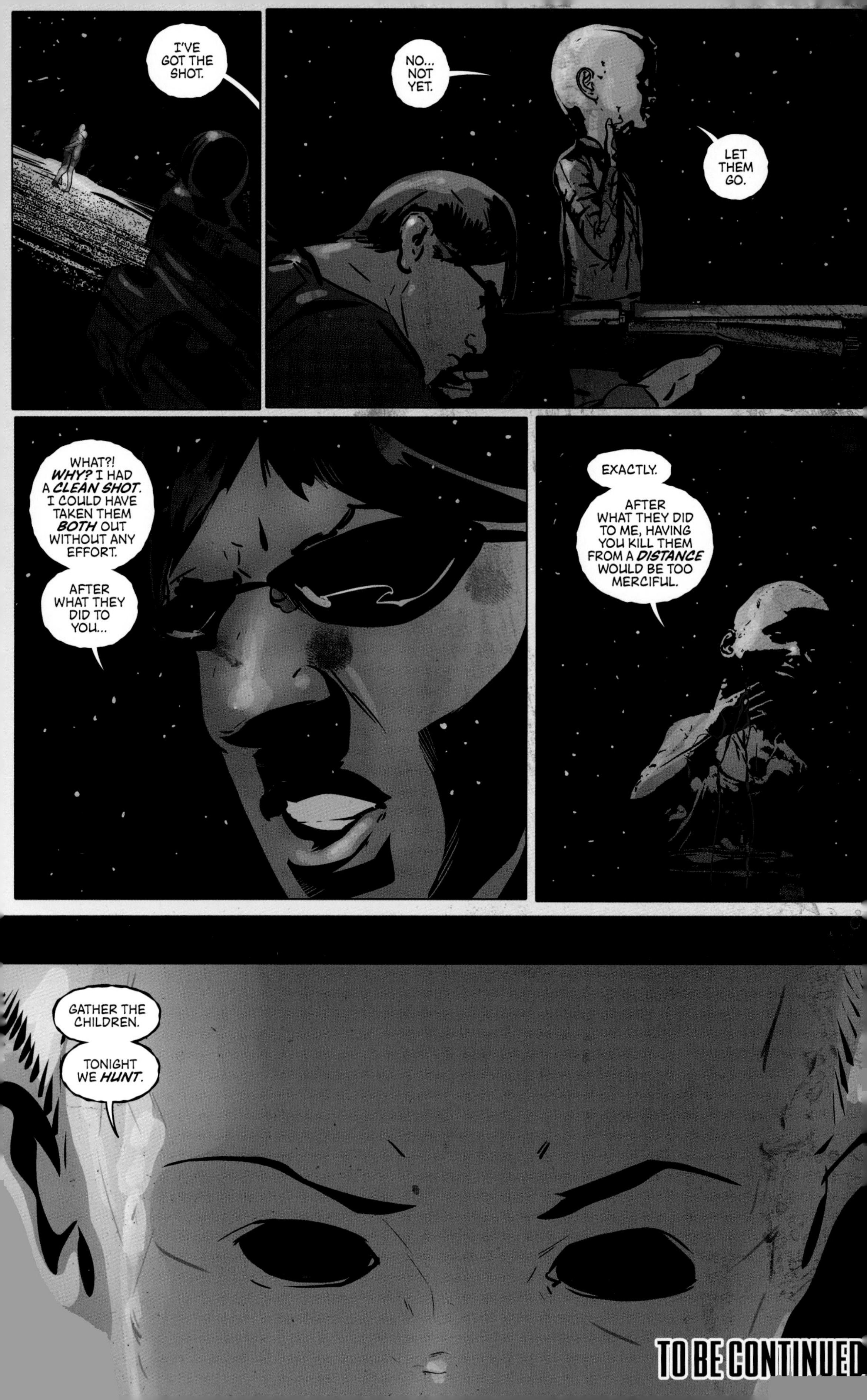
I'VE GOT THE SHOT.
NO... NOT YET.
LET THEM GO.
WHAT?! WHY? I HAD A CLEAN SHOT. I COULD HAVE TAKEN THEM BOTH OUT WITHOUT ANY EFFORT.
AFTER WHAT THEY DID TO YOU...
EXACTLY.
AFTER WHAT THEY DID TO ME, HAVING YOU KILL THEM FROM A DISTANCE WOULD BE TOO MERCIFUL.
GATHER THE CHILDREN.
TONIGHT WE HUNT.
TO BE CONTINUED

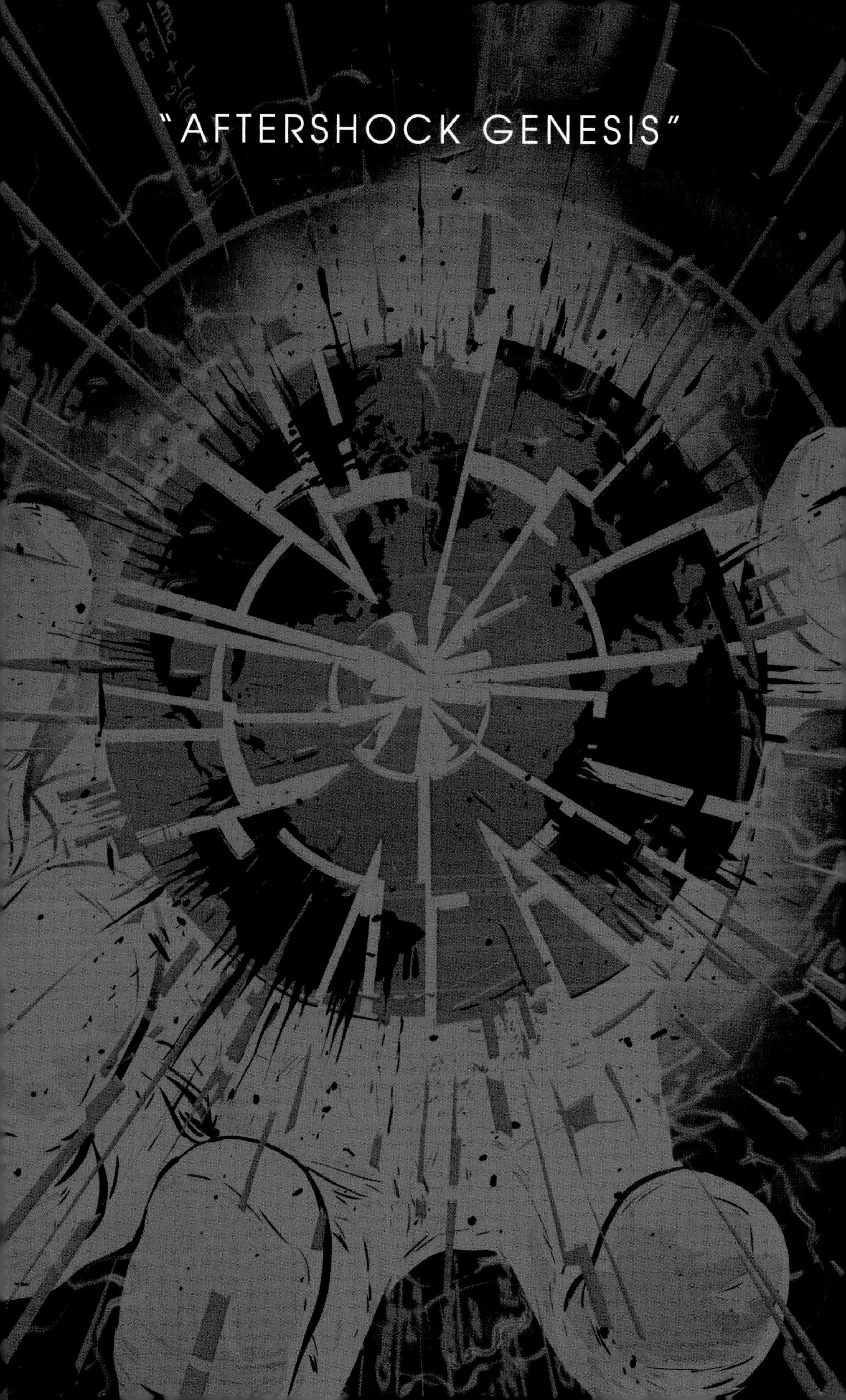
"AFTERSHOCK GENESIS"

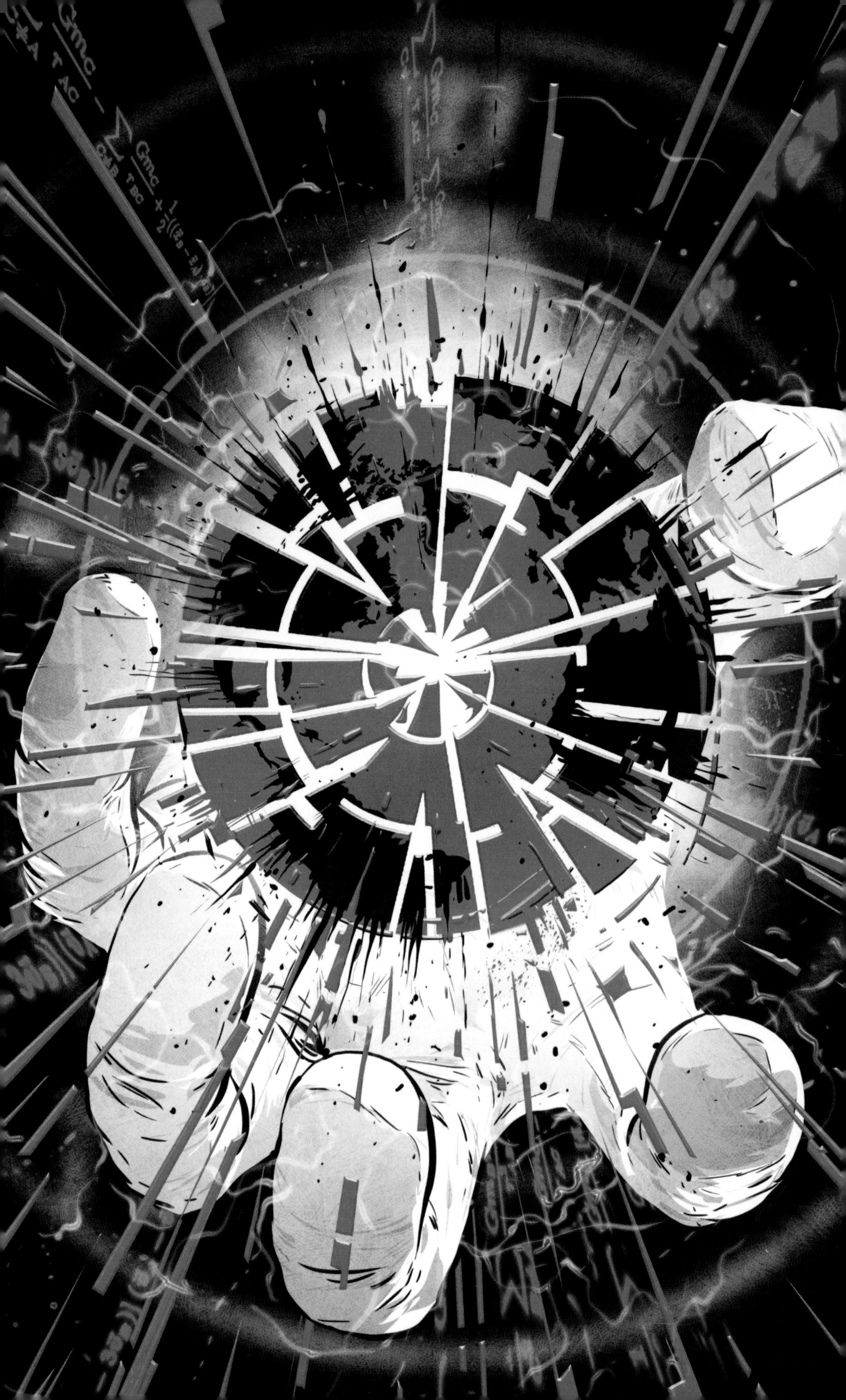

An EXCLUSIVE BLACK EYED KIDS™ short story

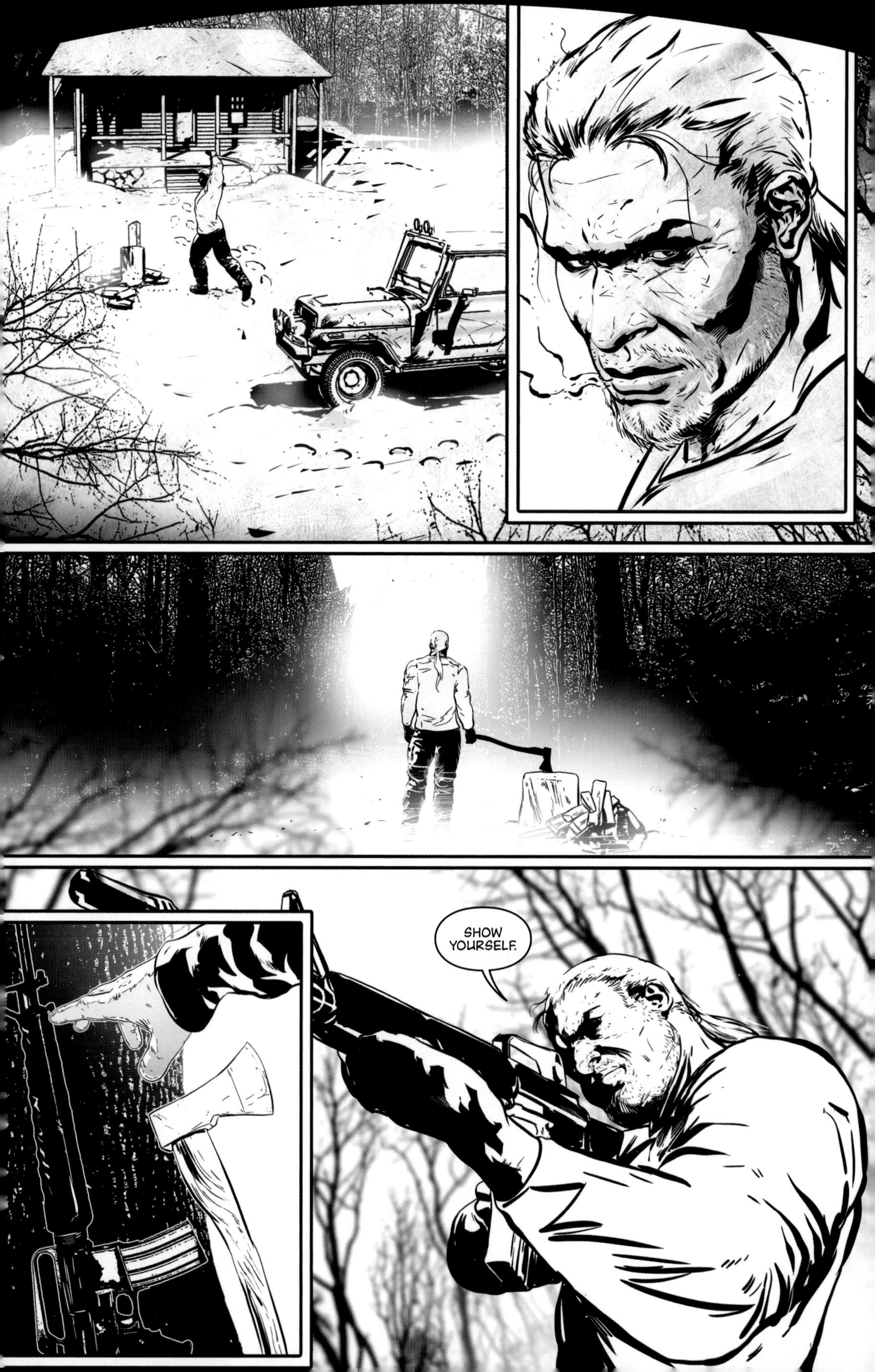
SHOW YOURSELF.

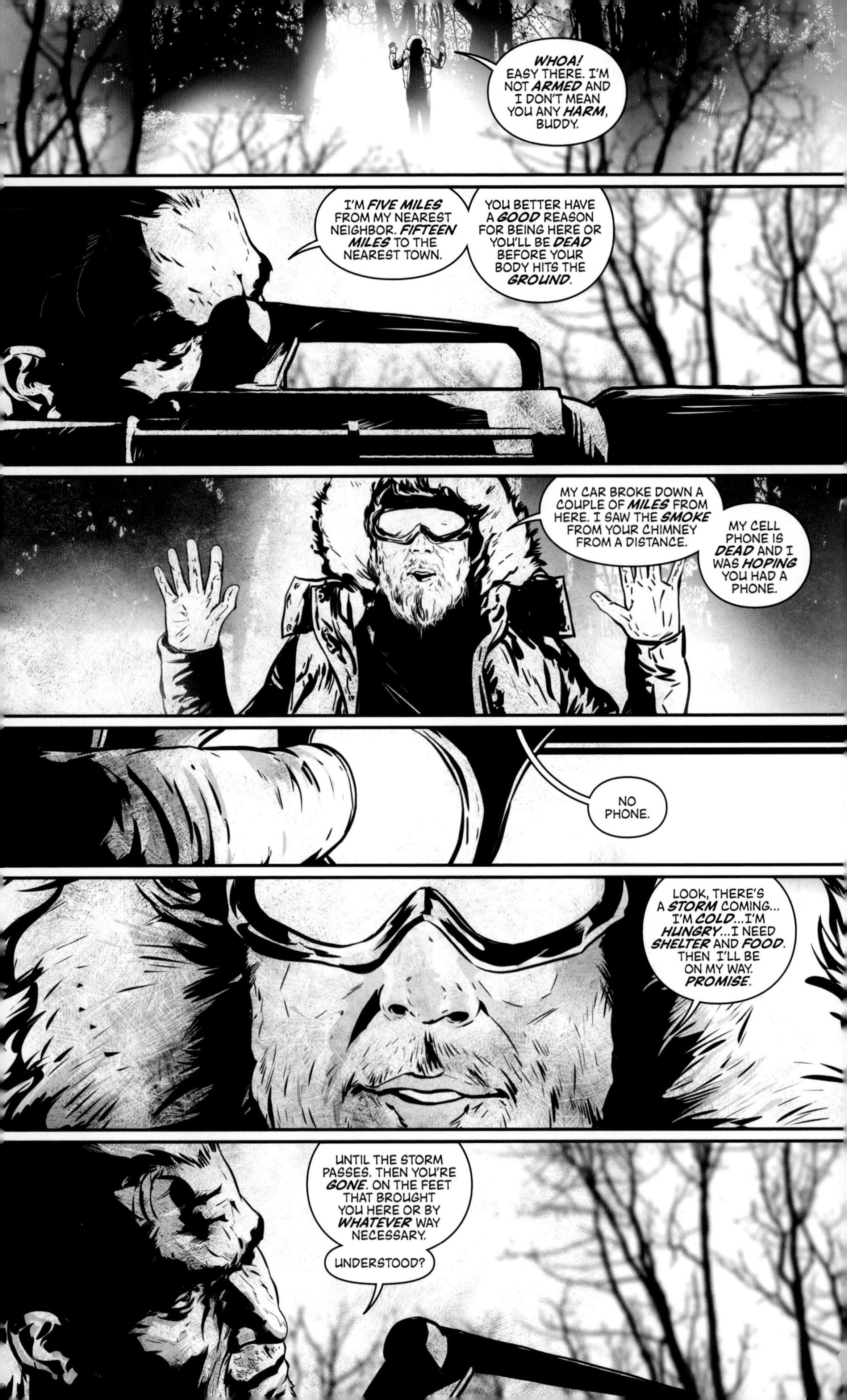
WHOA! EASY THERE. I'M NOT ARMED AND I DON'T MEAN YOU ANY HARM, BUDDY.
I'M FIVE MILES FROM MY NEAREST NEIGHBOR. FIFTEEN MILES TO THE NEAREST TOWN.
YOU BETTER HAVE A GOOD REASON FOR BEING HERE OR YOU'LL BE DEAD BEFORE YOUR BODY HITS THE GROUND.
MY CAR BROKE DOWN A COUPLE OF MILES FROM HERE. I SAW THE SMOKE FROM YOUR CHIMNEY FROM A DISTANCE.
MY CELL PHONE IS DEAD AND I WAS HOPING YOU HAD A PHONE.
NO PHONE.
LOOK, THERE'S A STORM COMING... I'M COLD...I'M HUNGRY...I NEED SHELTER AND FOOD. THEN I'LL BE ON MY WAY. PROMISE.
UNTIL THE STORM PASSES. THEN YOU'RE GONE. ON THE FEET THAT BROUGHT YOU HERE OR BY WHATEVER WAY NECESSARY.
UNDERSTOOD?

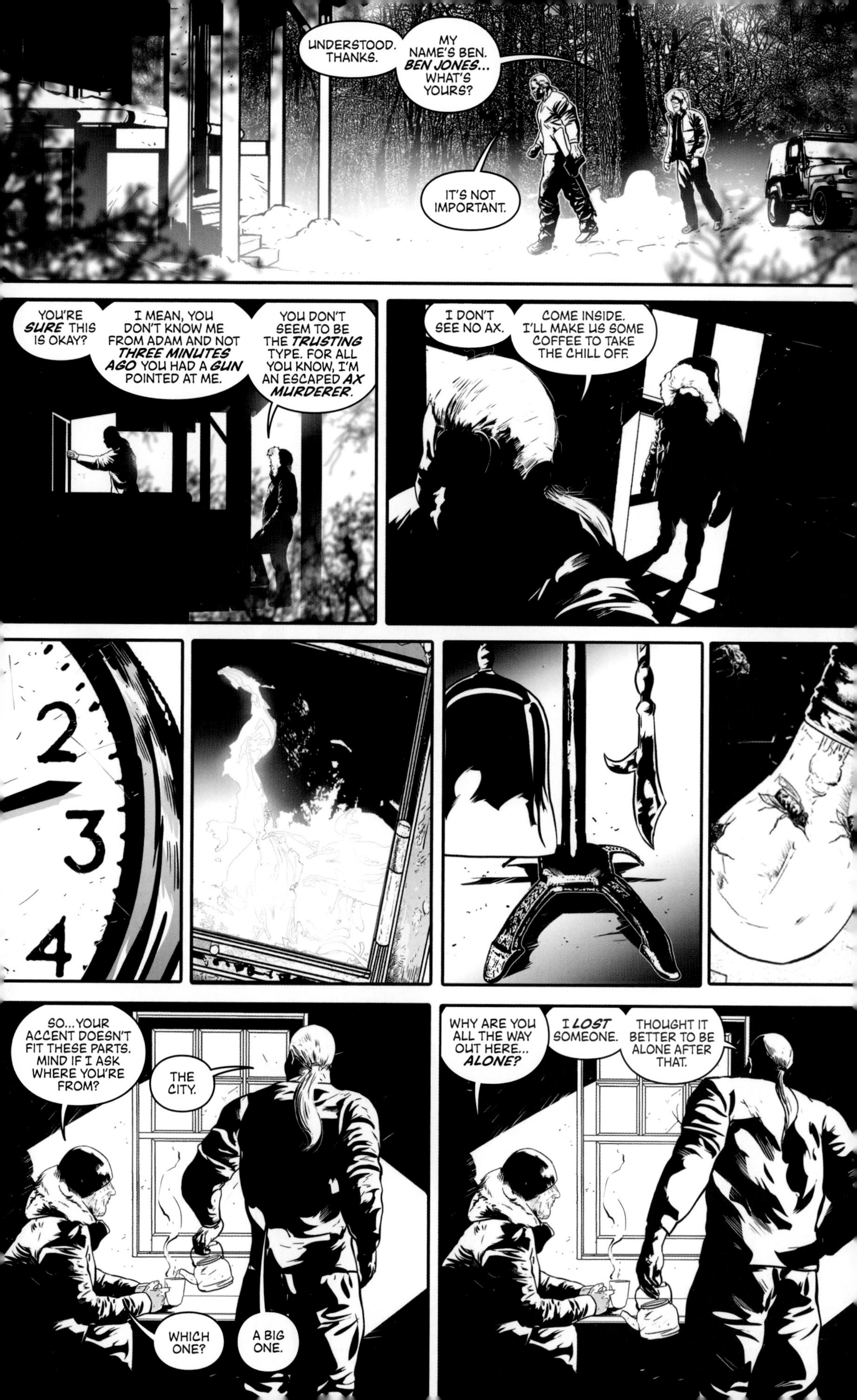
UNDERSTOOD. THANKS.
MY NAME'S BEN. BEN JONES... WHAT'S YOURS?
IT'S NOT IMPORTANT.
YOU'RE SURE THIS IS OKAY?
I MEAN, YOU DON'T KNOW ME FROM ADAM AND NOT THREE MINUTES AGO YOU HAD A GUN POINTED AT ME.
YOU DON'T SEEM TO BE THE TRUSTING TYPE. FOR ALL YOU KNOW, I'M AN ESCAPED AX MURDERER.
I DON'T SEE NO AX.
COME INSIDE. I'LL MAKE US SOME COFFEE TO TAKE THE CHILL OFF.
SO...YOUR ACCENT DOESN'T FIT THESE PARTS. MIND IF I ASK WHERE YOU'RE FROM?
THE CITY.
WHICH ONE?
A BIG ONE.
WHY ARE YOU ALL THE WAY OUT HERE... ALONE?
I LOST SOMEONE.
THOUGHT IT BETTER TO BE ALONE AFTER THAT.

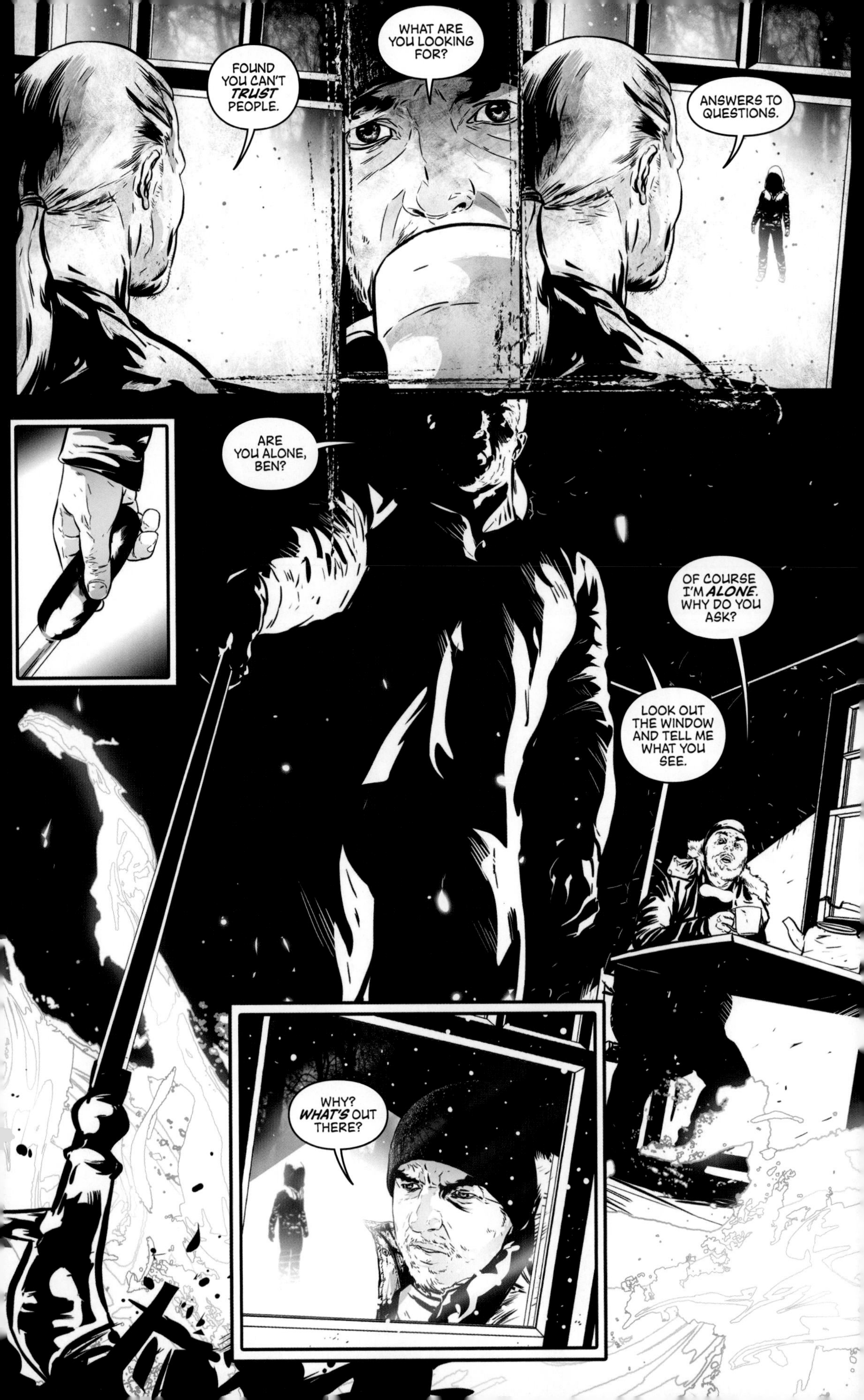
FOUND YOU CAN'T TRUST PEOPLE.
WHAT ARE YOU LOOKING FOR?
ANSWERS TO QUESTIONS.
ARE YOU ALONE, BEN?
OF COURSE I'M ALONE. WHY DO YOU ASK?
LOOK OUT THE WINDOW AND TELL ME WHAT YOU SEE.
WHY? WHAT'S OUT THERE?

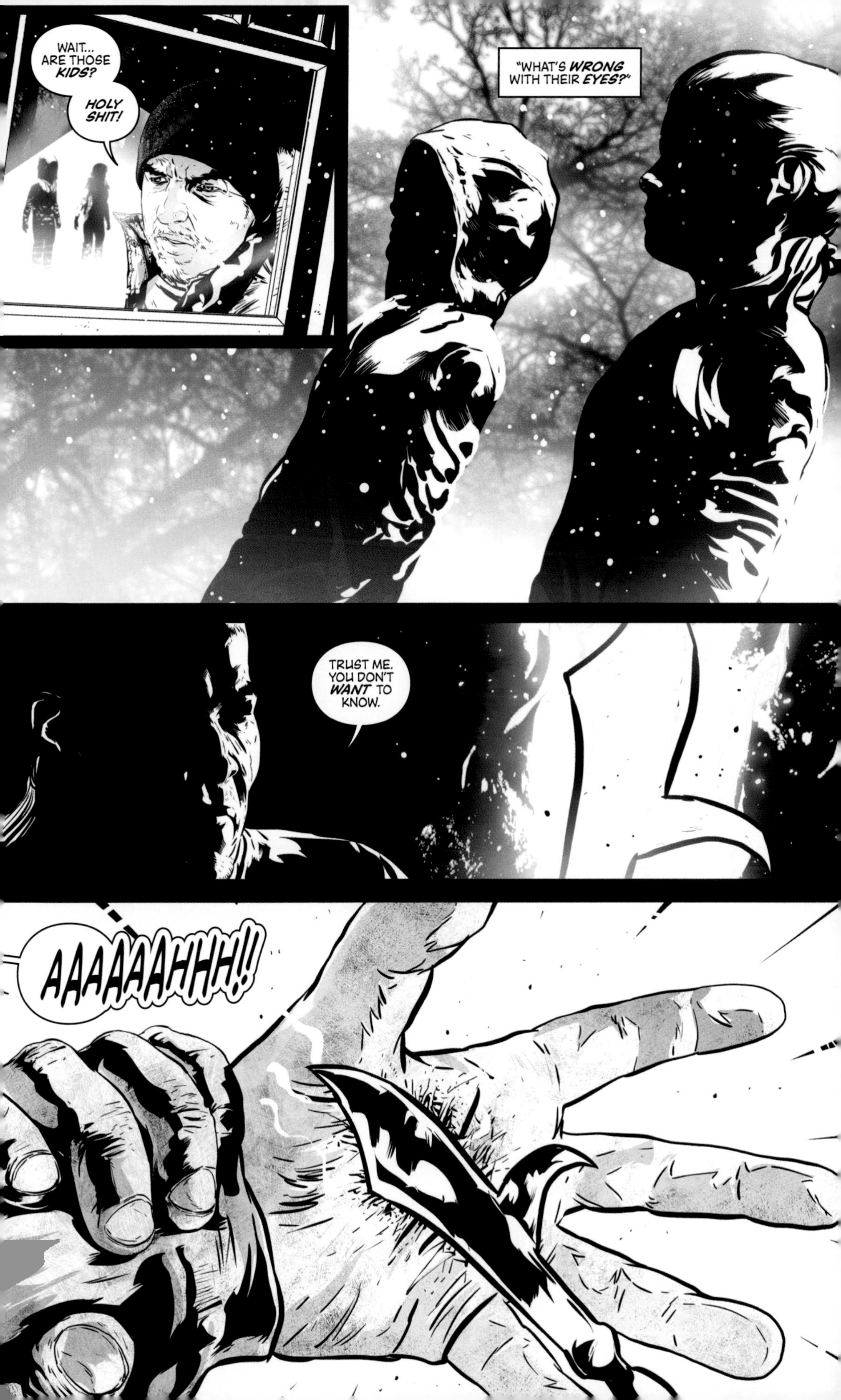
WAIT... ARE THOSE KIDS?
HOLY SHIT!
"WHAT'S WRONG WITH THEIR EYES?"
TRUST ME. YOU DON'T WANT TO KNOW.
AAAAAAAHHH!!

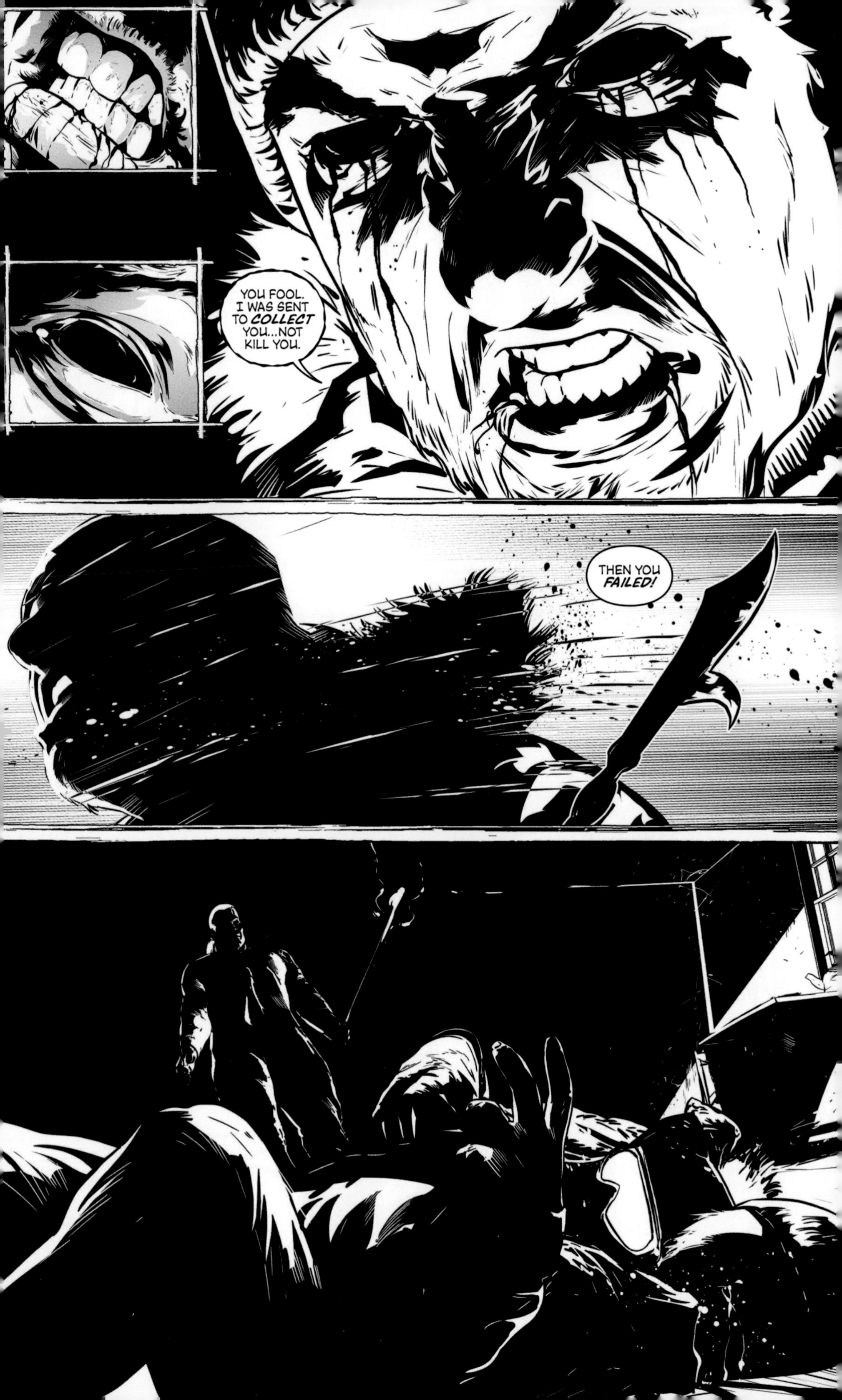
YOU FOOL. I WAS SENT TO COLLECT YOU...NOT KILL YOU.
THEN YOU FAILED!

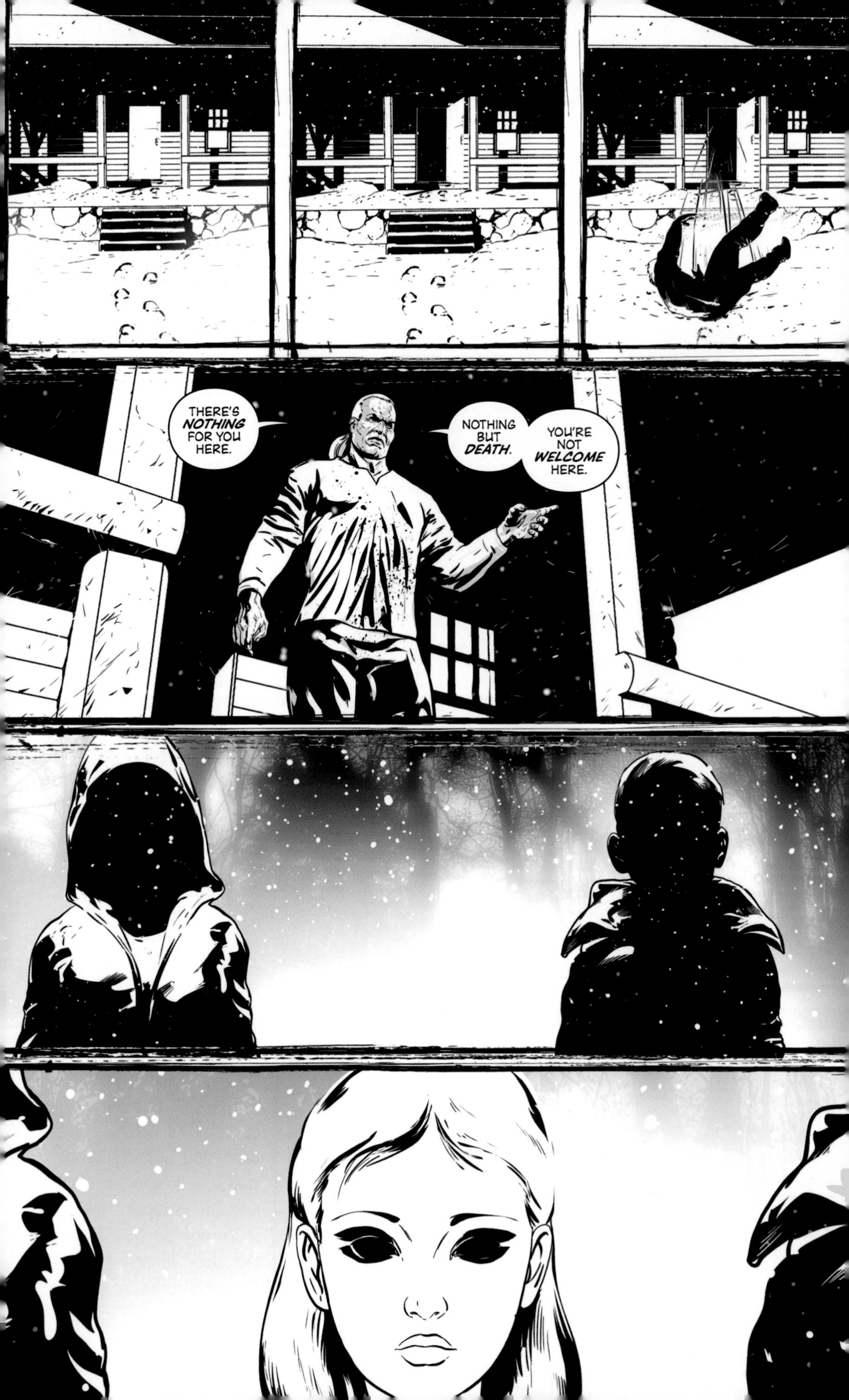
THERE'S NOTHING FOR YOU HERE.
NOTHING BUT DEATH.
YOU'RE NOT WELCOME HERE.

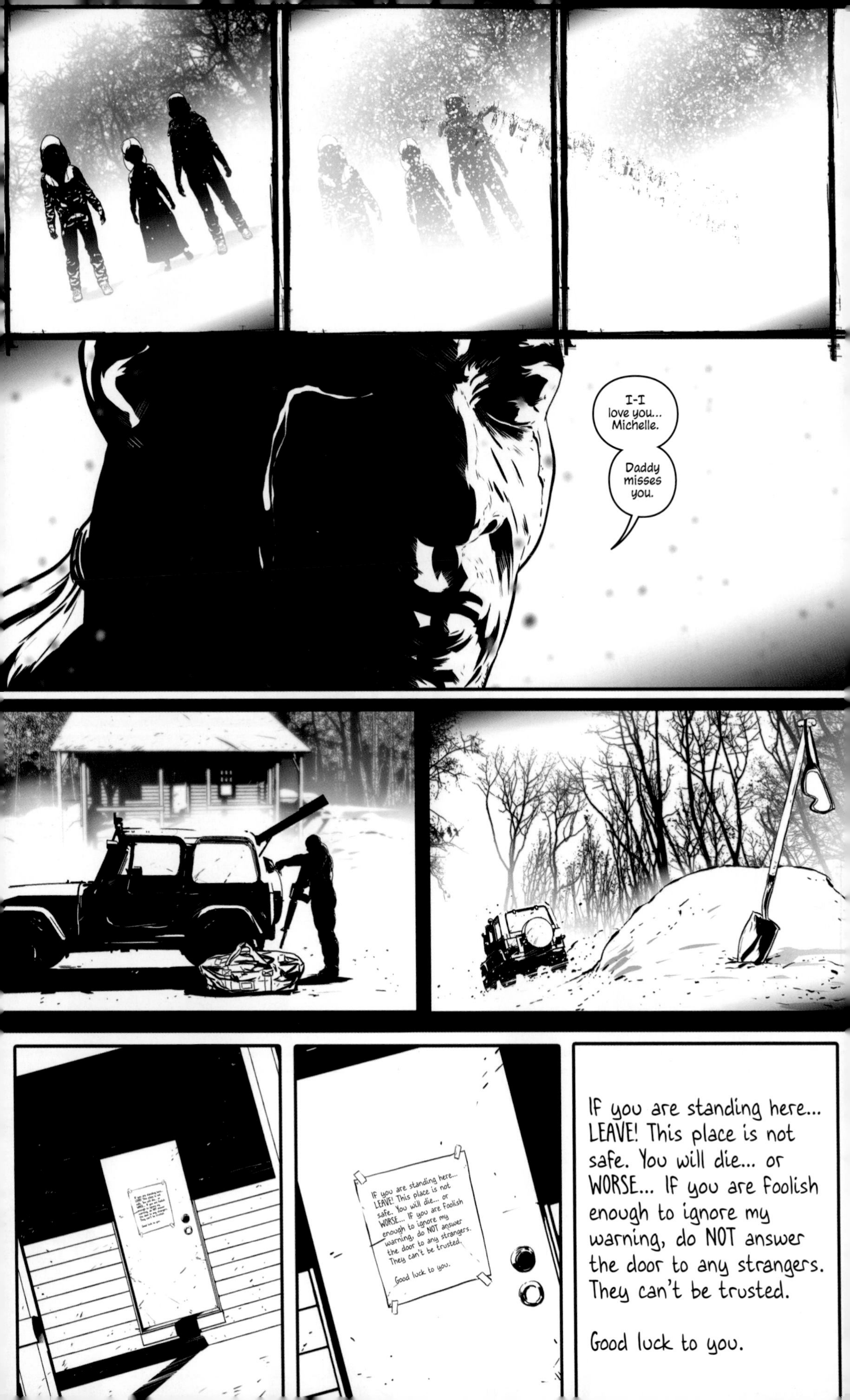

I-I love you... Michelle.
Daddy misses you.
If you are standing here... LEAVE! This place is not safe. You will die... or WORSE... If you are foolish enough to ignore my warning, do NOT answer the door to any strangers. They can't be trusted.
Good luck to you.

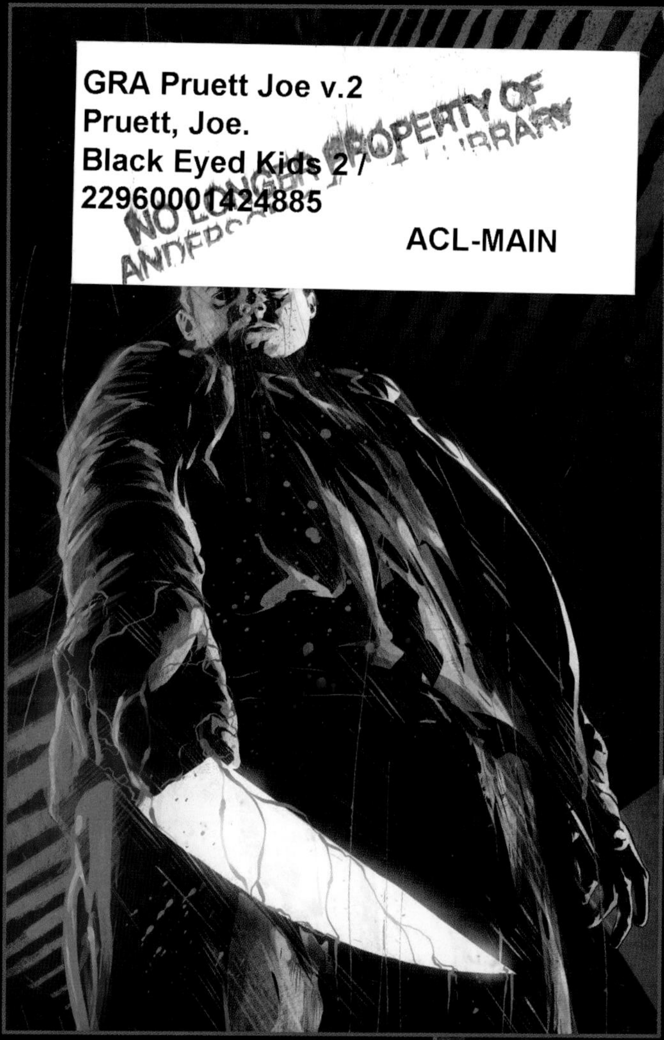

issue 6
Ssalefish variant cover
SZYMON KUDRANSKI

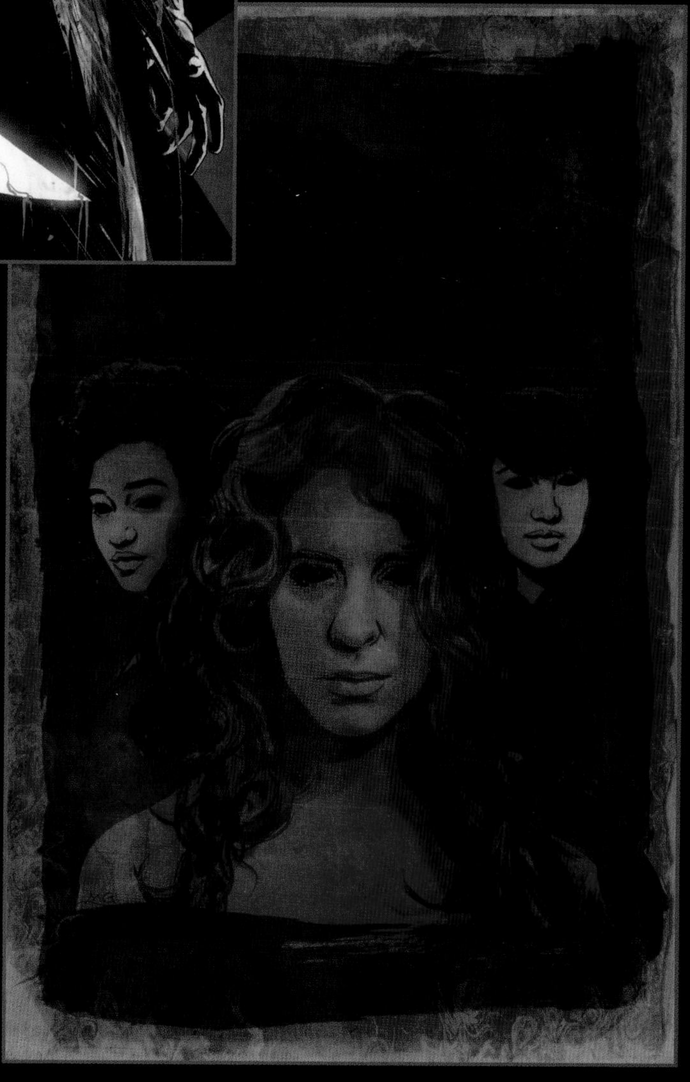

issue 7
Incentive variant cover
MICHAEL GAYDOS

JOE PRUETT writer

@pruett_joe

Joe Pruett is an Eisner Award-winning comic book editor, publisher, and writer, having been nominated for numerous Eisner, Harvey and Eagle awards for his work on *Negative Burn* at Caliber Comics. He is also known for his writing work at Marvel, where he wrote for *X-Men Unlimited, Cable* and *Magneto Rex*. In addition to his X-Men writing work, Joe has written for virtually every other major comic publisher, including Image, Vertigo and IDW.

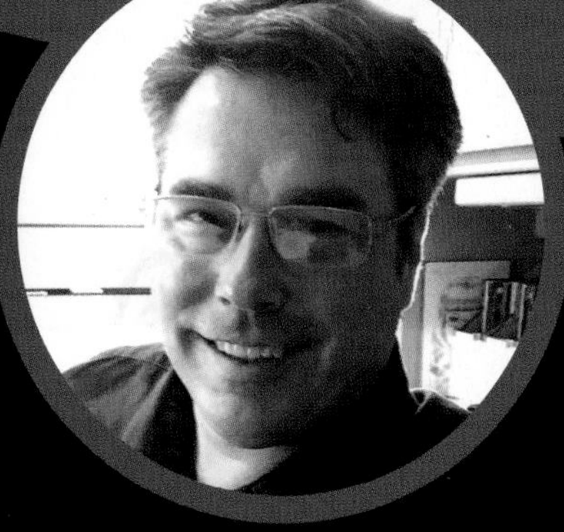

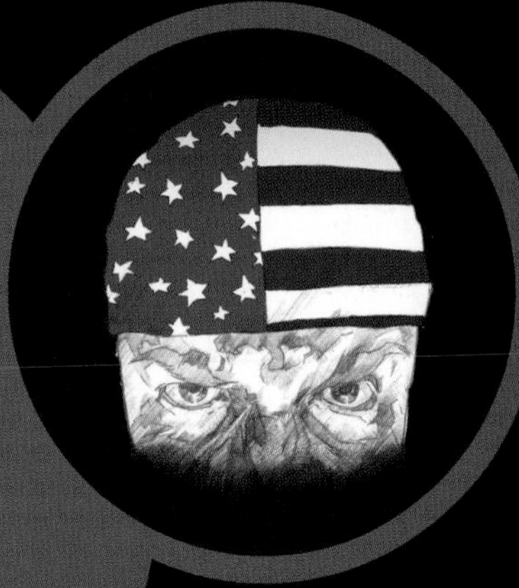

SZYMON KUDRANSKI artist

@SzymonKudranski

Born in Poland in 1986, Szymon got his big break into comics eighteen years later when writer Steve Niles asked him to draw a story featured in 2004's *30 Days of Night Annual*. Since then, Szymon has worked with many other comic publishers, including DC Comics *(Green Lantern, The Dark Knight)*, Marvel Comics *(Daredevil/Punisher)* and Image Comics, where he was personally asked by Todd McFarlane to take over art duties on the long-running *Spawn* series.

GUY MAJOR colorist

@guymajor

Guy Major is an artist and photographer who has been working in comics since 1995, when he responded to an add looking for colorists for Wildstorm's *WildC.A.T.S.* series. He worked for Homage Studios until 1998 when he became a freelance color artist. He has worked on just about every character from Batman to Barry Ween. When not working on comics or out with his camera, he is studying about, tasting or drinking wine. He currently lives in Oakland, CA with two amazing women—his wife Jackie and their daughter Riley.

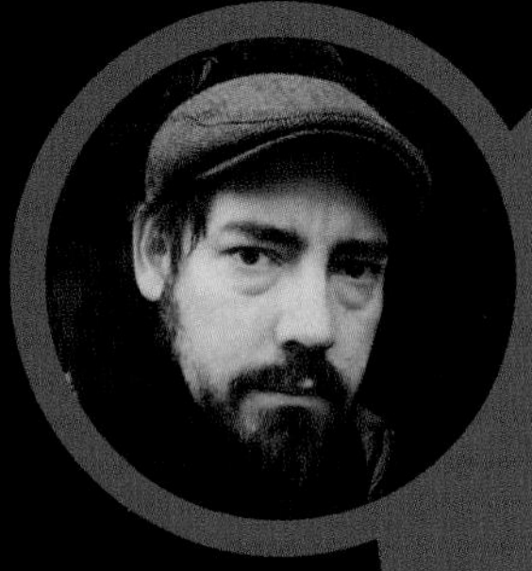

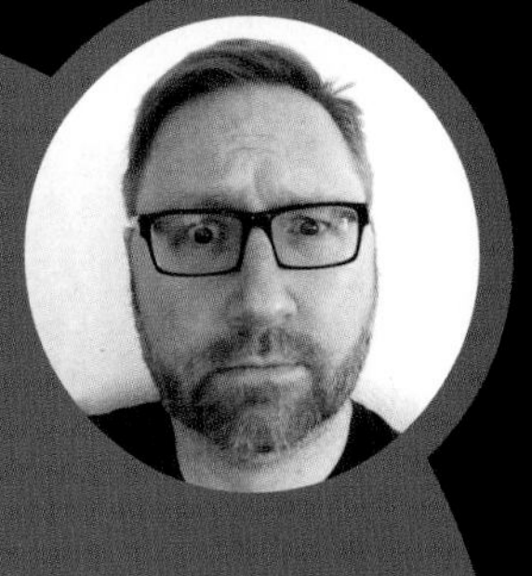

MARSHALL DILLON letterer

@MarshallDillon

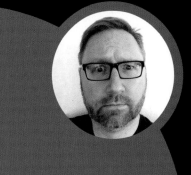

A comic book industry veteran, Marshall got his start in 1994, in the midst of the indy comic boom. Over the years, he's been everything from an independent self-published writer to an associate publisher working on properties like *G.I.Joe, Voltron* and *Street Fighter*. He's done just about everything except draw a comic book, and has worked for just about every publisher except the "big two." Primarily a father and letterer these days, he also dabbles in old-school paper & dice RPG game design. You can catch up with Marshall at firstdraftpress.net.